Language Use in Business and Commerce in Europe

# DUISBURGER ARBEITEN ZUR SPRACH- UND KULTURWISSENSCHAFT

## Duisburg Papers on Research in Language and Culture

Herausgegeben von
Ulrich Ammon, René Dirven und Martin Pütz

Band 78

PETER LANG
Frankfurt am Main · Berlin · Bern · Bruxelles · New York · Oxford · Wien

Gerhard Stickel (ed.)

# Language Use in Business and Commerce in Europe

## Contributions to the Annual Conference 2008 of EFNIL in Lisbon

PETER LANG
Internationaler Verlag der Wissenschaften

**Bibliographic Information published by the Deutsche Nationalbibliothek**
The Deutsche Nationalbibliothek lists this publication in the Deutsche Nationalbibliografie; detailed bibliographic data is available in the internet at http://dnb.d-nb.de.

ISSN 0934-3709
ISBN 978-3-631-58803-1



www.peterlang.de

# Vorwort

Industrie und Handel sind die Domänen, in denen sich die wirtschaftliche und kommunikative Globalisierung besonders stark auswirkt. Für EFNIL, das Netzwerk aus Sprachakademien und zentralen Sprachinstituten der EU-Staaten und darüber hinaus, lag es deshalb nahe, den Sprachgebrauch in diesen beiden Domänen europäischer Länder auf einer Jahrestagung zu diskutieren. Damit setzte EFNIL auf ihrer sechsten Jahrestagung am 13. und 14. November 2008 in Lissabon die alljährliche Behandlung wichtiger sprachpolitischer Themen fort, die sie auf ihrer Gründungstagung 2003 in Stockholm begonnen hat. Beiträge zu den ersten vier Jahrestagungen sind im Internet auf der Webseite von EFNIL zu finden: www.efnil.org. Die Vorträge, die auf der fünften Tagung in Riga gehalten wurden, sind als Buch erschienen.[1] Und dies geschieht nun auch in diesem Band mit den Beiträgen zur Tagung in Lissabon. Das Generalthema *Sprachgebrauch in Industrie und Handel* war im Einvernehmen mit dem gastgebenden Institut, dem Instituto Camões, ausgewählt worden.

Auf die einführenden Reden folgen sowohl generelle Überlegungen und Übersichtsdarstellungen zum Generalthema als auch Berichte über die spezifische sprachliche Situation in mehreren europäischen Ländern. Generelle Erörterungen bieten vor allem die Beiträge von Stephen Hagen und Martin Stegu. Die Verhältnisse im eigenen Land bzw. die Situation der eigenen Sprache behandeln die Berichte von José Paulo Esperança (Portugiesisch), Pirkko Nuolijärvi (Finnland), Charlotte Rønhof und Lisbeth Verstraete-Hansen (Dänemark), Guðrun Kvaran (Island), Sopie Bressé (Frankreich), Guy Berg (Luxemburg), Walery Pisarek (Polen), und František Čermák (Tschechien). Angesichts der verfügbaren Zeit konnte nur eine Auswahl aus den europäischen Ländern behandelt werden. Wichtig war uns aber, die Auswahl unter anderem nach der Größe der Staaten und ihrer längeren oder kürzeren Zugehörigkeit zur EU bzw. Nichtzugehörigkeit zu treffen.

Die Beiträge werden hier in der Abfolge, in der sie in Lissabon vorgetragen wurden, wiedergegeben. Eine Resolution „zum Sprachgebrauch in Industrie und Handel in Europa“ schließt die thematischen Teile des Bandes ab. Sie wurde von der Generalversammlung von EFNIL am 14. November 2008 beschlossen. Hier wird sie in 26 europäischen Sprachen geboten, darunter den 23 offiziellen Sprachen der Europäischen Union. Damit soll auch ein Beispiel praktizierter europäischer Mehrsprachigkeit gegeben werden, deren Bewahrung und Weiterentwicklung EFNIL sich zum Ziel gemacht hat. Wir hoffen, dass neben den Vortragstexten diese Resolution auch die Aufmerksamkeit politischer Akteure in den Bereichen nationaler und europäischer Sprachpolitik wie auch bei Vertretern der Wirtschaft finden wird. Der Anhang bietet als Liste einen Überblick über die Mitgliedsinstitutionen von EFNIL.

Gerhard Stickel

---

[1] G. Stickel (ed.): National and European Language Policies. Contributions to the Annual Conference 2007 of EFNIL in Riga. Frankfurt a.M./Berlin/Bern etc.: Peter Lang, 2009.

## Preface

Business and commerce are the domains that are especially affected by economic and communicative globalization. EFNIL, the network of language academies and central language institutes of the EU countries and beyond, decided to discuss the use of languages in these domains at one of its annual conferences. By this at its sixth Annual Conference in Lisbon on 13 and 14 November, EFNIL continued the annual treatment of important themes on language politics and policies that it started at its founding conference at Stockholm in 2003. Contributions to the first four annual conferences can be found on the website of EFNIL: www.efnil.org. The papers that were read at the fifth conference in Riga 2007 have appeared as a book (see fn. 1).Now, the contributions to the conference in Lisbon are also published as the present book. The general theme *Language Use in Business and Commerce in Europe* was selected in agreement with the hosting institution, the Instituto Camões.

The introductory statements are followed by general consideration and surveys concerning the theme of the conference as well as reports on the specific linguistic situations in several European countries. General discussions are offered mainly by Stephen Hagen and Martin Stegu in their contributions. The conditions within their own countries or the situation of their proper language are being treated by José Paulo Esperança (Portuguese), Pirkko Nuolijärvi (Finland), Charlotte Rønhof und Lisbeth Verstraete-Hansen (Denmark), Guðrun Kvaran (Iceland), Sopie Bressé (France), Guy Berg (Luxembourg), Walery Pisarek (Poland), and František Čermák (Czech Republic). In view of the limited time available, only a selection of countries could be considered for the conference and for this book. It was, however, important for us to make the choice among other reasons according to the size of the states and the time of their membership within the European Union.

The contributions are presented here in the sequence they were read in Lisbon. A resolution on „Language use in business and commerce in Europe" concludes the thematic parts of the volume. It was passed by the General Assembly of EFNIL on 14 November 2008. Here, the resolution is being presented in 26 European languages, including the 23 official languages of the European Union. By this, an example of practised multilingualism is being presented, the preservation and further development of which has been chosen by EFNIL as a main goal. We hope that this resolution – beside the various papers – will also find the attention of both political agents in the fields of national and European language politics and of representatives of economy. The appendix offers a list of EFNIL's member institutions.

Gerhard Stickel

## Contents

Simonetta Luz Afonso
Presidente do Instituto Camões

## Notas de Boas Vindas

É com o maior prazer que o Instituto Camões, na sua longa vida, quase octogenária, acolhe, em Lisboa, a 6ª Conferência Anual da EFNIL, saudando o Professor Gerhard Stickel pelo empenho e modo como tem conduzido a vida desta nossa Federação.

Cabe-me, perante esta prestigiosa assembleia, deixar expressa alguma reflexão que temos vindo a fazer sobre *As Línguas no Século XXI. Novos Valores*, abordando a importância e os desafios que as Línguas poderão e deverão representar na Idade da Globalização e focando, ainda, a importância e os desafios das Línguas Europeias, nomeadamente pela sua dimensão de partilha entre países e outros povos, pela sua dimensão, também, global.

Porque o IC é o executor externo da política linguístico-cultural de Portugal, sobre que vectores temos vindo a assentar o nosso posicionamento em termos de uma *política para o multilinguismo*?

### 1. Primeiramente, o do novo paradigma das relações entre Estados e as suas implicações a vários níveis, nomeadamente o linguístico-cultural

Descrito este novo paradigma como um espaço de negociação e de concertação entre Estados soberanos, em que as relações internacionais não se esgotam em conexões interestatais, ganhando relevo a dimensão transnacional na interacção entre as sociedades, nas suas diversas dinâmicas, é-nos exigida uma nova cultura na maneira de pensar e de agir. A par dos Estados, também novos actores agem na arena das relações internacionais: Associações (como a EFNIL ou a EUNIC), cientistas, pensadores, agentes culturais e humanitários entre outros, a par da malha empresaria, dos investimentos e das firmas a nível internacional.

Hoje, tendo como premissas, por um lado, a ideia de globalização e, por outro, a importância crescente dos diversos agentes no desenvolvimento interno e nas relações externas de cada Estado, assiste-se a novos modelos de diplomacia, assentes em princípios de identidade cultural, de diálogo intercultural, em estreita conexão com estratégias de desenvolvimento económico programadas por convénios ou organizações internacionais.

Assim, por exemplo, no seio da União Europeia, encontros e concertações entre os seus Estados-Membros ditam o que se vai defender perante terceiros, face aos diferentes níveis da conjuntura internacional.

Sob o ponto de vista educativo, a União Europeia tem vindo a construir mecanismos que determinam, como resultado de atitudes cooperativas, o estatuto da Europa enquanto centro de excelência no âmbito da educação e da formação em contexto internacional.

Sob o ponto de vista linguístico, através do Comissariado para o Multilinguismo, cuja criação se demonstrou imperativa, a União Europeia tem vindo a reforçar a defesa, no seu seio, do multilinguismo, como factor de promoção da diversidade linguística na sociedade e de uma economia multilingue dinâmica.

Enquadrado por este novo paradigma das relações entre Estados, o Instituto Camões projecta o seu agir em função da pertença da Língua Portuguesa a vários "espaços", estes entendidos como agrupamentos de países que se organizam em estruturas intergovernamentais.

Neste contexto, a Língua Portuguesa integra-se, naturalmente,

– no espaço europeu – **é uma Língua Europeia**,

mas também, sendo o Português Língua Oficial da **Comunidade dos Países de Língua Portuguesa**, é uma **Língua Africana** e uma **Língua Americana**, veículo de culturas e língua de diálogo de outras grandes organizações internacionais, como:

– a União Africana

e

– o Mercosul,

sendo ainda uma das duas línguas da área ibero-americana.

**2. O segundo vector sobre o qual temos vindo a assentar o nosso posicionamento em termos de uma *política para o multilinguismo*, relaciona-se com a natureza profunda do processo da globalização que radica na formação e funcionamento de mercados globais, ainda que não se esgote, é evidente, nesta dimensão**

Tendo em conta os dois vectores que acabei de identificar, o Instituto Camões, enquanto veículo de promoção e ensino da Língua Portuguesa no estrangeiro, posiciona-se face a uma política para o multilinguismo, com ópticas resultantes da conjugação de factores geopolíticos, geoeconómicos e geoculturais.

Assim:

As Línguas da União Europeia só podem existir plenamente, expressando todas as singularidades culturais e toda a sua relatividade, se os conceitos disfóricos de desintegração, marginalização, exclusão e desestruturação não forem conjugados. Esta premissa conduz-nos à defesa, na senda das propostas do Grupo de Intelectuais para o Diálogo Intercultural, constituído por iniciativa da Comissão Europeia, apresentadas sob o título *Um Desafio Salutar – Como a multiplicidade de Línguas poderia consolidar a Europa*, das seguintes medidas:

a) a preconização, pela União Europeia, da noção de *língua pessoal adoptiva*;

b) o uso, nas relações bilaterais entre os povos da União Europeia, das Línguas de cada um dos países;

c) o princípio da intercompreensão como base do alargamento da aprendizagem e da comunicação.

Dir-me-ão: tarefa impossível dados os custos e meios que acarretaria!

Deixo aqui, por isso, um desafio à EFNIL, que representa, no momento, 23 Línguas Europeias:

> Criar um programa segundo o qual os membros da EFNIL, individualmente ou por idiomas, de forma faseada e sistemática, em função do calendário desse programa, possam disponibilizar, on-line, nos seus sítios oficiais, matérias de aprendizagem e de ensino das Línguas que representam, constituindo, ainda, um gabinete de apoio pedagógico que pudesse responder às dúvidas dos professores estrangeiros que adoptassem os seus materiais.
>
> Os materiais de aprendizagem seriam feitos tendo em conta, por um lado, o Quadro Europeu Comum de Referência para as Línguas e, por outro, não só os níveis etários da população escolar – da educação pré-escolar ao ensino secundário –, mas também da população adulta, promovendo a aprendizagem ao longo da vida.

Deixando aqui este desafio, também expresso a disponibilidade do Instituto Camões para integrar o grupo de trabalho que concretizasse o programa que enquadraria esta iniciativa da EFNIL, indo ao encontro da tese defendida por Amin Maloouf, que presidiu ao Grupo de Intelectuais para o Diálogo Intercultural:

> Cada língua é o produto de uma experiência histórica única, cada uma é portadora de uma memória, de um património literário, de uma habilidade específica e constitui o fundamento legítimo de uma identidade cultural. As línguas não são permutáveis, nenhuma é dispensável, nenhuma é supérflua.
>
> Afinal, a multiplicidade de Línguas poderia consolidar a Europa.

Sintetizando o já mencionado, se cada Estado-Membro da União Europeia desenvolve as suas agendas de relações bilaterais, a União Europeia, como um todo, vem marcando as suas relações com várias "regiões" do mundo, negociando interesses comuns ou planetários, seja ao nível da segurança ou do ambiente, seja ao nível dos direitos humanos ou da economia.

E, chamo à colação, de novo, o trabalho *Um Desafio Salutar – Como a multiplicidade de Línguas poderia consolidar a Europa*, que afirma: *Que as relações com os diversos países sejam geridas principalmente por europeus que estudaram a língua do país em causa, a sua cultura, a sua sociedade, a sua história, as suas leis e as suas instituições é uma evolução desejável, que só pode trazer vantagens à União, a todos os níveis.*

Aqui, relevo a existência de Línguas Europeias que a História determinou serem Línguas também Africanas, Americanas, Asiáticas. Falo do Inglês, mas também falo do Francês, do Espanhol e do Português.

A população da União Europeia ascende a 495 milhões de cidadãos. O Francês, o Espanhol e o Português, mundialmente, são Línguas Maternas ou Línguas Segundas de mais de 850 milhões de falantes. O Português é de cerca de 240 milhões, enquanto realidade e ponte de diálogo das grandes economias ditas emergentes.

Contudo, não se entenda, através desta asserção, a defesa de uma política multilingue restritiva a um núcleo de *Línguas Europeias de Comunicação Global*.

A realidade cultural e histórica mundial, construída pelos mais diversos ciclos de mobilidade, deu origem a uma partilha de outras Línguas Europeias indissociáveis de matrizes culturais de grande relevância no pensamento e inspiração europeus. A tal propósito, cite-se o Alemão, o Neerlandês, o Polaco, o Italiano...

Para argumentar o segundo vector sobre o qual o Instituto Camões se posiciona para o seu agir, o da inter-relação globalização e mercados globais, irei apenas socorrer-me de um excerto do Relatório Final/Resumo do grupo de Alto Nível sobre o Multilinguismo.

Cito:

> Na sua comunicação de 2005, a Comissão, em conformidade com a Estratégia de Lisboa, reiterou a sua convicção de que a existência de competências em diversas línguas é importante para o desempenho económico de toda a EU, para a competitividade de cada empresa e para as perspectivas de emprego dos trabalhadores. Ainda, em finais de 2005, a Comissão solicitou a realização de um estudo intitulado "Efeitos na Economia Europeia da Escassez de Competências em Línguas Estrangeiras nas Empresas", ELAN. Este estudo à escala europeia, que confirmou a importância das competências linguísticas e interculturais para as exportações, foi o ponto de partida para o debate no Grupo acerca da importância das línguas para as empresas.
>
> O seguinte aspecto foi considerado particularmente relevante para o desenvolvimento das políticas e acções:
>
>> O ELAN deve ser complementado por estudos mais específicos a nível nacional ou regional, tendo em vista a apresentação de factos e números que possam impressionar e convencer tanto os organismos de natureza comercial como as autoridades públicas.

Neste contexto, o Instituto Camões encomendou, em Setembro de 2007, a uma instituição universitária portuguesa, o Instituto Superior de Ciências do Trabalho e da Empresa, um estudo sobre o *Valor Económico da Língua Portuguesa*, cuja metodologia, entre outros, o Professor José Paulo Esperança apresentará na sua comunicação: *Uma abordagem eclética do valor da língua: o uso global do Português*.

Neste estudo, o ISCTE lançou um inquérito aos estudantes e formandos da rede de docência do IC, que à altura integrava cerca de 250 instituições, com objectivos vários, destacando-se o de identificar os motivos por que os referidos estudantes investem no estudo da Língua e Cultura Portuguesas.

Lançaria agora um novo convite à EFNIL: desenvolver este estudo em rede, com a mesma metodologia ou uma metodologia próxima, de forma a EFNIL poder, como actor na nova diplomacia, intervir junto da Comissão Europeia no sentido de ***a Europa transformar a sua diversidade linguística numa vantagem verdadeiramente competitiva***. "As línguas são a alma do negócio; As línguas facilitam o funcionamento das empresas."[1]

[1] Fórum Empresarial para o Multilinguismo (*Languages mean business. Companies work better with languages.* Recommendations from the Business Forum for Multilingualism established by the European Commission. 2009).

## Welcome Notes

It is with the greatest pleasure that the Instituto Camões, now nearly eighty years old, hosts and opens the 6th Annual Conference of EFNIL in Lisbon by saluting Professor Gerhard Stickel for his dedication and the way in which he has led our Federation.

It falls to me, before this prestigious gathering, to express some thoughts about our work regarding *Languages in the 21st Century – New Values* and to address both the importance of and the challenges that languages can and must present in the age of globalisation, and specifically the European languages, particularly in view of the global scale on which they are shared between different countries and peoples.

Why is the IC the overseas carrier of Portugal's linguistic and cultural policy, and against which coordinates have we set out our position in terms of a *policy for multilingualism?*

### 1. Firstly, those of the new paradigm of the relations between States and their implications at various levels, particularly the cultural and linguistic level

This new paradigm has been described as a space for negotiation and agreement between sovereign States, in which international relations are not the be all and end all. A space in which they acquire transnational dimensions in societal interaction and are subject to their various dynamics. This demands of us a new way of thinking and acting. As with the States, new players are also active in the field of international relations: associations (such as EFNIL or EUNIC), scientists, thinkers, cultural and humanitarian players and indeed others, such as corporate networks of investments and firms at an international level.

Today, taking as premises on the one hand the idea of globalisation, and on the other hand the growing importance of the various agents in the internal development and external relations of each State, we are seeing new models of diplomacy, based on principles of cultural identity and intercultural dialogue, in close connection with economic development strategies planned by international conventions or organisations.

Thus, for example in the European Union, meetings and agreements between the Member States dictate what is to be defended vis-a-vis third parties, given the different levels of the international situation.

From an educational perspective, the European Union has been constructing mechanisms that determine, via collaboration, the status of Europe as a centre of excellence in the field of education and training in an international context.

From a linguistic perspective, through the Commission for Multilingualism, whose creation was shown to be imperative, the European Union has been strengthening the defence, within its boundaries, of multilingualism as a factor for promoting linguistic diversity in society, and a dynamic multilingual economy.

Framed by this new paradigm of relations between States, the Instituto Camões plans its activities as a function of the Portuguese language in various "spaces", these being understood as groups of countries that are organised into intergovernmental structures.

In this context, the Portuguese language naturally falls:

– in the European space **— it is a European language**,

However, as Portuguese is the official language of the **Comunidade dos Países de Língua Portuguesa** (Community of Portuguese-speaking Countries) it is also an **African Language** and an **American Language**, a vehicle of culture and the language of dialogue of other major international organisations, such as:

– The African Union

and

– Mercosul,

It is also one of the languages of Ibero-America.

**2. The second coordinate on which we have based our positioning in terms of a *policy for multilingualism* relates to the profound nature of the globalisation process, which has its roots in the formation and operation of global markets, although it is not confined, clearly, to this dimension**

Bearing in mind the two vectors that I have just identified, the Instituto Camões, as a vehicle for the promotion and teaching of Portuguese abroad, is well placed to manage a policy for multilingualism, with aims resulting from the combination of geopolitical, geo-economic and geo-cultural factors.

Thus:

The languages of the European Union can only exist fully, expressing all their cultural singularities and all their relativity, if the dysphoric concepts of disintegration, marginalisation, exclusion and destructuring do not come together. This premise leads us to defend, along the lines proposed by the Intellectuals' Group for Intercultural Dialogue, constituted at the initiative of the European Commission under the title *A Salutary Challenge – How the multiplicity of languages could consolidate Europe,* the following measures:

a) The advocating, by the European Union, of the notion of *an adoptive personal language*;

b) The use, in bilateral relations between the peoples of the European Union, of the languages of each of the countries concerned;

c) The principle of mutual understanding as the basis for widening communication and learning.

You will tell me that this is an impossible task, given the costs and resources that would be involved!

I now, therefore, throw down the gauntlet and challenge EFNIL, which currently represents 23 European languages:

> to create a programme by means of which EFNIL members, individually or by languages, in a phased and systematic form, as a function of this programme, could provide, online, on their official websites, material for teaching and learning the Languages that they represent, whilst also forming a pedagogic support office that could respond to any doubts voiced by foreign teachers who adopt their materials.
>
> The learning materials would be produced bearing in mind, on the one hand the Common European Frame of Reference for Languages, and, on the other hand, not only the age levels of the student populations – from pre-school education to secondary teaching – but also the adult population, thereby promoting lifelong learning.

Leaving this challenge here, I would also say that the Instituto Camões is willing to form part of the working party that would put together the programme of which this EFNIL initiative would form part, along the lines of the thesis proposed by Amin Maloouf, who chaired the Intellectuals' Group for Intercultural Dialogue:

> Every language is the product of a unique historical experience: each one carries a memory of a literary heritage, of a specific ability and constitutes the legitimate foundation of a cultural identity. Languages are not interchangeable, none is indispensable, none is superfluous.
>
> Finally, the multiplicity of languages could consolidate Europe.

In summarising the above, though each Member State of the European Union develops its agenda for bilateral relations, the European Union, as a whole, has been marking out its relations with various "regions" of the world, negotiating common or planetary interests, whether at a security or environmental level, or at an economic level.

I again draw to the conference's attention the work entitled *A Salutary Challenge – How the multiplicity of languages could consolidate Europe*, which asserts *that relations with the various countries are managed mainly by Europeans who have studied the language of the country in question, its culture, its society, its history, its laws and its institutions, is a desirable development, which can only bring advantages to the Union, at all levels.*

Here, I emphasise the existence of those European languages that history has determined would also be African, American and Asiatic languages: I am talking about English, but also about French, Spanish and Portuguese.

The population of the European Union stands at 495 million. French, Spanish and Portuguese, worldwide, are the mother tongues or second languages of more than 850 million speakers. Portuguese is spoken by about 240 million and in reality serves as a dialogue bridge for the major so-called emerging economies.

However, this assertion should not be understood to defend a multilingual policy restricted to a nucleus of *European Global Communication Languages*.

Worldwide cultural and historical reality, built up by the most diverse mobility cycles, has given rise to the sharing of other European languages that are inseparable from the cultural patterns of greatest relevance in European inspiration and thought. In this connection, we may cite German, Dutch, Polish or Italian, etc.

In arguing for the second vector on which the Instituto Camões positions itself in its activities, that of the interrelationship between globalisation and global markets, I will simply draw upon an excerpt from the Final Report/Summary of the High Level Group on Multilingualism.

I quote:

> In its 2005 communication, the Commission, in accordance with the Lisbon Strategy, reiterated its belief that the existence of skills in various languages is important for the economic performance of the EU as a whole, for the competitiveness of each company and for the employment prospects of workers. Also, in late 2005, the Commission arranged for a study to be carried out entitled "The Effects on the European Economy of a Scarcity of Skills in Foreign Languages in Companies" – ELAN. This study on a European level, which confirmed the importance of linguistic and intercultural skills for export, was the starting point for the debate in the Group about the importance of languages for companies.
>
> The following aspect was considered particularly relevant to the development of policies and actions:
>
>> The ELAN must be complemented by more specific studies at national or regional level, with the aim of presenting facts and figures that could impress and convince both bodies of a commercial nature and the public authorities.

In this context, in September 2007 the Instituto Camões commissioned a Portuguese University Institute, the Instituto Superior de Ciências do Trabalho e da Empresa, (Higher Institute of Work and Company Sciences) to produce a study of the *Economic Value of the Portuguese Language,* whose methodology, amongst others, will be introduced by Professor José Paulo Esperança in his speech entitled *An eclectic approach to the value of the language: the global use of Portuguese.*

In this study, the ISCTE conducted a survey of students and teachers on the IC teaching network, which at the time involved about 250 institutions, with various objectives, emphasising that of identifying the reasons why these students invested in studying Portuguese language and culture.

I would now make a new invitation to the EFNIL: to carry out this study in networked form, with the same methodology or a similar methodology, so that the EFNIL may, as a player in the new diplomacy, intervene with the European Commission in the sense of ***Europe transforming its linguistic diversity into a truly competitive advantage.*** "Languages are the soul of business; Languages facilitate the working of companies."[2]

---

2 Business Forum for Multilingualism (*Languages mean business. Companies work better with languages.* Recommendations from the Business Forum for Multilingualism established by the European Commission. 2009).

Gerhard Stickel

# Abertura / Opening

Senhora Secretaria de Estado,

excelências,

senhoras e senhores,

caros colegas:

tenho o prazer de saudá-los na abertura do sexto encontro anual da EFNIL, *Federação Européia das Instituições Nacionais para as Línguas.* Assim como há cinco anos, escolhemos novamente um tema especialmente importante para a situação lingüística em nossos países, bem como para a política de línguas nacional e européia: *A Utilização da Língua nos Negócios e no Comércio na Europa.* A Comissão Européia já tem se ocupado deste tema há algum tempo. Por esta razão, alegro-me com a presença dos vários representantes de instituições públicas européias. Tenho também o prazer de saudar os representantes de organizações européias aos quais o tema seja provavelmente ainda mais próximo do que a nós lingüistas e planeadores. Alegra-nos também que colegas de organizações lingüísticas afins tenham atendido ao nosso convite. Àqueles que não estão diretamente envolvidos pode parecer estranho que diversas organizações de especialistas estejam engajadas a favor da diversidade lingüística européia. Em vista dos muitos aspectos e da complexidade de nossas línguas, não existe concorrência, mas uma contínua divisão de trabalho. Contudo, até o momento não há um trabalho conjunto em termos concretos. Seria do interesse de nosso objetivo comum se pudéssemos utilizar este encontro também para discutir possibilidades concretas de cooperação.[1]

(Let me now stop pretending to be fluent in Portuguese and change to English.)

Before I make a few comments on our present topic, I will briefly recall the general themes of our previous conferences in order to demonstrate a certain thematic coherence and continuity of the activities of EFNIL. At the founding conference in Stockholm in 2003, we heard and discussed reports on changes of linguistic domains and on

[1] I salute you to the 6th Annual Conference of EFNIL, the *European Federation of National Institutions for Language.* As in the previous five years, we have chosen again a theme of special importance for the linguistic situation in our countries and, correspondingly, for national and European language policy: *Language Use in Business and Commerce in Europe.* Since some time, the European Commission has also been occupying itself with this topic. I am very glad, therefore, that several representatives of European authorities have come to this conference. I am also glad to welcome representatives of European professional organizations who have an even closer connection to this theme than we linguists and language planners. We are also pleased that colleagues from similar language organizations accepted our invitation. For an outsider, it may be surprising that several organizations of language specialists are dealing with the European linguistic diversity. In view of the many aspects and the complexity of our languages, there is, however, no competition but rather division of labor. Until now, there has been little co-operation. It would be fortunate in the interest of our common goals if this conference could also be used to explore avenues for concrete co-operation.

language legislation in several European countries. In Paris 2004, we dealt with co-operation in terminology work and translation. The theme of our conference in Brussels 2005 was *Plurilingual Europeans in multilingual Europe: language learning and language policy*. In Madrid 2006, we treated *Pluricentric languages in multilingual Europe*, and finally, in Riga 2007, our topic was *National and European language policies*. The contributions to last year's conference have recently appeared as a book publication that was included in your conference documents.

Now, at this conference, the general theme is *Language Use in Business and Commerce in Europe*. The esteemed previous speakers already stressed the importance of this topic from a European perspective and the perspective of our hosting country. Let me briefly discuss the interest that EFNIL and its member institutions take in this topic. At first sight, none of our members are particularly engaged in business and commerce. Some of us produce dictionaries, grammars, or teaching materials for the instruction of our languages as first or foreign languages. The commercial aspect of these activities is, however, in most cases only peripheral. Some of us co-operate also in the development of terminologies for various fields of industry and trade, again without being directly involved in industrial or commercial processes. Thus, why should we care about the linguistic aspects of business and commerce? The answers come from linguistics as a descriptive science and from the fields of language planning and language policy. One of the fathers of modern linguistics Ferdinand de Saussure conceived language as a 'fait social', a social fact. Contemporary linguistics does not limit the description of a language to just a repertoire of sounds, words, and grammatical patterns, but also studies the actual use of language within the domains of a linguistic community, that is, within the different social and situational contexts with regard to the purposes for which the language is being used. Because of their importance for a society, the various realms of business and commerce are especially interesting domains of language use. All speakers of a language are, in some way or another, subject to communication in business and/or commerce, be it as workers, administrators, or managers of a production firm, as employees of a bank or a trading company, or most often as customers of the products and services offered by industry and commerce. Thus, the specific linguistic forms and uses of language within industry and trade are interconnected with verbal communication in other domains. The phenomena of the professional uses of language have been studied in linguistics since the late 19th century under headings such as *languages for special purposes* (*LSP*), *langues techniques*, *lenguajes técnicos*, *Fachsprachen*, *vaktaalen*, etc.

In LSP linguistics, we sometimes make a rough distinction that might also be useful for our discussion at this conference, the division into three spheres or subdomains of language uses of an industry or a trade:[2] (1) First, the language of theory, that is, primarily the terminology of the science or sciences relevant for a particular industry or trade, for instance, the linguistic specifics of physics, chemistry, engineering, etc. relevant for

[2] See: Hahn, Walter v. (1973): Fachsprachen. In: *Lexikon der Germanistischen Linguistik*. Hg. v. Altmann, Hans Peter u.a. Tübingen, p. 283-269. Ischreyt, Heinz (1965): *Studien zum Verhältnis von Sprache und Technik*. Düsseldorf, p. 41ff.

the automobile industry, or the terminology of business administration and economics used by trading companies or banks. (2) The second subdomain is the language of workshops, that is, the language use among insiders, for instance, in a chemical factory laboratory, in the workshop of an automobile plant, or in the offices of a trading company or a bank. (3) The third subdomain, finally, is the language of distribution, that is, the use of language for selling products or services to customers, many of whom are laymen in the particular field of an industry or trade. Language of distribution, of course, also includes the language use in advertising.

Research in many languages has found ample evidence that language use in the various professional domains and the general use of a language mutually influence each other. Traditional linguistics has concentrated on languages for special purposes as varieties of one and the same language and considered other languages only when lexical items of a technical vocabulary were taken as loan words from another language. The planned and unplanned development of terminologies for the various domains of business and commerce took an important role in the development of those languages that are also used as official standard languages in our countries, one of the reasons why our topic is relevant for EFNIL.

As with natural sciences, technologies, and humanities, the special terminologies of business and commerce have, for centuries, been subject to exchange and borrowing between European languages. One has only to remember that parts of the banking terminology of several European languages were taken from Italian or that a great number of terms in the automobile and railway industry of many countries originated in French or English. The common Latin roots of many items of the technical terminologies of almost all European languages have also to be mentioned.

Since several decades, the linguistic situation of business and commerce has become more complex in most countries. The influence of other languages on the professional communication in these domains as in some other fields is no longer limited to the borrowing and adaptation of single foreign words or phrases, but extends to the use of other languages, especially English, besides or instead of the individual national language. This is of special interest not only for descriptive linguistics but also for language planning and language policy in the various countries and regions because it concerns also the terminology work done for the official language(es) of each country. If another language is used for professional communication in particular domains, terminology work for the individual standard language would become superfluous and pointless. But there are even more important reasons for our interest in the linguistic conditions of business and commerce in our countries.

It took several centuries to emancipate the various European languages from Latin and to develop them into standard languages that can be used in all domains for all communicative purposes. We all know that until the early modern age the common language of political, religious, and scientific domains of most European countries and regions was Latin. The rise of national languages was a slow process that took for some languages until the 19th century to develop into *Ausbausprachen*, as the German sociolinguist Heinz Kloss[3] used to say, that is, into fully developed languages that exist not just in regional varieties limited to local and private domains but are also used as standard varieties for literature, science, politics, business, and trade. They are the languages the members of EFNIL are mainly concerned with.

Since not later than the middle of the last century, the process of developing language varieties into comprising standard languages for all communicative purposes seems to be being gradually reversed, that is, the traditional European standard languages have begun to lose some of their domains of professional communication to English or a globalised variety of English. This has been described and discussed in detail for the language use in science. As we know, most physicists, chemists, biologists, and other natural scientists do not publish in their native languages any longer but in English. Some of them even teach in English and – as I do now – read their conference papers in English. I will not discuss this here. However, it should be plausible that if this process goes on, European languages such as Swedish, German, Portuguese, Polish, and others that developed their professional varieties over centuries will lose certain professional domains and after some time cannot be used any longer for communication in these domains. Since the language use in professional domains also has influence on the general use of a language, the future development of various European languages will not be mainly influenced by language internal processes of their professional domains but increasingly by English as an international LSP. This is considered by many linguistic patriots, as we may call them, as detrimental to the present and future development of their native languages. Cultural critics see it as a danger for the linguistic diversity of Europe as a whole that is essential for the cultural diversity and wealth of our continent.

On the other hand, there are obvious practical reasons for the use of other languages besides or instead of the individual national language, especially in business and commerce. Many industries and trades are internationally interlaced and have an increasing demand for communication with partners and customers in other linguistic communities. Thus, the use of a common vehicular language, a *lingua franca*, seems to suggest itself for contacts between speakers of different native languages. And this way out is, apparently, being taken by an increasing number of industries and trade companies of our countries that use English as a universal auxiliary language for their international business contacts, and in some cases, also for internal communication. In this connection, one of the questions we would like to have answers for is: To what extent is English being used in business and commerce **besides** the official languages of the various countries and to what extent is it being used **instead** of the national language of the countries. The answers will, probably, differ not only depending on the type of industry or trade and on the various countries but also on the three subdomains of the LSPs I sketched before, that is, communication in the field of professional theory, within the actual workshops, and in the distribution of goods and services.

---

[3] Kloss, Heinz (1978): *Die Entwicklung neuer germanischer Kultursprachen seit 1800*. 2. erw. Aufl. Düsseldorf: Schwann.

Recent studies showed that the tendency towards professional bilingualism of the individual official language and English in business and commerce may not only be detrimental to the national languages of the countries in question but may also have economical disadvantages. Due to the international interconnection and interlacement of most industries and trades in Europe and beyond, these disadvantages cannot, of course, be avoided by going back to national monolingual communication. On the contrary, there are, apparently, findings and arguments for an increased use of more than just two languages in business and commerce. Some of them have been recently presented under the heading *Languages mean business. Companies work better with languages* as *Recommendations from the Business Forum for Multilingualism established by the European Commission.*[4] I will refrain from quoting or summarizing these recommendations. Some of you are familiar with them and others can easily find them on the internet. For us, the actual research behind these recommendations is of greater interest, especially the ELAN report. Therefore, I am very glad that we could win several scholars who were engaged in research for ELAN and in similar studies as speakers for this conference. It is my pleasure to welcome these guest speakers and to thank them for presenting us some of their findings and the conclusions drawn from them. Let me also give our thanks in advance to those of our colleagues from several member institutions who will report on the situation in their countries with regards to the general theme of this conference.

In order not to steal from the time of the following speakers, let me hasten to give our thanks, last but by no means least, to our member organization, the Instituto Camoes, for hosting this conference. Final thanks will have to wait until the closing session tomorrow afternoon before many of us will depart. However, the fact that so many of us have come and are here in this hall now is convincing empirical proof that the preparation of this event has been successful. Let me also take the occasion to give special thanks to the president of the Instituto Camoes Simonetta Luz Afonso. She is guilty, I should better say, responsible for having EFNIL meet here, because she invited us two years ago to hold our annual conference 2008 here in Lisbon, the city that is also known in all member states of the Union as the city of the European Reform Treaty.

Let us now continue our work on this year's theme.

Thank you for your attention.

Vielen Dank!

Merci beaucoup!

Muite obregado!

---

4 The recommendations can be found on the Internet under: http://ec.europa.eu/commission_barroso/orban/docs/business_papers/davignon_en.pdf.

Stephen Hagen

# Mapping successful language use in international business: How, when and where do European companies achieve success?

In 2006, the first major all-Europe study ('ELAN') was undertaken of the use of languages by 2000 companies in 29 countries engaged in international business and commerce. The objective was to review the extent to which language skills were being managed by companies across Europe and the extent to which they enhanced trading prospects and business performance. The study revealed some startling findings: firstly, a significant amount of business may be being lost as a result of missing skills in languages and intercultural competence. Secondly, there is an apparent correlation between how more successful companies manage their use of languages. Thirdly, future growth trends in the study suggest which language skills will be needed for global (and local) markets and there may be changes in the role of English as the world's current *lingua franca* of business. While the study provides useful information on a wide spectrum of language use in European business, it also offers key recommendations for policy initiatives at European level, as well as for business and education, on ways of addressing language gaps and improving cross-border trade.

## 1. Studies which measure language and intercultural barriers as trade tariff equivalents

At the national level, different languages may be thought of as *a tax on trade*, according to Foreman-Peck (2007). For this reason, ELAN has incorporated data on companies' own evaluation of their lost business. For example, if a company's language skills are inadequate, they can reduce the opportunity for identifying profitable trade. The 'tax' is less, the more widespread the existence of language competence is in potential trading partners. The common language effect captures some of the trade diversion of language barriers. For example, in the case of the UK, the boost to well being from the reduction of even a one percent tax on British exports, that amount to one quarter of GDP, can be substantial, for it is equivalent to a similar rise in productivity; 1% of 25% of GDP is 0.25 percent, more than 4.4 billion Euro, from the 2005 GDP figure. On top of the direct effects of reducing the 'tax effects' of language deficiencies on exports are the productivity gains from accessing a wider market (Foreman-Peck 2007).

Frankel (1997), Frankel/Rose (2002), and Helliwell (1999) measure language differences as *trade barriers* and have quantified the costs of language barriers as between 15%-22% in terms of tariff equivalents. They also estimate that sharing a common language can increase bilateral trade by between 75% and 170%. However, Noguer/Siscart (2003) estimate that the tariff equivalent of language as a trade barrier is a modest 6% and the value of sharing a common language to be just 11%. The Noguer/Siscart (2003) model, however, points to a series of key variables:

- Measures of political and colonial association are likely determinants of current trade flows and are potentially correlated with sharing a common language;

- Price indices are implicit functions of bilateral trade barriers and any measure of the impact of language barriers on trade should account for their effect on the price indices;
- Adjacency: common languages are often spoken in countries sharing a common border;
- Political and free trade unions: we would expect the older members of the EU (who form a closer union) to have greater volumes of inter-trade.

Noguer/Siscart (2003) further argue that language barriers vary across sectors: the tariff equivalent of language barriers is close to zero they say in sectors such as agriculture, mining, petroleum refineries, iron & steel and food. However, there are large tariff equivalents of language barriers in printing & publishing (18%); clothing (14%); professional, scientific and controlling equipment (10%). Language barriers also adversely affect international integration through the effect on factor markets, notably migration and capital flows, and hamper intra-national social harmony.

The use of foreign languages in the export process can also be hypothesised as a separate variable in the successful internationalisation of SMEs within Westhead's definition of 'export capable' firms, though he does not refer to it specifically (Westhead et al. 2002). A fruitful method of enquiry is also to isolate the situations, or critical points of contact with the foreign customer at which use of the foreign language (or cultural competence) had its greatest impact. In ELAN, for example, a series of such situational variables (or *tipping points*) are tested to identify at which points individuals in companies are more likely to lose trade. There are, however, other factors at play; for example, cultural differences and the behavioural characteristics of managers.

## 2. Cultural and behavioural factors

Significant work has taken place in defining cultural differences and a series of analytical frameworks exist (Shenkar 2001). Following the example of such figures as Hofstede and Trompenaars, many academic researchers have done work in the field of cross-cultural management. Transnational firms no longer have a single national culture, in the present global communication age collaborative cross-cultural learning is increasingly necessary to generate real understanding.

According to Langhoff (1977), a firm's competence in dealing with managerial issues across markets is based on three different, but related abilities:
- coping with cultural heterogeneity across different international markets,
- harmonizing its products and services and their marketing with the symbolic learning which target markets in different cultures assign them, and
- identifying and exploiting new opportunities in foreign cultural contexts in expectation of gaining longer lasting competitive advantage.

Intercultural problems arising from the use of IT have been identified relatively recently. Russo/Boor (1993) suggest ways in which programme interface designers might develop their products for optimal use by people from different cultures.

While SMEs in the transition economies of eastern Europe identified price, product uniqueness and quality as the main competitive advantage in exporting, establishing good *customer relationships* is a key feature. For example, this can translate into customer relations. When the low-cost economies in eastern Europe rise to price parity with western European, competitive advantage (and the companies' survival) will increasingly depend on quality of service; notably, how well they understand and treat their customers. In other words, whether they can operate successfully in the customer's culture of expectation.

The language component is only one of many factors in successful exporting, Wolff/ Pett (2000) have previously suggested that organisational factors and environmental conditions play a key role in successful exporting, alongside linguistic competence. The *British Chambers of Commerce language survey* (BCC 2004), however, placed a particular emphasis on the attitude of individual managers in companies. It identified and segmented the different behaviours and attitudes held by individual exporters based in the UK in relation to trading in overseas markets and profile them, taking into account their motivations, ambitions, education and language competence.

## 3. Is there an impact on companies' bottom-lines?

The BCC study found that different behaviours on the part of export managers, including use of languages, are associated with different types of export performance in their companies. It identified four different profiles of export managers based in the UK, taking into account their motivations, ambitions, education and individual language competence and classifying them as (from the least proactive to the most): *opportunist*, *developer*, *adaptor* and *enabler*. These behavioural styles were then linked with different types of export performance in their companies. The survey found there was a direct correlation between the value an individual export manager placed on language skills within their business and annual turnover.

The most important finding of the *British Chambers of Commerce language survey* was the direct correlation between the value an individual export manager places on language skills within their business and their annual turnover. Only 33% of *Opportunists* have an annual export turnover above €750,000. This increases to 54% for *Developers*, 67% for *Adapters* and 77% for *Enablers*, who place the most value on language skills within their business. Moreover, export sales by *Opportunists* (the segment that least values language skills) are declining by an average of €75,000 a year per exporter, while *Enablers*' (the segment placing the highest value on language skills) exports are increasing by an average of €440,000 a year per exporter.

## 4. The ELAN research findings

The critical findings for the study are whether companies report having experienced loss of trade as a result of language and/or cultural deficiencies. Similar survey and studies have taken place (Hagen 1988, 1993, 1999, 2005), but ELAN is the most comprehensive of these that has sought to measure the impact of language skills on the success of individual companies, as well as offering a hypothesis on the macro-European economic perspective.

The questions on this aspect were phrased in a very direct manner, requiring respondents to identify lost contracts due to language and cultural problems. This contrasts with earlier studies which tended to measure 'communication barriers' rather than estimating impact. Not unexpectedly, it is a mixture of recent accession, candidate members (Romania, Turkey) and Scandinavian countries (three over 20%: Finland, Denmark, Sweden; and Norway lower at 16%, but still high) which tended to score more highly on this particular index than western European members. In the case the Nordic countries, there have always been greater awareness of the need to speak other people's languages, since their languages are not widely spoken. Turkish (and Finnish) exporters appear to have the greatest difficulties at 26%. However, across the sample, there is evidence that between 11% and 15% of SMEs in Spain, Italy, Sweden, Bulgaria and Norway appear to be losing trade due to language deficiencies. Evidence of loss is far less marked in the cultural domain (on average 4%), where, with the exception of Sweden (12%), Finland (10%) and Iceland (9%), the incidence of lost contracts is in single percentages for most countries. However, when companies were asked about encountering cultural barriers, as opposed to *losing contracts*, there was a significant upward shift in awareness in (notably) the Scandinavian/Nordic countries (Norway 42%; Iceland 39%; Sweden 37%; Finland 30%), where the European average was 18%. There was also an above-average response in more recent accession members, namely, Romania, Czech Republic and Hungary. There appears to be greater concerns in the more recent and geographically peripheral members of the European Union.

## 5. Potential loss of trade across Europe

The survey of SMEs in ELAN found that this could potentially add up to a significant amount of business is being lost to European enterprise as a result of lack of language and/or cultural skills. Across the sample of nearly 2000 businesses, 11% of respondents (195 SMEs) had lost a contract as a result of lack of language skills. Many were unable or unwilling to indicate the size of the contract lost, but 37 businesses declared they had lost actual contracts which together were valued at between 8 million and 13.5 million Euro. A further 54 businesses had lost potential contracts worth in total between 16.5 million and 25.3 million Euro. At least 10 businesses had lost contracts worth over 1 million Euro. Clearly, the survey identified only those situations where companies were aware of the actual business lost or potentially lost, and the real unknown, or undeclared, figure is likely to be much greater. Hypothetically, if the proportion of businesses losing trade through lack of language skills were repeated across the whole EU exporting SME sector, we could calculate conservatively that at least 945,000 European SMEs may be losing trade as a result of lack of language competence. The average loss per business over a three year period is 325,000. If we multiply this by the number of businesses we estimate to be losing trade, the total losses to the EU economy through lack of language skills in the SME sector are in the region of 100 billion per year. SMEs experience intercultural as well as language barriers when operating across borders. In all but eight countries out of 29, more than 10% of respondents were aware of having encountered intercultural difficulties *additional to* linguistic problems.

## 6. Future language needs

Many companies in the samples recognise they will need to acquire additional language skills and, to a lesser extent, intercultural communication skills to enable them to meet their future trading plans (see Table 1).

This question is perhaps a clearer indicator of how companies assess their own language needs against their future export plans. Again, the recent accession members and candidates consistently expect a higher demand for language skills than most established member-countries. There are expectations of the need to export into new markets which will require new linguistic expertise. For example, 88% of Romanian and 71% of Bulgarian companies in the sample acknowledge they will need export-related language skills in future markets (and 69% in Turkey) where the average for the European sample is 42%. In a surprisingly high number and range of other countries (Spain, Latvia, Austria, Cyprus, Finland, Germany, Iceland, Hungary, Iceland) 50% or over expect they will need new language skills. Their need for particular languages is reflected in the all-European sample below.

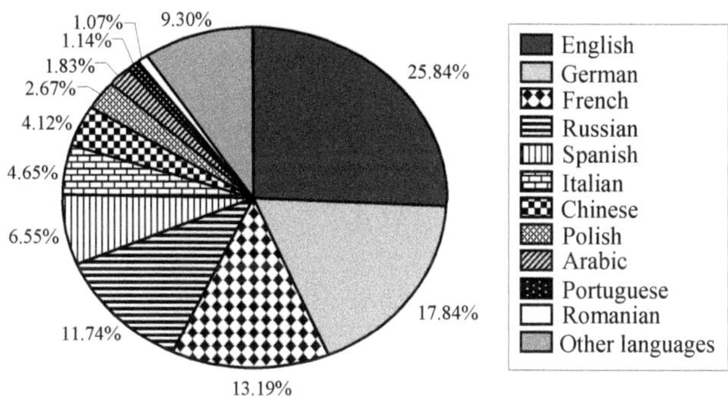


Table 1: The future language needs of SMEs in ELAN survey

If we compare SME language needs with future multinational company needs (defined in ELAN as operating in at least 10 European countries), we see that English is relatively stable between the two groups: SME 26%; multinational (over 250 personnel): 29%. German will apparently not be needed by multinational companies (SME: 18%, large: 0%); French is needed by 13% of SMEs, but only 6% of multinational companies; Russian very similar to French. However, four languages, apart from English, appear to be in greater need: Spanish (SME: 7%, multinational: 20%); Chinese (SME 4%, multinational: 17%); Arabic (SME: 2%, multinational: 10%) and Portuguese (SME: 1%, multinational: 6%).

Individual SME respondents mentioned that English might be used for initial market entry, but longer-term business partnerships depended upon relationship building. Thereafter, cultural and linguistic knowledge of the target country were essential. There was, however, widespread evidence of Anglophone complacency, an over-reliance on English, which is not restricted to Anglophone countries.

Skills in understanding business ways in particular countries, i.e. new intercultural skills, are also likely to be required, averaging one in five of the companies. Need is strongest amongst recent or candidate countries, i.e. Romanian and Bulgarian companies (over 40%), while Iceland is even higher (53%), again, there is an element either of geographical isolation or, for new and recent member of the EU, the recognition of the need to understand the cultures of future European trading partners better.

## 7. Solutions to overcoming barriers: The language (or communication) strategy

There is widespread recognition of the value of language strategies across most countries, except the UK where there is apparent evidence of complacency. There is now a significant body of evidence which points to the economic value of companies adopting a language, or communication strategy. Defined in ELAN as "having in place planned mechanisms for dealing with language and cultural problems in given markets", nearly half Europe's international companies argue they already have a language strategy in place. Moreover, it is clear that there are a range of actions which companies and organisations can take that will enhance their export performance.

The ELAN Report shows that there is a correlation between a company adopting four specific elements of language management and disproportionately higher success. In other words, companies which have *a developed language strategy*, *appointed native speakers*, *recruited staff specifically with language skills and used translators/interpreters*, appear to be more successful at trading. However, it should always be borne in mind that correlation is not causation. Conversely, the main reasons given for companies losing trade are: *lack of staff speaking languages*, *lack of follow-up* and *lack of confidence* (*to deal with foreign customers*). They also report particular situations, or tipping points, where loss of business due to communication is more likely: switchboard problems, difficulties handling agents and distributors; lack of cultural affinity. However, the conclusion is that the greater the awareness of the issues the better, but then exporters need guidance on how to implement the particular strategy for their environment.

How does the proportion of sales abroad vary by country and by resources invested in languages? All four language investments (*a language strategy*, *employment of nationals*, *language skills acquisition*, *and use of translators*) help boost sales abroad, but agents do not (nor are they a hindrance). Taking the variable 'acquiring or training staff with language skills' as an example, with a coefficient of 0.7 in the 'proportion of export sales' equation, at the sample mean, the export sales proportion is driven up by 16.6 percentage points by this variable. An SME with all four investments may hypothetically achieve an export sale proportion 44.5 percentage points higher than an SME with none of these investments.

Bulgaria, Sweden, Luxemburg, and Iceland show positive country effects. That is they sell more abroad, controlling for skills and other language resources. Italy, France, Spain, Romania, Portugal, Latvia, Greece and Hungary show significant negative effects. These (generally negative) country effects can be even larger than the impact of individual types of foreign language investments.

Individual country effects estimated in the export sales equation can be compared with *Eurobarometer* scores on the grounds that the likelihood of nationals already possessing foreign language expertise may influence export performance. The *Eurobarometer* survey of the number of other languages spoken by the population in European countries placed the UK at the bottom and Luxembourg at the top with 244 percent as the aggregate of percentages claiming to speak non-mother tongues. Hungary came next to the UK and then Ireland – a matter of more significance for Hungary than for Ireland and the UK, who can deal in a widespread international language. Portugal, Poland and Turkey all score under 50% on the *Eurobarometer* scale. Consistent with this score, Portugal has the largest negative country effect in our analysis, followed by Spain (low on *Eurobarometer* with 54%) and then the UK. Luxemburg also has the second largest positive country effect consistent with Eurobarometer (Iceland is not recorded). Sweden has a high *Eurobarometer* score (126%) and shows a positive country effect in the first 'sales abroad 'model. The surprise is the Bulgarian country effect when the Eurobarometer records only 51%. One source of divergence between the *Eurobarometer* and the export model is of course that having a population able to speak a language will not help exports if it is not the language of the target markets for exports.

## 8. Other measures taken by companies to address communication gaps

If the market is working, then SMEs will acquire language skills when their value to the firm exceeds their cost. This will depend on SMEs' export markets, both current and projected, as well as on the skills of their established staff. The UK, Iceland, Cyprus and Lithuania are less likely to have acquired language skilled staff – perhaps because they do not need to, whereas the Czech Republic, France, Romania, Spain, and Hungary are more likely to have done so. Possessing a language strategy increases the likelihood of acquiring language skills, as does employing nationals, translators and agents, as well as sales abroad. For those countries that affirmed having hired staff with specific languages skills due to export needs: 18% of the firms hired staff with German knowledge for export needs to German, while 9% of the firms hired staff with French skills for exporting to France. It is worth noticing that the companies also hired staff with English skills for exporting needs to Germany, the Middle East and Netherlands.

Nearly half of companies in the total ELAN SME (49%) sample already offer language training to their employees. Some appear more committed than others. There is a discrepancy between companies that *offer* and those *undertaking* language training. The latter is much lower. The major users of language training appear to be companies in: Czech Republic (79%), Spain, Austria, Slovakia, Luxembourg, Finland and Germany. A number of interviewees from smaller companies identified that language training was mainly a pastime of the 'larger' companies. The medium sized and small companies could simply not afford to invest in this training and thus their profits suffer. Of those interviewed in the Czech Republic, 40% mentioned the problem of small and medium sized companies not having the resources for language training. Furthermore, 60% of those interviewed from Lithuania commented upon the problem. One said that now not only the larger companies in Lithuania but also the medium sized ones were waking up to the idea of a language strategy, which was clearly only a luxury that the larger companies could afford before this.

On average, 22% of the firms have employed native speakers who also support their foreign communication needs. This is a growing trend and it is being encouraged by higher mobility across the EU and the impact of globalization on jobs.

## 9. Are large companies very different?

Dhir/Goke-Pariola (2002) analyse multinational language planning in large corporates and the development of language policies. They identify how managing cultural diversity and linguistic complexity can be turned into a critical asset for large companies in the global knowledge-based economy. Knapp (1997) illustrates that the difficulties of communication between employees of the German headquarters of a large business company and the staff of its British subsidiary.

Indeed, with the projected growth of international operations, additional international business education programs would need to be developed, particularly programs with a focus on Asia. At the very least, they argued, all business graduates needed to have an *appreciation for cross-cultural differences* and *a global perspective*. Additional training programs, both degree and non-degree, were also needed to provide management personnel with the higher levels of knowledge needed to address the competitive challenges of the global business environment.

Large companies in the ELAN study (with a sample of 30) also prefer to recruit staff with language skills rather than train pre-existing staff. Of the companies, 73% of them had a widely practised scheme of recruiting language-skilled employees whereas only 45% had a programme of intercultural training for managers. Companies are clearly aware of language skills but they would rather employ staff with language skills than undertake possibly expensive training schemes for managers and employees. In an analysis of the language of business transactions, English is not so exclusively used for international trade transactions as might be imagined: while English may be the predominant language in international business for most of these European companies, there is also significant use of French, German, Italian and Spanish as foreign languages; clear evidence of the importance of the use of Scandinavian languages in Denmark; and small, but noticeable use of East Asian languages, such as Chinese and Japanese, in Scotland.

However, only half of the multinational companies surveyed regularly audited their available language skills against their needs. This would certainly suggest a lack of language planning and strategising on the part of these Companies, and some SMEs were further ahead in this regard. Furthermore, 73% had no language departments or had tried to start one, but abandoned it. However, they usually had a vigorous and watchful recruitment strategy.

Prior to ELAN, the most recent work on language policies and their implementation in larger, or global, companies is *Talking Sense*, a research study into the management of language skills in major companies. (Feely/Winslow, 2005). The analysis is based on a sample of 151 companies, the majority having their global headquarters based in the UK, Germany and France. Respondents to the survey evaluated each of these nine modes of language management on a scale from 1 (the company has not employed this method) to 4 (the method is widely practised throughout the company). An aggregate Language Management score was then calculated by summing the nine responses and reducing the totals to a scale of 1 to 10. The study found that French and German companies were generally more flexible than the UK companies, offering to work in a mix of languages or in neutral English, where they could not work in their partners' language. Only a handful of French and German companies expected to work in their own language and this applied not only to customers and joint venture partners, but also to suppliers and subsidiaries.

## 10. Comments from study participants

There were a range of comments from participants from different countries, which give important personal insights into how important some companies view language competence:

- "The personal contact with foreign customer is necessary for every method of trade; it is not just a question of the language capabilities of negotiators, but also of the technical support of the product" (Czech Republic).
- "Improved communication (written and verbal) in foreign languages and a better understanding of cultural differences will have an important impact on doing business abroad successfully" (Belgium).
- "They enable to receive better information about the business environment and new ideas about production, raw materials, marketing and trade channels" (Estonia).
- "It will lead to an increased volume of the export activity and also to a more professional and smooth business communication within international business partnerships" (Romania).
- "Those who are involved in foreign relations are – as the survey showed – able to hire the employees with the necessary language skills" (Hungary).

## 11. Conclusions

Lack of a common language is a barrier to trade. Overcoming the barrier is costly but there are widespread benefits from doing so that may warrant public intervention. Information shortcomings, network effects, problems arising from the indivisibility of substantial investments in language skills, complementarities between firm-specific skills and languages, and uncertainty, all suggest that underinvestment in overcoming the language barrier to exporting may be particularly marked for smaller firms. The payoff from effective intervention in language investment could be large (Foreman-Peck 2007).

These payoffs normally cannot be measured by market returns to individuals' investment in language skills. In the absence of barriers, higher than 'normal' returns will encourage more investment that will, in due course, eliminate excess payoffs. Moreover, Studies in the dynamics of the small firm have suggested that, in general, SMEs are less productive than large companies. Research also indicates, though, that exporting SMEs are more productive than those which do not export and that there is often a hidden bonus for exporting companies through exposure to increased technical know-how, market-awareness and cost or efficiency savings.

Given that SMEs account for more than fifty percent of employment within the European Union, it would thus appear that, if a greater number of SMEs were to become successful exporters, and if those currently exporting were to expand their markets, there would be a significant impact on the European economy and also that there could be considerable additional benefits in terms of greater innovation and market-awareness, which in turn could impact on productivity within national economies.

ELAN's findings support the argument for investment in language skills for a range of SMEs. Investment in language skills represents one of the fixed costs of exporting to certain countries. Thus the analysis of the management and impact of this investment by business represents critical information for governments and support agencies concerned with the economic health of the small business sector. The outcomes of the Study, moreover, demonstrate the real possibility of measuring the impact of language skills on economic performance. Four elements of language management were found to be correlated with successful export performance: *having a language strategy, appointing native speakers, recruiting staff with language skills and using translators/interpreters*.

An SME investing in these four elements was calculated to achieve a potential export sales proportion 44.5% higher than one without these investments. Assuming a model where SMEs accounted for 45% of output (the range across the EU is 30%-60%) and supposing that half of the SMEs responsible for that output adopted the four language management elements listed above, we could speculate that exports would rise by an astonishing 10% of GDP – equivalent to more than 1 trillion Euro. Furthermore, it is likely that there would be productivity gains from exporting which would wash back to the internal economy. Total Factor Productivity for exporters can be as much as 3.7% higher than the industry mean. A 3.7% productivity spill-over from exporting could imply a very substantial additional impact from these investments in language skills – 3.7% of 10% of GDP is 0.037% of GDP, which for the EU as a whole, is equivalent to over 4 billion Euro.

## 12. References

Brake, T./Medina Walker, D./Walker, T. (1995): *Doing business internationally – the guide to cross cultural success*. New York/London: McGraw-Hill.

British Chambers of Commerce (BCC) (2003, 2004): *The impact of foreign languages on British business*. British Chambers of Commerce/LSC November 2003 (Qualitative results) and May 2004 (Quantitative results).

Centre for Information on Language Teaching and Research (CILT) (2005): *Talking World Class: the impact of language skills on the UK economy*. London: CILT.

Dhir, K.S./Goke-Pariola, A. (2002): The Case for Language Policies in Multinational Corporations. In: *Corporate Communications: An International Journal*, 7, 4, 241-251.

ELAN Study (2006): *Effects on the European economy of shortages of foreign language skills in enterprise*. Report Commissioned by the European Commission, published by CILT and European Commission, December 2006. (PI: Stephen Hagen).

Eurobarometer: www.europa.eu.int/comm/education/policies/lang/languages/lang/europeanlanguages_en.html.

Feely, A./Winslow, D. (2005): *Talking sense: a research study of languages skills management in major companies*. London: CILT.

Foreman-Peck, J. (2007): *Costing Babel: the contribution of language skills to SME exporting and productivity in the UK*. Paper prepared and published by CILT, the National UK Centre for Languages, August 2007. London: CILT.

Frankel, J. (1997): *Regional trading blocks*. Washington, DC: Institute for International Economics.

Frankel, J./Rose, A.K. (2002): An estimate of the effect of common currencies on trade and income. In: *The Quarterly Journal of Economics*, 117, 2, 437-466.

Hagen, S. (Ed.) (1988): *Languages in British business. An analysis of current needs*. Newcastle: 'Unique' – University of Northumbria Publishers.

Hagen, S. (Ed.) (1993): *Languages in European business: A regional survey of small and medium sized companies*. London: CILT.

Hagen, S. (Ed.) (1999): *Business communication across borders. A study of language use and practice in European companies*. London: CILT.

Hagen, S. (2005): *Language and culture in British business*. London: CILT.

Helliwell, J. (1999): Language and trade. In: Breton, A. (Ed.): *Exploring the economics of language*. Ottawa: Official Languages Support Programs, Canadian Heritage, 26.

Hoffman, R.C./Gopinath, C. (1994): The importance of international business to the strategic agenda of US CEOs. In: *Journal of International Business Studies*, Third Quarter, 625-637.

Hofstede, G. (1997): *Cultures and organizations: Software of the mind. Intercultural cooperation and its importance for survival*. Revised ed. London/New York: McGraw-Hill.

Knapp, K. (1997): Cultural, organisational or linguistic causes of intercultural conflicts? A case study. In: Beneke, J. (Ed.): *Thriving on Diversity*. Bonn: Dümmler, 117-134.

Langhoff, T. (1997): The influence of cultural differences on internationalization process of firms. In: Bjorkman, L./Forsgren, M. (Eds.): *The Nature of the International Firm: Nordic contributions to international business research*. (= Copenhagen studies in economics and management series A, 11). Copenhagen: Handelshøjskolens Forlag, 135-164.

Nehrt, L.C. (1977): *Business and international education: International Education Project*. (= Occasional Paper No. 4). Washington, DC: American Council on Education.

Noguer, M./Siscart, M. (2003): *Language as a barrier to international trade? An empirical investigation*. Second Job-market Paper, November 2003.

Russo, P./Boor, S. (1993): How fluent is your interface? Design for international users. In: Ashlund, S./Mullet, K./Henderson, A./Hallengel, E./White, T. (Eds.): *Proceedings of the Conference on Human Factors in Computing Systems, Amsterdam April 1993*. Amsterdam: ACM Press, 342-247.

Shenkar, O. (2001): Cultural distance revisited: Towards a more rigorous conceptualization and measurement of cultural differences. In: *Journal of International Business Studies*, 32, 3, 519-535.

Truchot, C. (2002): *Key aspects of the use of English in Europe*. Unpublished Report, DGIV. Strasbourg: Council of Europe.

Trompenaars, F./Hampden-Turner, C. (1997): *Riding the waves of culture: understanding cultural diversity in business*. Second edition (reprinted with corrections). London: Nicholas Brealey.

Trompenaars, F./Hampden-Turner, C. (1998): *Riding the waves of culture: understanding cultural diversity in business*. Second edition. New York: McGraw-Hill.

Westhead, P./Binks, M./Ucbasaran, D./Wright, M. (2002): Internationalization of SMEs: a research note. In: *Journal of Small Business and Enterprise Development*, 9, 1, 38-48.

Wolff, J.A./Pett, T.L. (2000): Internationalisation of small firms: an examination of export competitive patterns, firm size, and export performance. In: *Journal of Small Business Management*, 38, 2, 34-47.

José Paulo Esperança

# An Eclectic Approach to Language Valuation: The Global Influence of the Portuguese Language*

**Resumo: Uma Abordagem Ecléctica ao Valor da Língua: O Uso Global do Português**

Apesar de ter um valor significativo, a língua é um activo intangível cuja medição permanece difícil e imprecisa. O efeito da globalização e da aprendizagem ao longo da vida conduz a um desenvolvimento assimétrico com um conjunto reduzido de idiomas em expansão.

A língua portuguesa tem um número crescente de utilizadores, sobretudo como segunda língua, sendo mesmo de aprendizagem obrigatória em diversos países. Para a sua avaliação, baseamo-nos numa abordagem ecléctica que inclui a perspectiva das externalidades de rede, do peso na actividade económica (em % do PIB) e da notoriedade das pessoas e marcas do espaço lusófono. Este estudo assenta num questionário dirigido a estudantes de português no mundo, na recolha de elementos estatísticos e na medição do peso da língua nas actividades económicas que integram o PIB nacional.

## Abstract

Although it enjoys a significant value, language is a hard to measure intangible asset. Globalization and life long learning lead to an asymmetrical development, with only a few expanding languages.

The Portuguese language has a rising number of users, especially as a second language, having become required in the school curricula of several countries. To contribute to its valuation, we use an eclectic approach, including the network externalities approach, the weighted share of GDP and the recognition of people and brands from the Portuguese speaking world. This study is based on a questionnaire mailed to Portuguese language students throughout the world, the collection of statistical data and the measurement of the language allocated value of economic activities that make up the Portuguese GDP.

## 1. Introduction

The economic analysis of language has attracted a rising attention, not least due to the role played by language in the global flows of ideas, people, capital and goods. The social implications are obvious and many governments define policies that promote some languages, domestically and abroad, and provide advice and support to the learning of others, regarded as a valuable knowledge for both the citizens and the nation. Karim (1995) states that governments have long recognized the impact of languages on international trade and commerce, although other intangible benefits should also be taken in consideration. One evidence is presented by the number of students of the French language, whose relative weight is well above the level it should have on purely economic considerations.

* This is a first draft based on a study on the value of the Portuguese language conceived and financed by Instituto Camões (IC). IC has also organized the distribution and collection of the questionnaire sent to its many students worldwide. The research team includes António Firmino da Costa, Fernando Luís Machado and Mohammed Azzim Gulamhussen. We acknowledge the assistance provided by Andrea Freitas, Helena Torres, Sérgio Estevinha and Jorge Horta Ferreira. Last but not least, this study would not been possible without the the guidance of the Institute's President, Simonetta Afonso, who first proposed this theme, and ISCTE's President Luís Reto.

The concern with language implications is not bounded to the social or state level. Krishna (2005) analyses the challenges facing corporate planners in managing language as a corporate asset due to the evolution of the knowledge economy, the globalization of businesses, and the increasing diversity of the workforce. Multinational corporations, in particular, require and often sponsor diversified language skills among their employees.

Early studies on the economics of languages concentrated on the intrinsic characteristics and the impact on future expansion or decline. Grin (1990) quotes Marshak (1965) who suggested that more efficient languages, with the ability to transmit a certain amount of information in less time, had a larger chance of survival. However, Grin observes that there is no empirical evidence that confirms this prediction.

The functionalist approach led to the view of second (or $n^{th}$) language learning as a form of investment in human capital, whose instant costs bring benefits that are spread over time (Karim 1995). The return on this investment can find an objective measurement by comparing similarly skilled individuals with and without a given language skill.

A potentially powerful explanation for the interest in specific second languages deals with the network externalities approach. Languages are a public good whose value rises with the further use by other people. Therefore, languages enjoy the critical mass properties that are typical of telecommunications networks – most customers prefer to join a network with a large number of users, as within the network communication tends to be cheaper and easier.

Empirical studies have provided plenty of evidence of the network effect that attracts consumers to large operators. For instance, Doganoglu and Grzybowski (2006) have observed that the quick adhesion to dominant operators could not be explained by price factors alone. Other network effects such as quality signalling are also at play.

Belonging to a given social group enhances the network effect, accelerating adhesion through a process that is described as a "wave effect". Becker (1991) studies the economic impact of social interactions, a field exploited by an expanding body of the economics literature.

The size of economic literature on the role of social interactions and network effects has not translated into significant empirical research. We lack the capacity to measure the economic impact of a language, predict its evolution and evaluate the social engineering policies that impact the individual choices on language learning investment. In this study we try to shed light on the individual goals and motivations expressed by students of Portuguese from many different origins. The questionnaire that obtained about 2,500 answers asks the professional and personal aims, as well as the reflection of their learning on the identification of Portuguese brands and celebrities. Furthermore, we used a methodology borrowed from Martin Municio (2003) to identify the value of the language as a percentage of the Portuguese GDP.

This study is organized as follows. Section 2 addresses the presence of the Portuguese language in the world, analysing the number of native speakers and the possible motives for its learning. Section 3 provides some insights into its network effects, including the economic impact on trade and migration. Section 4 measures the value as a percentage of Portuguese GDP. Section 5 presents some questionnaire results on people and brands identification. Finally, section 6 summarizes the main conclusions and suggests some venues for future research and possible extensions of this study.

## 2. Portuguese around the world

The maritime expansion of the 15th and 16th centuries led a language first used by less than a million people to spread to many continents, especially South America, Africa and Asia. Besides Portugal, Portuguese became the official language of Angola, Brazil, Cape Verde, Guinea- Bissau, Mozambique, São Tomé and Príncipe and Timor, as portrayed in table 1:

| Portuguese speaking countries | Population (millions) | World ranking |
|---|---|---|
| Brazil | 191.6 | 5 |
| Mozambique | 21.4 | 49 |
| Angola | 17.0 | 56 |
| Portugal | 10.6 | 74 |
| Guinea-Bissau | 1.7 | 145 |
| East Timor | 1.1 | 151 |
| Cape Verde | 0.5 | 161 |
| Saint Tome and Prince | 0.2 | 182 |
| **Total** | 244 | |
| **Percentage of world population** | 3.7% | |

Table 1: Portuguese native speakers around the world (millions). Source: World Bank (2006)

A few native speakers still remain in other small regions such as Goa (Índia) and Macau (China), not to mention the Portuguese migrants that are even more spread, estimated at about 5 million people.

Linguists (Calvet 2002) classify Portuguese as a supercentral language, a second tier level, after English and at a level equivalent to French, Spanish and others.

The Portuguese language has also inspired a community – Comunidade dos Países da Língua Portuguesa, joining all Portuguese speaking countries. This association is similar to the Commonwealth (English speaking countries, La Francophonie (French speaking countries) or the League of Arab States (Karim 1995).

Portuguese has also become a prominent language on the emerging mega–media provided by the internet. From the Internet World Statistics (2008), we see that Portuguese is placed on the 8th position, and is bound to rise as it enjoys one of the highest growth rates:

| 10 top languages | % of total Internet users | Internet users (millions) | Internet access | Internet growth (2000-2008) | Language users in 2008 (millions) |
|---|---|---|---|---|---|
| English | 30.4% | 427 | 21.0% | 201.1% | 2.039 |
| Chinese | 16.6% | 233 | 17.1% | 622.0% | 1.365 |
| Spanish | 8.7% | 122 | 27.1% | 395.7% | 452 |
| Japanese | 6.7% | 94 | 73.8% | 99.7% | 127 |
| French | 4.8% | 67 | 16.4% | 451.8% | 410 |
| German | 4.5% | 64 | 66.0% | 129.6% | 96 |
| Arabic | 4.2% | 60 | 16.7% | 2062.2% | 357 |
| Portuguese | 4.1% | 58 | 24.3% | 668.0% | 240 |
| Korean | 2.5% | 34 | 47.9% | 82.9% | 73 |
| Italian | 2.4% | 34 | 57.9% | 155.4% | 58 |
| TOP 10 | 84.8% | 1.194 | 22.9% | 263.6% | 5.218 |
| Other | 15.2% | 213 | 14.6% | 556.7% | 1.458 |
| **World total** | 100.0% | 1.408 | 21.1% | 290.0% | 6.676 |

Table 2: Internet users and total speakers, by language (millions)

## 3. Network effect

Given the network effect, the larger the number of native speakers and secondary users, the larger is the reward for learning a given language. Moreover, the cumulative wealth of its users is also important for reinforcing the network effect. The recent explosion of interest for Mandarin, a very difficult language for non native learners, is certainly related with the continuous double digit growth of the Chinese economy during at least the past two decades. Grin (2001: 68) suggests that "the relative position of a language, *ceteris paribus*, is positively correlated with the aggregate purchasing power of its speakers".

Therefore, it is interesting to compare the relative size and wealth of the native Portuguese speaking community. For that we have added the population of CPLP member states and the first generation Portuguese migrants. We assume that their individual wealth equals the average of per capita income in the hosting nations. This measurement may slightly underestimate the size and wealth of the Portuguese speakers living in other nations, as some citizens from other CPLP members have also migrated to non Portuguese speaking countries – Brazil and Cape Verde, for instance, have a significant number of emigrants. Table 3 presents the relative share of native Portuguese speakers, on the world's population and wealth:

| | Total (€ million) | % of world values |
|---|---|---|
| CPLP population | 244,049 | 3.7% |
| Portuguese emmigrants | 4,442 | 0.1% |
| **Total** | 248,491 | 3,8% |
| CPLP GDP | 1,090,549 | 2.9% |
| GDP of Portuguese Emmigrants | 107,997 | 0.3% |
| **Total** | 1,198,546 | 3.2% |

Table 3: Share of native Portuguese speakers. Source: World Bank (2006)

The average wealth of Portuguese speakers (3.2%) is slightly lower than the world average, as they represent 3.8% of the total world population.

### 3.1 Immigration

The network effect has a significant impact on migration and the integration of migrants. The migrant has lower adaptation costs in a host country whose language he shares. Employers also face lower communication barriers.

Recently, Portugal has attracted a large number of immigrants. Indeed, the resident population has expanded even despite a sharp decline of fertility rates. The following table shows the relative share of Portuguese immigrants:

| Country of origin | Immigrants (thousands) | % |
|---|---|---|
| Cape Verde | 65 | 16% |
| Brazil | 65 | 16% |
| Angola | 33 | 8% |
| Guinea-Bissau | 25 | 6% |
| UK | 20 | 5% |
| Spain | 17 | 4% |
| Saint Tome and Prince | 11 | 3% |
| US and Canada | 10 | 2% |
| China | 10 | 2% |
| Mozambique | 6 | 1% |
| Other in Latin America | 72 | 18% |
| Other in Africa | 10 | 2% |
| Other | 65 | 16% |
| **Total** | 409 | 100% |
| **Total from CPLP countries** | 205 | 50% |

Table 4: Immigration in Portugal, by country of origin

About 50% of Portuguese immigrants come from other CPLP countries. This contrasts with a much lower share of foreign trade, as Europe represents about 70% of the total. The next largest group is made up of Spanish speaking citizens from Latin American countries, a group with little difficulty to learn and fluently use the host country's language. Analysing the behavior of immigrants to the US, Lazear (1999) observes that the value of assimilation is larger to an individual from a small minority than to one from a large minority group. When a society has a very large majority of individuals from one culture, individuals from minority groups will be assimilated more quickly. From this point of view, Portugal should have less difficulty with assimilation, as immigrants from very different languages don't constitute large communities. Indeed, there is anecdotal evidence of extremely quick learning by adult immigrants from several Slavic countries, and even more so by their children of school age.

## 3.2 Outward migration

A large number of Portuguese born citizens live in other countries, namely Europe and North America, as portrayed in table 5:

| World ranking | Main host countries | Number (thousands) | Pop. (millions) | % of Portuguese | GDP (€ million) | Migrants' share (€ million) |
|---|---|---|---|---|---|---|
| 1 | US | 973 | 302 | 0.3% | 9,395,759 | 30.319 |
| 3 | Germany | 130 | 82 | 0.6% | 2,243,108 | 3.536 |
| 5 | UK | 350 | 61 | 0.6% | 1,855,726 | 10.642 |
| 6 | France | 950 | 62 | 1.5% | 1,743,125 | 26.824 |
| 8 | Spain | 108 | 45 | 0.2% | 972,302 | 2.340 |
| 9 | Canada | 594 | 33 | 1.8% | 902,334 | 16.265 |
| 15 | Australia | 57 | 21 | 0.3% | 559,013 | 1.523 |
| 22 | Switzerland | 166 | 8 | 2.2% | 282,676 | 6.247 |
| 28 | South Africa | 274 | 48 | 0.6% | 188,838 | 1.088 |
| 34 | Venezuela | 590 | 27 | 2.1% | 155,157 | 3.333 |
| 63 | Luxembourg | 85 | 0.5 | 17.7% | 32,615 | 5.776 |
| | Asia | 163 | 1520 | 0.01% | 978,675 | 105 |
| | **Total** | 4440 | 2209 | | 4071,61 | 107.998 |
| | **Share of world GDP** | | | | | 0.3% |

Table 5: Outward migration from Portugal, by hosting country

This was an earlier migration wave, far less influenced by language factors. Geography and economic opportunities were the main triggers for migration.

### 3.3 User's benefits

Our questionnaire has a specific section about the main interests of students of the Portuguese language. The following tables summarize those interests, confirming that work and social relations come on the top of the list. We confirm also that the super-central nature of Portuguese may be at play in the motivations of many respondents, as they regard foreign languages as a valuable type of human capital.

| **Reasons for learning Portuguese:** | **%** |
|---|---|
| To learn other languages (important for the future) | 60.9 |
| To learn more about the Portuguese culture | 39.1 |
| To earn more culture | 32.9 |
| To find or progress in my job | 29.1 |
| This is my country's official language | 25.3 |
| To communicate with friends | 23.6 |
| To study in a Portuguese speaking country | 23.2 |
| This is the official language in many countries | 22.2 |
| The language is rising | 18.1 |
| To communicate with my family | 14.2 |
| This is the official language in many international organizations | 8.2 |
| This is my parents/grand parents language | 7.9 |
| To do business | 7.3 |

Table 6: Motivations for learning Portuguese

A more specific question on the using context (current and future) shows similar results:

| **Situations in which I speak Portuguese** | **%** |
|---|---|
| To talk to friends / colleagues | 55.4 |
| To travel | 48.1 |
| At home | 34.4 |
| In my work | 30.8 |
| In the future I plan to speak Portuguese to: | (%) |
| To travel | 77.6 |
| In my work | 60.6 |
| Leisure | 43.2 |
| Study | 39.7 |
| International events | 25.3 |

Table 7: Current and future uses of the Portuguese language

### 3.4 Value in the labor market

Several studies have produced a concrete measurement of the benefit of learning a foreign language, based upon the income differencial for people with the capability to speak a certain language. These studies have benefited from the availability of census data. Rendon (2007) studied the wealth differencial for Catalunya residents with the capacity to speak Catalan. This study took advantage of a favourable setting – the change of regulation that required Catalan for the exercise of a number of jobs and the availability of data. It showed that people with understanding of spoken and written Catalan had a 3 to 5% higher probability of finding a job.

Grim (2001) looks at Swiss citizens with the distinct capability of speaking English. In a multilingual context, with several official languages, English knowledge was found to raise the average income by 12 to 30%. This approach is objective but raises some methodological concerns. Both examples provide clear evidence that language knowledge is correlated with higher probability of finding a job or with average salary. However, other factors may be at play as Catalan speakers may enjoy better connections that raise the odds of finding a job. In general, people who speak several languages may also be better educated, enjoying other skills that may facilitate selection for attractive jobs.

## 4. Valuation as a share of GDP

There is no doubt that language played a crucial role in enhancing the productivity of society as a whole. The division of labor is possible due to the communication skills developed by mankind. A common culture and language is a facilitator of trade (Lazear 1999) while individuals who know only different languages face strong barriers to both trade and interaction within a firm.

The importance of communication and understanding is very high in some activities such as teaching or radio, while in others like mining or manufacturing, it plays a smaller role. This logic may lead to the valuation of the language as a share of GDP for a given country. Martin Municio (2003) led a team who carried a thorough study on "The Economic Value of the Spanish Language". This was a very detailed analysis of all economic activities carried out in Spain, estimating a coefficient for the value of language for each activity.

In this method, we need to identify first those activities or products in which language is a key component. These include such traditional activities as the press, radio, TV, publishing or telecommunication as well as the support activities that render these possible. Research and development for telecommunications, telephone rooters, editing, translation, data mining and other activities that contribute to writing or broadcasting information are an example of these. Next, Martin Municio consider those activities that are closely linked, as suppliers of inputs such as the paper industry or the manufacturing of radios or TV sets. At the opposite end come activities that have a much lower language content such as mining or agriculture. The study gives much attention to detail. One example is the distinction between advertising based on outdoors (low language content) and news paper texts (high content).

The coefficients range from high levels such as Printing (91%), Mail and Telecommunications (95%) and Education (82%), to medium levels such as Recreation, Culture and Sports (40%) and Public Administration (25%) and to low levels of language content such as Agriculture (0.6%), Electricity and Gas (0.04%) or Waste disposal (0.07%). These coefficients were multiplied by the value of each activity, obtaining a total that was divided by the Spanish GDP yielding a percentage of approximately 15%.

We replicated this study for the Portuguese economy. We benefitted from the fact that the National Accounts of both countries follow the *Nomenclature des Activités Économiques* (*NACE*) defined by the European Union in 1986. The Spanish *Clasificación Nacional de Actividades Económicas* (*CNAE93*) and the Portuguese *Classificação das Actividades Económicas* are identical. Small differences remained as the level of specification is higher in Spain, with a total of 70 activities versus only 60 for Portugal. However, we expect that the adoption of the coefficients used in Martin Municio (2003) must provide a reasonable estimation of the value of the Portuguese language, under the very same methodology. Moreover, we benefit from a higher uniformity as Portugal has only one language. In Spain one is measuring the value of the Spanish languages rather than the value of Spanish or Castilian.

The next table presents the aggregate value of the Portuguese language, under this methodology:

| | **Language coefficient** | **GDP** | **$GDP_L$** |
|---|---|---|---|
| Agriculture, forests and fishing | 0,544% | 3729 | 20 |
| Electricity | 0,063% | 3816 | 2 |
| Manufacturing | 8,699% | 21584 | 1878 |
| Building and construction | 0,078% | 8884 | 7 |
| Market services | 14,931% | 55011 | 8214 |
| Other services | 29,297% | 46673 | 13674 |
| **Total** | | 139697 | 23795 |
| $GDP_L$ | 23.794,7 | | |
| $GDP_L$/GDP | 17,033% | | |
| $Taxes_L$ | 3.917,2 | | |
| $GDP_L$ | 27.711,9 | | |
| $GDP_L$/GDP | 17,010% | | |

Table 8: Value of the language as a % of Portuguese GDP. Source: GDP by industry was obtained from INE (National Statistics Institute) data

The value of the Portuguese language is close to 17%, a higher value than in Spain reflecting the slightly different structure of the Portuguese economy, as the relative weight of activities with a high language content is higher.

## 5. Famous Portuguese speakers

Interest for a foreign language is both determined and a cause of interest for local writers, artists, sportsmen and brands. In our questionnaire we asked respondents to freely name Portuguese speaking celebrities and brands. The following table gives a list of the spontaneous responses obtained:

| **Personalities** | **Number of references** |
|---|---|
| *1º Lula da Silva* | *241* |
| **2º Ronaldinho Gaúcho** | 237 |
| **3º Figo** | 232 |
| *4º José Saramago* | *220* |
| **5º Ronaldo** | 215 |
| **6º Cristiano Ronaldo** | 213 |
| *7º Fernando Pessoa* | *207* |
| *8º Paulo Coelho* | *198* |
| *9º Camões* | *187* |
| *10º Mariza* | *170* |
| *11º Durão Barroso* | *133* |
| *12º Amália* | *130* |
| *13º Mia Couto* | *122* |
| *14º José Sócrates* | *119* |
| *15º Cesária Évora* | *107* |
| *16º Cavaco Silva* | *106* |
| **17º Pelé** | 104 |
| *18º Caetano Veloso* | *100* |
| *19º Roberto Carlos* | *81* |
| **20º Lurdes Mutola** | 78 |

Table 9: References of well known Portuguese speakers

Both Portuguese and Brazilian personalities were mentioned. It is interesting to note that a vibrant literary and artistic community is emerging in younger Portuguese speaking nations. Therefore, it is no surprise that some personalities from Angola, Cape Verde and Mozambique have also been mentioned. All names (in italic) refer to "language workers", people who became well known by being writers, singers or politicians. The next group is made up of sports stars, mainly from football.

We have also asked the Portuguese students about their knowledge of brands from the Portuguese speaking world. The results were poorer, probably showing that many respondents live in regions beyond the reach of these firms:

| Brands | Number of references |
|---|---|
| 1° Sagres | 50 |
| 2° Millenium BCP | 38 |
| 3° Pingo Doce | 37 |
| 4° Sonangol | 28 |
| 5° Jumbo | 25 |
| 6° Vodafone | 24 |
| 7° Jerónimo Martins | 23 |
| 8° Sumol | 17 |
| 9° PT Comunicações | 16 |
| 10° TAP e Compal | 15 |

Table 10: Brand recognition

A later stage of questionnaire analysis will enable the understanding of regional differences for both people and brand recognition. It is important to acknowledge that not all Portuguese or Brazilian firms use their brand names abroad. One interesting example is the case of Jerónimo Martins, who brands its subsidiary in Poland, the largest local retailer, Biedronka, the Polish word for "lady bug".

## 6. Summary and conclusions

Language is a public good whose use by one party enhances the value of the next user. Measuring the value of a language is elusive, but there are steps that can be made towards a more accurate assessment. First of all there are some activities that can be called language industries. Those enjoy the largest network effect and include the literature, cinema, press and education, well beyond language education itself, among others.

Languages with a large number of native and non native users provide a larger market for cultural goods than those that are understood by a smaller number of people. Next come other activities with a high language content. The growth of the service sector leads to a higher language content for the economy as a whole. Although some services such as cleaning have a low language content, most are more language intensive than manufacturing or agriculture and mining. These activities can be performed by virtually any worker, regardless of his language skills, while many services, including basic functions as performed by call centers, require a good knowledge of the client's language.

A language is also a facilitator and a beneficiary of its speakers' wealth. Portuguese has enjoyed much recent attraction as a second language due to the rising demand of Angolan and Brazilian produce. We found evidence that people flows and trade are significantly influenced by language. The measurement of the language content of the

Portuguese economy, provided a significant value, reflecting the high share of service industries. Finally, we observed that interest for a foreign language is correlated with the knowledge of influential personalities, with a high visibility for "language workers" such as writers and singers.

In this study we tried an eclectic approach to language valuation with contributions from different theories. Some of the analysis is more preliminary, requiring further and more robust observation and testing. One example is the impact of language on trade and FDI. We expect that a systematic comparison will show that trade and FDI are more intense among Portuguese speaking countries. Moreover the higher the language differences the less relative trade and investment should exist. Again, "language distance avoidance" should be more significant in language intensive industries. For instance, trade in raw materials and agricultural products should be less sensitive than trade in services or goods with a high language content. Indeed, one interesting exercise would bc the test of the impact of language coefficients as defined by Martin Municio (2003).

However, a truly advance in the learning of language value would require a comparative study including different languages, local and global, or hypercentral, super central, central and local in Calvet's (2002) classification. The benefits of one such study are twofold – academic progress in the valuation of an intangible asset with strong network externalities and identification of efficient policies by members of a given language zone.

## 7. Bibliography

Becker, G. (1991): A note on restaurant pricing and other examples of social influence on price. In: *Journal of Political Economy*, 99 (5), 116-31.

Calvet, L.-J. (2002): *Le marché aux langues. Les effects linquistiques de la mondialisation.* Paris: Plon.

Dalmazzone, S. (2000): Economic of language: a network externalities approach. In: Breton, A.: *New Canadian perspectives*. Toronto: University of Toronto.

Delgado, J.L.G. (2007): *El valor económico del Español – una introducción.* Barcelona: Fundación Telefónica.

Doganoglu, T./Grzybowski, L. (2006): Estimating network effects in mobile telephony in Germany. In: *Information Economics and Policy*, doi:/10.1016/j.infoecopol.2006.11.001.

Galito, M.d.S. (2006): *Impacto Económico da Língua Portuguesa Enquanto Língua de Trabalho, Tese de Doutoramento*. Centro de Investigação e Análise em Relações Internacionais, Instituto de Estudos Políticos, Universidade Católica Portuguesa. Unpublished Dissertation.

Grin, F. (2001): English as economic value: facts and fallacies". In *World Englishes*. Vol. 20, n. 1 (March 2001), 65-78.

Karim, K.H. (1995): Economic dimension of minority and foreign language use: An international overview. In: *Languages and the Economy: Canada in an International Perspective.*

Krishna, S.D. (2005): The value of language: concept, perspectives, and policies. In: *Corporate Communications: An International Journal*, Vol. 10, n°4, 358-382.

Lazear, E.P. (1999): Culture and Language. In: *Journal of Political Economy*, Vol. 107, no. 6, 95-126.

Martin Municio, Á. (2003): *El Valor Económico de la Lengua.* Madrid: Fundacion Santander Central Hispano.

Rendon, S. (2007): The Catalan premium: language and employment in Catalonia. In: *Journal of Population Economics*, n. 20, 666-686.

Sophie Bressé

# L'usage des langues étrangères dans les entreprises françaises

En France comme ailleurs, dans les entreprises, et tout particulièrement dans celles qui travaillent à l'international, la capacité d'utilisation par les salariés d'une langue véhiculaire du commerce, qui permette aux acheteurs et aux vendeurs de communiquer et de se comprendre, est un enjeu économique de taille. Une enquête sur les pratiques linguistiques de 500 entreprises françaises travaillant à l'international réalisée en 2003,[1] montre que l'anglais est la langue parlée par environ neuf sur dix de leurs clients non francophones et que la moitié d'entre elles considèrent que l'anglais représente un des facteurs clés de la réussite à l'international. 52% d'entre elles déclaraient avoir réalisé au moins la moitié de leur chiffre d'affaire grâce à leur commerce avec la clientèle non francophone. Le volet Salariés de l'enquête Changements Organisationnels et Informatisation (COI) réalisée fin 2006 auprès d'un échantillon représentatif de plus de 14.000 salariés d'entreprises de 20 salariés et plus (voir encadré 1) confirme en effet que parmi ceux qui sont amenés à utiliser une langue étrangère dans le cadre de leur activité professionnelle, neuf sur dix ont recours à l'anglais. Au-delà de la nécessité de recourir à cette langue pour les échanges commerciaux, ce qui ne concerne qu'une certaine catégorie de salariés, l'anglais est aussi utilisé dans d'autres cadres à l'intérieur de l'entreprise. Certains salariés reçoivent des instructions relatives à leur travail en anglais (notes de services dans des entreprises internationales par exemple); d'autres sont contraints de lire des documents rédigés en langue étrangère comme des notices ou des modes d'emploi nécessaires à la mise en œuvre de leurs tâches. En France, où la loi du 4 août 1994 a introduit l'obligation pour l'employeur de rédiger en français "tout document comportant des obligations pour le salarié ou des dispositions dont la connaissance est nécessaire à celui-ci pour l'exécution de son travail" afin que les salariés maîtrisant mal une langue étrangère ne soient pas pénalisés, mais aussi dans le souci de limiter les risques de litige et de protéger la santé et la sécurité des personnes, ces nouvelles pratiques mettent certains salariés en difficulté et peuvent être source de tensions.

Dans un contexte de mondialisation des échanges, de plus en plus d'entreprises s'efforcent donc, pour améliorer leurs performances, d'adapter leur main d'œuvre à ces nouveaux enjeux. Elles disposent alors de deux leviers, non exclusifs l'un de l'autre: la formation de leurs salariés à l'usage des langues étrangères et/ou le recrutement de nouveaux salariés compétents en langues, et plus particulièrement en anglais.

En contrepied d'une approche visant à appréhender les stratégies mises en œuvre par les entreprises pour augmenter leurs performances sur les marchés internationaux, via l'amélioration de leurs compétences linguistiques, cette étude mobilise de premiers résultats du dispositif d'enquêtes couplées Employeurs/Salariés COI 2006 (voir encadré)

---

[1] Cette enquête a été réalisée par l'Observatoire de la Formation, de l'Emploi et des Métiers, la Direction des Relations internationales de l'Enseignement de la Chambre de Commerce et d'Industrie de Paris, et la Délégation Générale à la Langue Française et aux langues de France.

pour aborder la question de l'usage des langues étrangères au travail à travers le prisme des salariés, et tenter d'identifier les répercussions de ces nouvelles attentes et de ces nouvelles pratiques sur ces derniers dans les entreprises françaises.

Quelle proportion d'entre eux est confrontée à l'usage d'une langue étrangère dans le cadre de son activité professionnelle? Quelles formes prend cet usage? Quel est le profil des salariés capables de répondre à ces attentes de compétences linguistiques? Et à l'inverse, qui sont ceux qui souffrent de cette nouvelle contrainte de performance et de ces nouvelles pratiques de travail? Les générations de salariés plus âgées sont-elles plus concernées?

Pour répondre à ces questions, des données issues de l'exploitation statistique du volet Salariés de l'enquête COI 2006 seront mobilisées. Ce dispositif d'enquêtes couplées employeurs/salariés constitue une ressource nouvelle et originale pour appréhender les changements qui affectent l'organisation des entreprises et leurs conséquences sur les postes de travail et les conditions de travail des salariés. Outre que les résultats sur les salariés et ceux qui concernent les entreprises au sein desquelles ils travaillent peuvent être mis en regard et s'enrichir mutuellement, c'est aussi l'ampleur des échantillons d'entreprises et de salariés enquêtés qui fait la richesse de ce dispositif d'enquêtes, garantissant ainsi la représentativité et la robustesse des résultats obtenus. Les données sur lesquelles repose cette étude portent ainsi sur plus de 14.000 salariés stables dans leur emploi depuis au moins un an, du secteur privé (issus d'entreprises d'au moins 20 salariés).

Dans le but de pouvoir disposer de données fiables et représentatives de l'ensemble des salariés des entreprises françaises sur leur utilisation, au travail, des langues étrangères, la Délégation Générale à la Langue Française et aux Langues de France a financé le volet linguistique de l'enquête COI 2006 auprès des salariés, soit un ensemble de questions relatives aux langues apprises dans l'enfance et aux langues utilisées dans le cadre de l'activité professionnelle, posées de façon transversale au questionnaire. Ce sont ces questions (voir encadré 2) qui permettent d'identifier et d'étudier les différentes catégories de salariés utilisateurs de langues étrangères au travail.

Sur l'ensemble des salariés des entreprises françaises de 20 salariés et plus, 25%, soit environ 1.840.000 individus, ont un travail impliquant de s'exprimer (à l'oral et/ou à l'écrit) dans une langue étrangère: 11% le font fréquemment, et 14% occasionnellement. La langue principalement utilisée est alors le plus souvent l'anglais (dans 89% des cas), plus rarement l'allemand (5% des cas), l'espagnol (2% des cas), ou encore l'italien (1% des cas)… Parallèlement, 31% des salariés sont amenés à lire dans le cadre de leur travail des documents, comme des notices ou des modes d'emploi par exemple, qui ne sont pas rédigés en français: pour 11% cet usage est fréquent, et pour 20% il est occasionnel.

Au total, dans le secteur privé des entreprises de 20 salariés et plus, quatre salariés sur dix sont confrontés, d'une manière ou d'une autre, à l'utilisation d'une langue étrangère dans le cadre de leur activité professionnelle. Mais les formes que prennent cet usage sont multiples; la fréquence (fréquemment, occasionnellement, jamais ou presque) et les modalités (expression dans la langue ou usage réceptif de la langue) de cet usage diffèrent objectivement d'un salarié à l'autre. Le tableau 1 distingue plusieurs profils d'utilisation des langues étrangères dans le cadre de l'activité professionnelle.

| **Dans le cadre de leur activité professionnelle:** | |
|---|---|
| Parlent et/ou écrivent dans une langue étrangère<br>- fréquemment<br>- occasionnellement | 25%<br>11%<br>14% |
| Lisent des documents rédigés dans une langue étrangère<br>- fréquemment<br>- occasionnellement | 31%<br>11%<br>20% |
| Parlent et/ou écrivent fréquemment dans une langue étrangère ET lisent fréquemment des documents rédigés en langue étrangère | 7% |
| Parlent et/ou écrivent occasionnellement dans une langue étrangère ET lisent occasionnellement des documents en langue étrangère | 6% |
| Ne parlent ni n'écrivent jamais mais lisent occasionnellement dans une langue étrangère | 11% |
| N'ont jamais l'usage d'une langue étrangère | 61% |

Tableau 1: Proportions de salariés concernées par les différentes configurations d'usage d'une langue étrangère dans le cadre de leur activité professionnelle
Source: Enquête COI couplée 2006, Statistique Publique, INSEE-DARES-CEE.
Champ: salariés stables (au moins un an d'ancienneté) des entreprises françaises de 20 salariés ou plus.

En outre, une troisième dimension permet de caractériser l'usage d'une ou plusieurs langues étrangères au travail par les salariés, à savoir les difficultés qu'il génère, ou non. En effet, parmi ceux qui sont amenés à utiliser une langue étrangère dans le cadre de leur activité professionnelle, certains en éprouvent une gêne. Leur part est difficile à quantifier et très probablement sous-estimée par l'enquête COI puisque nous ne disposons pour les identifier que d'une question ("Cela gêne-t-il le bon déroulement de votre travail?"), posée exclusivement aux personnes ayant répondu qu'elles étaient amenées à lire des documents en langues étrangères dans le cadre de leur activité professionnelle. En conséquence, les personnes dont le travail implique de parler et/ou écrire dans une autre langue que le français, mais pas de lire cette langue étrangère (soit 7% des salariés des entreprises de 20 salariés ou plus), n'ont pas été interrogées sur leur éventuelle difficulté à le faire. Par ailleurs, il faut rappeler que la perception qu'ont les salariés de cet usage et de son impact sur le bon déroulement de leur travail est forcément subjective et que le recueil de données déclaratives implique de s'en remettre aux répondants pour apprécier cet impact. Des personnes ayant des niveaux de langue un peu différents mais aussi des façons différentes d'apprécier leur propre niveau de langue et les difficultés qu'il génère, sont donc susceptibles de se retrouver dans la même catégorie d'utilisateurs (voir tableau 2).

| **Salariés dont l'activité professionnelle...** | ...implique de s'exprimer souvent dans une langue étrangère | ...implique de s'exprimer occasionnellement dans une langue étrangère | ...n'implique pas de s'exprimer dans une langue étrangère | Total |
|---|---|---|---|---|
| ...n'implique pas de lire des documents rédigés en langue étrangère | 2% | 5% | 61% | 68% |
| ...implique de lire des documents rédigés en langue étrangère et en sont gênés dans leur travail | 1% | 2% | 4% | 7% |
| ...implique de lire des documents rédigés en langue étrangère et n'en sont pas gênés dans leur travail | 8% | 7% | 10% | 24% |
| Total | 11% | 14% | 75% | 100% |

Tableau 2: Catégories d'utilisateurs selon le mode d'usage et le niveau de difficulté ressenti.
Source: Enquête COI couplée 2006, Statistique Publique, INSEE-DARES-CEE.
Champ: salariés stables (au moins un an d'ancienneté) des entreprises françaises de 20 salariés ou plus.

Néanmoins, malgré les quelques limites de ces données, nous disposons aujourd'hui d'un ensemble d'informations inédites sur la question de l'usage des langues étrangères dans les entreprises françaises qui seront mobilisées pour répondre aux questions de cette étude et donc identifier les profils des salariés capables de répondre aux attentes de compétences linguistiques d'une part, et de ceux qui rencontrent des difficultés d'autre part. Les premiers, qu'on appellera les utilisateurs "compétents en langue", et dont les entreprises ont besoin pour relever leurs nouveaux défis, sont définis dans cette étude comme ceux dont le travail implique de s'exprimer fréquemment dans une langue étrangère, d'être amenés à lire des documents rédigés dans une autre langue que le français, et qui déclarent qu'ils n'en éprouvent pas de difficulté; les seconds sont ceux qui décarent au contraire qu'ils se sentent gênés dans leur travail par l'utilisation (au sens de "lecture") d'une langue étrangère.

Les salariés compétents en langues représentent 8% des salariés des entreprises de 20 salariés et plus, et un sur cinq des salariés dont le travail implique l'usage d'une langue étrangère, ce qui représente environ 575.000 individus. 93% d'entre eux utilisent principalement[2] l'anglais dans le cadre de leur activité professionnelle. 91% travaillent dans une entreprise ayant des liens avec l'international (c'est-à-dire intervenant sur des marchés internationaux (87%) et/ou dont le plus gros fournisseur est localisé à l'étranger (36%)). Pour autant, tous les salariés de ces entreprises ne sont pas nécessairement amenés à utiliser une langue étrangère dans le cadre de leur activité professionnelle: 16% d'entre eux ont un travail qui implique de s'exprimer fréquemment dans une langue étrangère; et 12% sont compétents en langues au sens où nous l'avons défini plus haut. Même si le fait de travailler dans une entreprise ayant des marchés ou des fournisseurs internationaux augmente la probabilité d'avoir (de devoir avoir) de bonnes compétences en langues, même au sein de ces entreprises, seules certaines catégories de salariés, occupant des postes stratégiques, doivent nécessairement en avoir. La proportion de salariés compétents en langue dans les entreprises, somme toute assez faible (8%), incarne donc la rencontre entre des besoins très spécifiques de l'entreprise pour certaines tâches stratégiques et un profil de salariés lui aussi très spécifique, dont nous allons à présent examiner les caractéristiques.

Les qualifications en langues de ces salariés s'inscrivent en effet dans un niveau de qualification globalement très élevé: ainsi 83% d'entre eux ont fait des études supérieures, et 36% sont diplômés d'une grande école, d'une école de commerce ou d'une école d'ingénieurs, contre respectivement 35% et 6% dans l'ensemble de la population salariée des entreprises de 20 salariés et plus. Près de sept sur dix sont des cadres, alors que ceux-ci représentent un cinquième de l'ensemble des salariés. Ces cadres sont par ailleurs plus diplômés que leurs homologues: 91% d'entre eux ont fait des études supérieures (contre 79%), et 48% d'entre eux sont diplômés d'une grande école (école de commerce, d'ingénieur), contre 28% de l'ensemble des cadres.

La conséquence directe de ce niveau de qualification très élevé est une association forte avec des fonctions d'encadrements dans l'entreprise puisque la moitié des salariés compétents en langue encadrent une équipe, contre 30% dans l'ensemble des salariés des entreprises de 20 salariés et plus; et 12% encadrent au moins 20 salariés et occupent donc des fonctions d'encadrement à des niveaux relativement élevés de l'entreprise, contre 6% de l'ensemble des salariés.

Le recours à l'utilisation d'une langue étrangère n'est pas réservé exclusivement aux relations des salariés avec des interlocuteurs extérieurs à l'entreprise. Les salariés dont le travail implique de s'exprimer dans une langue étrangère sont 35% à le faire dans le cadre de leurs relations avec leurs fournisseurs et 55% avec leurs clients. Mais 24% l'utilisent aussi avec leurs collègues et 13% avec leurs supérieurs hiérarchiques. Le constat est encore plus marqué pour les salariés compétents en langue (voir tableau 3) qui utilisent bien sûr une langue étrangère dans le cadre de leurs relations avec leurs clients (pour 57% d'entre eux) et leurs fournisseurs (pour 49% d'entre eux), mais aussi

[2] Dans le cas où les individus déclarent utiliser plusieurs langues étrangères dans le cadre de leur activité professionnelle, on leur demande de mentionner celle à laquelle ils recourent le plus fréquemment. Ainsi, parmi les individus qui utilisent "principalement" l'anglais, on compte ceux qui n'utilisent que cette langue et ceux qui l'utilisent parmi d'autres, mais plus fréquemment que ces autres langues.

dans leurs relations avec leurs collègues pour 44% d'entre eux, et avec leurs supérieurs hiérarchiques pour 24% d'entre eux. On peut observer deux phénomènes: plus ils sont haut placés dans la hiérarchie de l'entreprise, plus ils sont en relation avec les fournisseurs étrangers de l'entreprise: c'est le cas de 35% des salariés qui déclarent qu'ils sont amenés dans leur travail à s'exprimer dans une langue étrangère, de la moitié des salariés compétents en langue, de 57% de ceux qui sont compétents et occupent des fonctions d'encadrement, et parmi ceux-là c'est le cas de 70% de ceux qui encadrent au moins 20 salariés; par ailleurs, plus ils occupent des postes à responsabilité dans l'entreprise plus ils recourent parfois à une langue étrangère pour communiquer avec leurs collègues et leurs supérieurs hiérarchiques. L'utilisation de la langue dans les rapports avec des collaborateurs internes à la structure de travail est donc manifestement corrélé avec le niveau de qualification et de responsabilité des salariés (voir tableau 3): parmi les salariés compétents en langue et ayant au moins vingt personnes sous leur responsabilité, sept sur dix communiquent avec leurs collègues dans une langue étrangère. Globalement, plus les salariés compétents en langue occupent des postes à responsabilité, plus ils sont amenés à s'exprimer en langue étrangère dans des configurations multiples et qui dépassent largement le cadre traditionnel de la relation clients/ fournisseurs, et plus leurs compétences linguistiques semblent fondamentales et constitutives de leur activité professionnelle.

| **Salariés...** | ...amenés à s'exprimer en langue étrangère | ...compétents en langue | ...compétents en langue et encadrant des équipes | ...compétents en langue et encadrant au moins 20 personnes |
|---|---|---|---|---|
| Utilisent la langue pour communiquer avec les clients | 55% | 57% | 57% | 64% |
| Utilisent la langue pour communiquer avec les fournisseurs | 35% | 49% | 57% | 70% |
| Utilisent la langue pour communiquer avec les collègues | 24% | 44% | 50% | 69% |
| Utilisent la langue pour communiquer avec les supérieurs hiérarchiques | 13% | 24% | 30% | 42% |

| **Salariés...** | ...amenés à s'exprimer en langue étrangère | ...compétents en langue | ...compétents en langue et encadrant des équipes | ...compétents en langue et encadrant au moins 20 personnes |
|---|---|---|---|---|
| Utilisent la langue pour des relations avec d'autres personnes extérieures | 46% | 57% | 61% | 76% |

Tableau 3: L'utilisation de la langue avec différents interlocuteurs
*Note de lecture: parmi les salariés compétents en langue, 57% utilisent la langue étrangère pour communiquer avec les clients, 49% pour communiquer avec les fournisseurs, 44% pour communiquer avec les collègues etc...*
Source: Enquête COI couplée 2006, Statistique Publique, INSEE-DARES-CEE.
Champ: salariés stables (au moins un an d'ancienneté) des entreprises françaises de 20 salariés ou plus.

Outre ces cadres supérieurs dont les fonctions quotidiennes impliquent une bonne maîtrise d'une ou plusieurs langues étrangères, les entreprises françaises de 20 salariés et plus comptent aussi une proportion non négligeable (tout à fait comparable à celle des salariés compétents en langue) de salariés qui sont amenés dans le cadre de leur travail à utiliser une langue étrangère et qui en souffrent. On a vu plus haut que ces individus sont identifiés, dans l'enquête, via une question filtre qui cherche à identifier les personnes dont le travail implique de lire des documents rédigés en langue étrangère; les difficultés ressenties sont donc identifiées au niveau du déchiffrage de documents en langue étrangère et non au niveau du recours à l'expression orale et/ou écrite d'une langue étrangère. On sait ainsi que le tiers des salariés des entreprises de 20 salariés et plus est amené à lire des documents en langue étrangère et que parmi ces derniers, 22% trouvent que cela gêne le bon déroulement de leur travail. Ces salariés en difficulté dans leur usage d'une langue étrangère représentent 7% de l'ensemble des salariés, et comptent pour un peu plus de 500.000 d'entre eux.

Ces difficultés sont-elles liées à un décalage entre les performances attendues de ces salariés par leurs employeurs et leur niveau de qualification réel? Ce groupe est en fait composé de profils assez hétérogènes. D'un côté, le fait d'être exposé au "risque" de devoir lire des documents rédigés en langue étrangère peut être interprété comme le signal d'un certain niveau de qualification de ces salariés, lui-même associé à des postes de travail de niveau supérieur. Mais dans le même temps, les personnes qui sont peu exposées à l'utilisation d'une langue étrangère, mais y sont néanmoins confrontées, en éprouvent naturellement plus de difficultés. Le fait de se sentir en difficulté semble fortement associé à une utilisation réceptive plutôt faible (occasionnelle) d'une langue étrangère: celle-ci n'est pas intégrée dans les tâches habituelles de travail, ne devient donc pas un automatisme, et requiert en conséquence un effort particulier, qui se traduit par le fait de se sentir gêné dans son travail. Ainsi 27% des salariés qui ne sont qu'occasionnellement amenés à lire des documents rédigés en langue étrangère en éprouvent une gêne, alors que ce n'est le cas que de 16% de ceux qui doivent le faire fréquemment.

Par ailleurs le fait de cumuler un usage réceptif et un usage actif (expression orale ou écrite) de la langue étrangère semble procurer un avantage non négligeable: les salariés qui lisent, et s'expriment aussi dans une langue étrangère sont 17% à se sentir en difficulté alors que c'est le cas de 30% de ceux qui doivent lire des documents en langue étrangère mais ne sont jamais amenés à s'exprimer par ailleurs.

Globalement, les personnes qui ne sont amenées qu'occasionnellement à lire des documents dans une langue étrangère, alors même qu'elles ne sont par ailleurs jamais ou peu sollicitées dans leur travail pour s'exprimer dans cette langue (qui la pratiquent peu, en résumé) se sentent bien davantage en difficulté (respectivement 26% et 29% des personnes concernées) que celles qui sont exposées régulièrement et souvent à cet usage: seuls 9% des salariés qui lisent et s'expriment fréquemment dans une langue étrangère dans le cadre de leur activité professionnelle se sentent en difficulté (voir tableau 4).

Les salariés qui déclarent que leur travail implique de lire des documents rédigés dans une langue étrangère et que cela gêne le bon déroulement de leur travail peuvent donc être répartis en deux groupes. Ceux dont l'exposition à la langue étrangère est faible (ils ne s'expriment jamais par ailleurs dans la langue en question), et qui représentent 61% des salariés en difficulté; et ceux qui se sentent en difficulté bien que leur travail implique également qu'ils puissent avoir à s'exprimer, à l'oral et/ou à l'écrit, dans la langue étrangère (l'anglais dans 92% des cas).

| **Proportion de salariés en difficulté pour la lecture de documents en langue étrangère** | | Exposition à la lecture d'une langue étrangère | |
|---|---|---|---|
| | | Personnes souvent exposées | Personnes occasionnellement exposées |
| Utilisation active de la langue étrangère | Personnes s'exprimant souvent en langue | 9% | 13% |
| | Personnes s'exprimant occasionnellement en langue | 18% | 26% |
| | Personnes ne s'exprimant jamais en langue | 32% | 29% |

Tableau 4: Proportion de salariés éprouvant des difficultés à la lecture de documents rédigés dans une langue étrangère selon le degré d'exposition à l'utilisation d'une langue étrangère
*Note de lecture: parmi les salariés souvent exposés à la lecture de documents en langue étrangère mais ne s'exprimant jamais en langue, 32% sont gênés par cette lecture; ce n'est le cas que de 9% de ceux qui sont souvent exposés à la lecture d'une part, et souvent amenés à s'exprimer en langue d'autre part.*
Source: Enquête COI couplée 2006, Statistique Publique, INSEE-DARES-CEE.
Champ: salariés stables (au moins un an d'ancienneté) des entreprises françaises de 20 salariés ou plus.

L'étude de la distribution de ces salariés selon leur diplôme et leur groupe socio-professionnel vient bien confirmer l'existence de deux catégories différentes: les premiers, gênés et peu exposés à l'usage d'une langue étrangère, comptent une proportion nettement plus importante de professions intermédiaires que la population salariée générale (44% contre 27%), moins d'employés, et des proportions comparables d'ouvriers et de cadres. En revanche, les seconds, gênés et plus exposés à l'usage d'une langue étrangère, sont beaucoup plus souvent cadres que dans la population générale (45% contre 20%) et comptent en revanche, proportionnellement, moins d'employés (6% contre 19%) et nettement moins d'ouvriers (7% contre 33%); les professions intermédiaires sont aussi surreprésentées parmi eux (41% contre 27%). Le fait que près de la moitié des salariés qui sont en difficulté tout en étant assez exposés à l'usage d'une langue étrangère soient des cadres explique qu'ils occupent des postes correspondant à un niveau élevé de compétences (dont les compétences linguistiques). Cependant, il est intéressant de souligner que le niveau de diplôme de ces cadres, exposés mais en difficulté, et celui des cadres que nous avons appelés "compétents en langue", c'est-à-dire exposés mais ne se sentant pas en difficulté sur le plan des performances linguistiques, est loin d'être homogène. Sur l'ensemble des cadres de la population salariée de référence, 79% ont fait des études supérieures, et 28% sont issus d'une grande école; parmi les cadres exposés et en difficulté sur le plan des performances en langue, en revanche, le niveau de diplôme est globalement nettement plus faible puisque 53% ont fait des études supérieures et 19% une grande école. Tout à fait à l'inverse, les cadres compétents en langue ont un niveau d'études supérieures pour 91% d'entre eux, et 48% sortent d'une grande école. Pour autant, les données montrent que les seconds n'ont pas plus de responsabilités que les premiers: 59% des cadres exposés en difficulté encadrent une équipe contre 57% des cadres compétents en langue. Mais les cadres gênés ayant un rôle de management encadrent des équipes plus importantes en nombre: 42% encadrent plus de dix personnes et le quart en gère au moins 45. Du côté des cadres compétents en langue, 28% de ceux qui occupent des fonctions d'encadrement ont en charge une équipe de plus de 10 personnes et seuls 25% d'entre eux encadrent plus de 15 personnes. Dans des entreprises ayant une activité à l'internationale, les cadres dont le travail implique de lire et de s'exprimer dans une langue étrangère, mais qui en éprouvent des difficultés occupent donc visiblement plus souvent des postes à responsabilité et encadrent des équipes numériquement plus importantes que les cadres compétents en langue; et ce tout en étant par ailleurs nettement moins diplômés. Ces résultats s'expliquent bien évidemment par une dimension générationnelle, les premiers étant globalement beaucoup plus âgés que les seconds: ils sont donc plus avancés dans leurs carrières, et ont parallèlement reçu une formation en langue moins complète. Ainsi 77% des cadres gênés sur le plan linguistique et qui encadrent une équipe sont âgés de 45 ans ou plus, alors que ce n'est le cas que de 46% de leurs homologues parmi les cadres "compétents en langue".

Pour les salariés qui éprouvent des difficultés en langue et qui ne sont pas cadres, les difficultés s'expliquent aussi par un décalage entre les compétences réelles des salariés et les compétences demandées par les entreprises puisque seuls un quart d'entre eux ont un niveau post baccalauréat, et 53% n'ont même jamais été au lycée.

**ENCADRÉ 1 : LE DISPOSITIF COUPLÉ EMPLOYEURS/SALARIÉS « CHANGEMENTS ORGANISATIONNELS ET INFORMATISATION » (COI) 2006**

C.O.I. 2006 est un dispositif d'enquêtes couplées employeurs/salariés sur les changements organisationnels et l'informatisation. La conception et la mise en œuvre de ce dispositif est le fruit d'une coopération des différents services ministériels, à savoir l'INSEE, la DARES, le DRESS et la DGAFP. Le CEE en a assuré la direction scientifique et la coordination. Ce dispositif permet d'évaluer les effets des changements dans l'organisation et l'outillage informatique des entreprises sur l'organisation du travail des salariés, leurs compétences, leur formation, leurs conditions de travail, leurs salaires. Sa mise en relation avec d'autres sources sur les entreprises, les services publics ou les établissements du secteur hospitalier permet d'étudier différents axes de performances associés aux nouvelles formes d'organisation et aux nouveaux outils informatiques et leurs effets sur la main-d'œuvre.

*Le volet « employeur » intègre trois enquêtes :*

- **L'enquête COI-TIC 2006** concerne les entreprises du secteur marchand. Elle cherche à cerner la manière dont l'entreprise mobilise les outils de gestion de l'organisation du travail et des ressources humaines et les outils techniques couramment regroupés sous les termes de TIC (Technologies de l'Information et de la Communication). Elle a été réalisée en 2005/début 2006 auprès un échantillon d'environ 17 000 entreprises de 10 salariés et plus des secteurs marchands, parmi lesquelles 14 000 entreprises de plus de 20 salariés ont aussi été interrogés.

- **Les volets « employeur » des enquêtes COI-Hôpitaux et COI-Fonction Publique** concernent le secteur hospitalier et certaines administrations de la Fonction Publique. Ces deux parties cherchent à mesurer les transformations en cours sur le plan de l'organisation (nouveaux outils managériaux, Loi d'Organisation de la Loi de Finance (LOLF), relations à l'usager, au patient, tarification à l'activité...) et des outils informatiques utilisés, et à observer l'effet de ces changements dans les secteurs concernés. Ces enquêtes ont été menées auprès de 400 unités employeurs de la Fonction Publique d'État et 800 établissements hospitaliers publics et privés.

*Le volet « salariés » est unique.*

L'enquête COI auprès des salariés apporte une information complémentaire au volet « employeur » sur les caractéristiques organisationnelles des postes de travail et sur les usages des TIC. Dans ce cadre, 20 000 salariés dans les entreprises du volet « entreprises » ont été interrogés fin 2006, ainsi que 2 000 salariés de la fonction publique de l'État et 2 000 pour le secteur hospitalier (pour environ 600 employeurs). Certains salariés avaient pu avoir quitté l'entreprise, l'administration ou l'établissement hospitalier pour lequel ils ont été tirés au moment de l'interrogation. En 1997, ces salariés avaient été exclus du champ de l'enquête. Pour l'édition 2006, ils ont été interrogés. C'est pourquoi le volet « salariés » comporte deux questionnaires :

- un questionnaire principal pour les personnes encore dans l'entreprise ou l'établissement public pour lequel ils ont été tirés au moment de l'interrogation
- un questionnaire secondaire pour celles qui auraient quitté l'entreprise, ou l'établissement en question.

L'étude présentée ici porte sur le seul questionnaire principal, auxquels n'ont répondu que les salariés stables (au moins un an d'ancienneté).

L'enquête a été réalisée par téléphone ou en face-à-face lorsque le numéro de téléphone n'a pas été retrouvé. Sa durée était de 40 minutes maximum pour le questionnaire principal, et de 15 minutes pour le secondaire. En outre, le dispositif a été conçu de manière à pouvoir être enrichi par d'autres sources, le plus souvent administratives, apportant des compléments d'information à la fois sur les entreprises ou les employeurs, mais aussi sur les salariés.

**Encadré 2 : les questions de l'enquête Changements Organisationnels et Informatisation 2006, volet Salariés, sur l'utilisation des langues étrangères au travail**

*(Question posée à tous les salariés)*
**Votre travail implique-t-il de parler ou écrire une autre langue que le français ?**

- ☐ 1. Fréquemment
- ☐ 2. Occasionnellement
- ☐ 3. Jamais ou presque

---

***(Question posée uniquement à ceux qui ont répondu « Fréquemment » ou « Occasionnellement »)***
**De quelle langue s'agit-il ?**
**(Si plusieurs langues étrangères utilisées, noter la plus fréquente)**

---

*(Question posée à tous les salariés)*
**Vous arrive-t-il de devoir utiliser des documents comme des notices, des modes d'emploi etc...qui ne sont pas rédigés en français ?**

- ☐ 1. Fréquemment
- ☐ 2. Occasionnellement
- ☐ 3. Jamais ou presque

---

***(Question posée uniquement à ceux qui ont répondu « Fréquemment » ou « Occasionnellement »)***
**Cela gêne-t-il le bon déroulement de votre travail ?**

- ☐ 1. Oui
- ☐ 2. Non

---

***(Question posée uniquement à ceux qui ont répondu qu'ils s'exprimaient dans une langue étrangère « Fréquemment » ou « Occasionnellement »)***
**L'utilisez-vous ?**

- ☐ 1. dans vos relations avec vos collègues
- ☐ 2. dans vos relations avec vos supérieurs hiérarchiques
- ☐ 3. dans vos relations avec vos fournisseurs
- ☐ 4. dans vos relations avec vos clients
- ☐ 5. dans vos relations avec d'autres personnes extérieures

Charlotte Rønhof

# Linguistic conditions in Danish industries

Language, both Danish and foreign, is a subject that concerns the Confederation of Danish Industry (DI) very much. In co-operation with Copenhagen Business School and Lisbeth Verstraete, we conducted a survey last year of the corporate sector's demand for skills in foreign languages – which linguistic and communicational challenges do enterprises in international business have and what consequences do these challenges pose for the enterprises.

I would like to begin with a short summary of the survey and its results. Afterwards, I will explain how DI sees the demand for language, and which initiatives we believe will strengthen foreign language skills in Denmark.

The fact that Denmark is a small economy which is dependent on the surrounding world was the starting point for our survey. Inter-state trade is crucial for our country's continuing growth and prosperity – and that requires ability both to penetrate the global market and to communicate with old and new trading partners.

This calls for enterprises and employees to possess inter-cultural understanding and great communication skills, which are decisive elements when enterprises compete in an increasingly globalised market.

There are many unwritten rules that enterprises must know and gain insight into: How does one behave at meetings? How does one address business associates? And how does one discuss and obtain good results?

In short: In order to trade at an international level, it is important to be able to make meaningful conversation. And the key to understanding a foreign culture is to understand and speak the language.

**Share of enterprises with international activities**

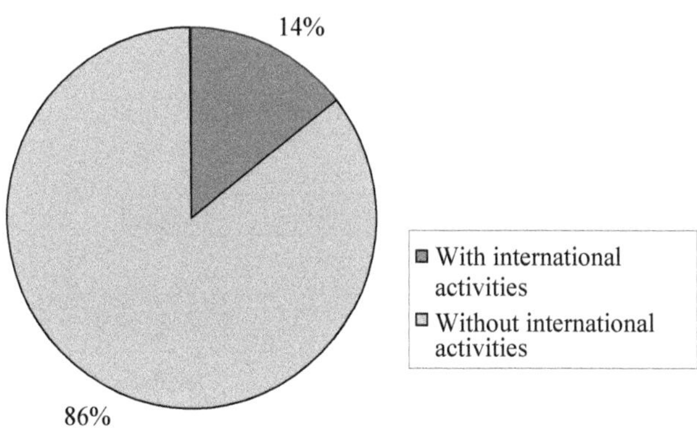

The international market constitutes the major part of the enterprise's business, for almost nine out of ten of the participants in our survey. 86 percent of the enterprises have international activities, such as trade, international collaboration, and subsidiary companies.

The trade of Danish enterprises takes place all over the world, but especially in Scandinavian, German, and English speaking areas.

**Foreign language skills represented in the enterprises**

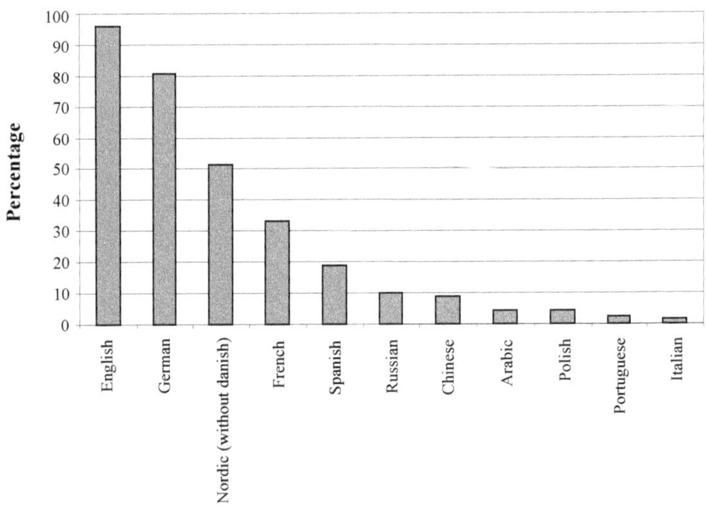


The international activities put forward a demand on enterprises and their employees, when it comes to communication and collaboration with different groups of languages. Basically all the participating enterprises have dual or multi-lingual employees.

**Which types of employees with foreign language skills are in demand?**

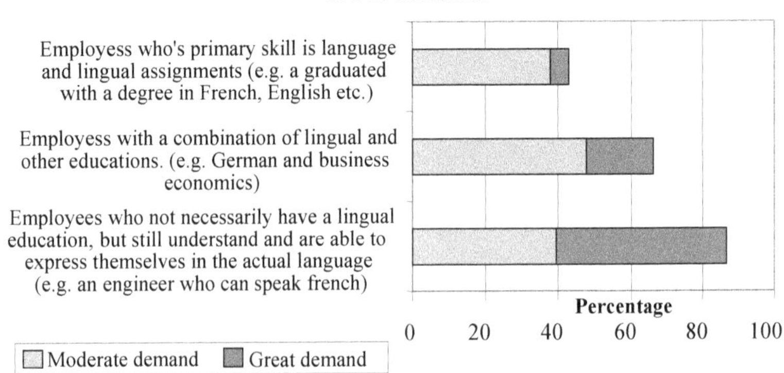

The enterprises are aware of the significance of foreign language skills. But it is not employees with a pure linguistic education that are the most sought after. Only three percent of the enterprises interviewed believe that they need employees with a pure linguistic education. It is, first of all, due to the fact that there are not enough assignments/tasks for employees with such an education. Instead, enterprises choose external consultants when the help of language experts is required. Therefore, one may say, there is a more indirect demand.

Concerning foreign language skills, the enterprises indicate that they need employees with double skills – in other words, an employee that is able to take part in the daily business operation or production, but at the same time has a high level of foreign language skills. For example, an engineer who is fluent in German or a graduate who speaks French.

These employees will be able to manage the daily contact with foreign partners, along with having meetings in foreign languages and understanding a foreign culture. But since these employees are not as such linguistic educated, they will not have the thorough knowledge and insight into a language and all its aspects. Therefore, there will still be a demand for experts.

**The primary language of communication which the enterprise uses in relation to the enterprise's largest business associates**

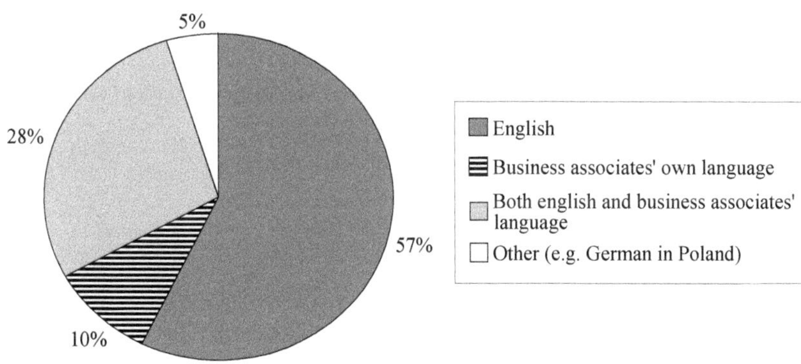


If we look closer at the languages in the different enterprises, we find that English is the dominant foreign language.

English is the language that basically all enterprises use when they communicate and trade at the international market. 96 percent of the enterprises have one or more employees who are able to communicate in English.

And English is the primary business language. More than half of the enterprises use English when they communicate with business associates, and about one third use both English and their business associates' local language. The enterprises' business associates are mostly able to communicate and negotiate in English, and that is the reason why most enterprises choose to communicate in English.

But not all speak English equally well. Enterprises therefore also meet communication challenges. About four out of ten of the participating enterprises have experienced communication issues with enterprises in other countries because of lack of foreign language skills.

**Countries where enterprises have faced communication difficulties**

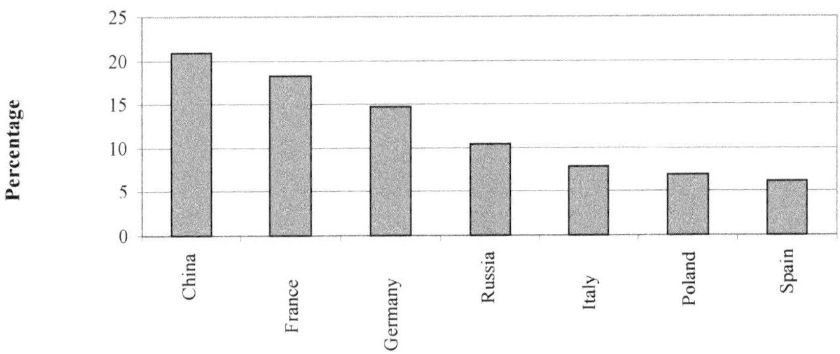


Especially Chinese enterprises are difficult to communicate with. But enterprises also experience communication difficulties in some of Denmark's biggest export markets, such as France and Germany.

**Problems the enterprises have experienced, due to lack of foreign language skills**

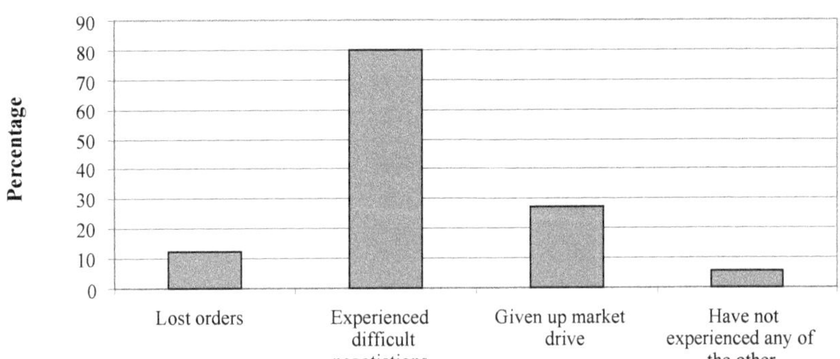


The consequences of communication difficulties vary: It is everything, from minor misunderstandings, to an enterprise loosing a contract. About one third of the enterprises in our survey have experienced that the lack of foreign language skills has had an impact for the enterprise at the international market.

Almost every fourth enterprise have experienced difficulties in negotiations.

Some of the participants in our survey have also directly experienced economic consequences due to the lack of foreign language skills. Nearly four percent of the enterprises have seen losses because of insufficient communication with a business associate, and nearly eight percent have given up ideas about expanding in new markets because of inadequate foreign language skills.

So it will appear that lack of foreign language skills may have very direct economic consequences for an enterprise.

There is, of course, a reason for our interest in this topic: DI's member enterprises need more employees with more foreign language skills.

We would like to correct the misconception that English skills alone are enough, because – as our survey showed – our enterprises need employees with various foreign language skills.

We need to focus on better foreign language skills, and we need to invest in foreign language skills in order to improve.

One way is to start much earlier with foreign language teaching.

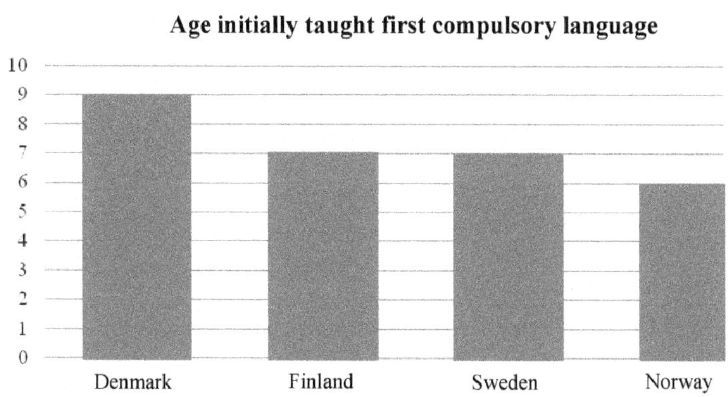


Source: Eurydice

In Denmark, children do not receive teaching in English until the age of 9. In comparison, all the other Scandinavian countries introduce the first foreign language 2-3 years earlier.

Holland has, for example, experimented with English lessons for 5-6 years old primary students, letting them "play" with the language at this early a point of their education.

Therefore, Confederation of Danish Industry believes that foreign language teaching in the Danish primary school should start much earlier. At the age of five or six, the children should start off with English teaching through play, fun, and games, and at the age of 11 or 12, Danish students should receive proper teaching in a second foreign language.

Such an initiative would be a good long-term investment in order to strengthen foreign language skills in Denmark.

But such an investment must not be lost. Today, it is not possible for students to maintain their language skills after they have graduated from secondary school (junior high school in the US) or upper secondary school (UK)/High School (US), unless they take a linguistic higher education.

Many of the students have several foreign language skills, when they start University. But because they no longer use their French, German, or other languages, the skills die as time passes, and that is a shame! Especially when our survey shows that enterprises have great need for employees that are able to speak more than just English.

That is why we work for students to get the opportunity to maintain their foreign language skills while they study engineering, economics, or design. In this way, they will be able to speak other languages than English – and thereby reduce the communication difficulties that enterprises meet.

Lisbeth Verstraete-Hansen

# En route vers le *tout-anglais*? Pratiques et représentations des langues étrangères dans les entreprises danoises


## Resumé

For danske virksomheder er international kommunikation et overvejende engelsksproget fænomen. Nærværende artikel søger – med afsæt i spørgeskemaundersøgelsen *Sproglige kompetencer i den globale økonomi* udarbejdet af Dansk Industri og Copenhagen Business School – at belyse årsagen til denne beskedne interesse for andre fremmedsprog end engelsk.

I artiklens første afsnit fokuseres på de holdninger og praksisser, der ligger bag virksomhedernes vurdering af deres fremtidige behov for fremmedsprog, hvorefter der ses på virksomhedernes oplevelse med sproglige barrierer i den internationale samhandel. Over 40% af de medvirkende virksomheder oplever problemer, som de tilskriver manglende sproglige kompetencer hos deres udenlandske samhandelspartnere.

Vi ser, at virksomhedernes oplevelse af sproglige barrierer forstærkes, når kilden til problemet identificeres som de udenlandske partneres manglende engelskkundskaber. Men trods disse erfaringer anser virksomhederne andre fremmedsprog end engelsk for at være den mindst nødvendige erhvervshumanistiske medarbejderkompetence i international samhandel, og de vurderer ikke, at de i fremtiden vil få større behov for medarbejdere med en sproglig uddannelse. På den baggrund foreslår artiklen at se danske virksomheders holdning til fremmedsprog som udtryk for "anglo-centrisme", således som det er defineret af R. Phillipson.

I artiklens sidste del perspektiveres virksomhedernes "anglo-centrisme" i forhold til den sprogopfattelse, man kan se udtrykt i officielle dokumenter (den danske regerings såkaldte *Globaliseringsrapport*) og institutionelle reformer som f.eks. den seneste gymnasiereform fra 2005.


Pour la plupart des entreprises danoises, la communication internationale est un phénomène largement identifié à l'anglais, qu'il s'agisse de leur pratique actuelle ou de l'évaluation de leurs besoins futurs. Certes, l'usage de l'anglais crée des problèmes dans les pays où cette langue n'est pas la langue maternelle, mais les entreprises n'envisagent pas pour autant un changement de stratégie. Comment expliquer cette absence de considération pour toute autre langue étrangère que l'anglais dans les entreprises danoises? Telle est l'interrogation fondamentale de la présente étude basée sur l'enquête électronique *Compétences linguistiques dans l'économie globale* réalisée en collaboration avec la fédération des entreprises danoises, Dansk Industri (DI).

Après une brève présentation de l'enquête, j'essaierai de dégager la représentation des langues étrangères qui sous-tendent la perception qu'ont les entreprises de leurs besoins linguistiques. Par la suite, ces besoins seront confrontés à la réalité des pratiques et des expériences des entreprises. Pour terminer, les résultats de l'analyse seront considérés à la lumière des discours politiques ayant précédé les récentes réformes du système de l'éducation danois.

Il convient de souligner, d'entrée de jeu, que le terme "besoin" n'est pas simple à manier dans le cadre d'une enquête quantitative fondée sur la perception subjective des répondants. En effet, rien ne permet d'affirmer que les entreprises sont toujours conscientes de leurs besoins. Pour mieux contourner le problème de l'éventuel décalage entre la perception subjective des répondants et les situations objectives qu'ils sont priés de commenter, il m'a paru nécessaire de faire une distinction entre trois types de besoins. Pour ce faire, je me suis inspirée – tout en la simplifiant quelque peu – de la catégorisation proposée par Sonja Vandermeeren (Vandermeeren 2003). On distinguera donc ici entre:

- Besoin *objectif* (les conditions requises pour réussir la communication dans une langue étrangère).
- Besoin *subjectif ou reconnu* (la perception qu'ont les entreprises interrogées de leur besoin futur en langues étrangères).
- Besoin *non reconnu* (l'écart entre les deux premiers évalué en fonction du nombre plus ou moins élevé de problèmes de communication).

## 1. Besoins linguistiques dans les entreprises danoises

L'enquête à la base de cette étude a été réalisée courant octobre-novembre 2007 auprès d'un échantillon représentatif des entreprises danoises membres de DI. Sur l'échantillon de 957 entreprises tirées aléatoirement en fonction de leur taille, 312 ont répondu, et de celles-ci 267 ont déclaré travailler à l'international. Ce sont ces 267 entreprises qui constituent la base de l'analyse ici présentée.[1] Le résultat est représentatif des entreprises membres de DI, mais par rapport au tissu global des entreprises danoises, la catégorie d'entreprises employant plus de 100 personnes est surreprésentée dans l'étude.

L'enquête était divisée en trois sections dont la première était consacrée au profil linguistique de l'entreprise, à l'estimation du futur besoin en langues et les stratégies de recrutement envisagées; la deuxième section concernait la formation et le niveau d'études des employés possédant des compétences linguistiques ainsi que la gestion courante des activités impliquant les langues étrangères. La troisième section, enfin, focalisait sur les pratiques et les expériences avec les langues étrangères dans un contexte international.

Un rapide aperçu des compétences linguistiques actuellement représentées dans les entreprises peut fournir un canevas utile pour évaluer aussi bien les besoins subjectifs que les pratiques réelles des entreprises: l'anglais est omniprésent, tandis que l'allemand est représenté dans plus de 80% des cas, aussi bien dans les petites et moyennes entreprises (PME: moins de 250 employés) que dans les grandes entreprises (GE: plus de 250 employés). En ce qui concerne les autres langues, elles sont généralement moins bien représentées dans les PME que dans les GE. Ainsi, plus de la moitié des GE affirment avoir des compétences lingustiques en français contre seulement un petit tiers des PME. La différence est encore plus prononcée quand il s'agit de l'espagnol et de l'italien (respectivement 47,5% et 29,5% dans les grands établissements contre 13,6% pour l'espagnol et 7,3% pour l'italien dans les PME).

---

[1] Le traitement statistique des données a été effectué en collaboration avec *UNI-C Danmarks IT-center for uddannelse og forskning* (Centre danois d'information technologique pour l'enseignement et la recherche).

En ce qui concerne le besoin futur en langues étrangères, plus de la moitié (53,2%) des entreprises interrogées travaillant à l'international déclarent avoir besoin de compétences linguistiques supplémentaires dans les années à venir (voir Tableau 1).

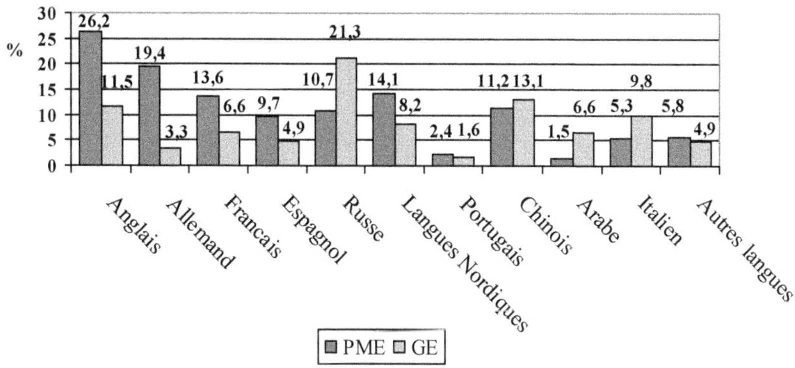


Tableau 1: "De quelle(s) langue(s) l'entreprise pourrait-elle avoir besoin dans les années à venir?" Basé sur les réponses des 52,3% des entreprises ayant déclaré avoir besoin de compétences linguistiques supplémentaires (Possibilité de cocher plusieurs cases)

Les PME recherchent avant tout des compétences en anglais (26,2%), puis en allemand (19,4%), en langues nordiques (14,1%) et en français (13,6%), tandis que le chinois et le russe sont recherchés respectivement par 11,2% et 10,7% des PME. Ce sont justement ces deux langues que les GE recherchent le plus actuellement: 21,3% des GE indiquent un grand besoin futur du russe, qui est suivi du chinois (13,1%). L'anglais est demandé par 11,5%, tandis que le français (6,6%), l'espagnol (4,9%) et surtout l'allemand (3,3%) sont moins demandés.

La question qui se pose automatiquement par la suite est celle de la stratégie de recrutement envisagée par les entreprises. À cet égard, les diplômés issus des filières langues n'entrent pas souvent en ligne de compte. C'est ce qu'indique le Tableau 2 (ci-dessous) qui, conjugué au Tableau 1, contribue à cerner ce qui a été défini plus haut comme le besoin subjectif (ou reconnu) des entreprises.

On observe ici la même tendance dans toutes les entreprises: quelque soit leur taille, elles ne recherchent que dans des proportions modestes le profil linguistique fort caractéristique des filières langues traditionnelles. En effet, les réponses témoignent d'une nette préférence pour des employés combinant des compétences linguistiques avec des compétences techniques.

On peut donner à ce choix plusieurs explications possibles dont d'aucuns sont d'ordre économique tandis que d'autres relèvent davantage de la représentation qu'on se fait des langues étrangères dans les entreprises.

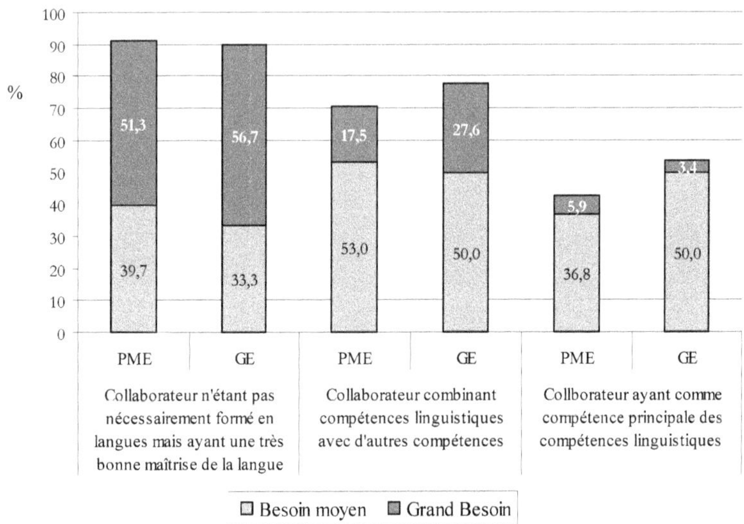


Tableau 2: "De quel type de collaborateur l'entreprise aura-t-elle besoin et comment estimez-vous ce besoin (grand, moyen)?"

En ce qui concerne l'aspect économique, il est probable que le recrutement d'un employé exclusivement occupé par des tâches linguistiques – lesquelles n'ont peut-être pas toujours un volume assez important pour justifier un poste à temps plein – représente un coût trop élevé, à moins que l'employé puisse participer à d'autres activités dans l'entreprise. Par conséquent, le profil idéal est plutôt pluridisciplinaire.

Une autre explication pourrait tenir au fait que les entreprises doutent de la valeur (non seulement dans le sens de rentabilité économique mais aussi dans celui de teneur académique) du savoir acquis dans les filières langues. À titre d'exemple, un répondant a déclaré: "Nous avons régulièrement besoin de compétences linguistiques, le plus souvent combinées avec d'autres compétences, puisque les langues, ça s'apprend".[2] Comment interpréter cette remarque, puisque le droit, les sciences politiques et économiques, la technologie, l'informatique, le génie civil, cela s'apprend aussi? Avançons l'hypothèse que ce qu'exprime ce répondant, c'est l'idée que, contrairement aux études techniques, scientifiques, économiques ou juridiques, une bonne maîtrise des langues s'obtient facilement en dehors de l'université (voyages, séjours à l'étranger, etc.).

On peut donc voir dans les réponses à la fois un doute sur la rentabilité des compétences en langues étrangères et une sorte de méconnaissance des efforts que demande effectivement une connaissance approfondie de tous les aspects (linguistiques, socioculturels et historiques) qui concourent à faire des études des langues étrangères des disciplines académiques à part entière. Envisagé sous cet angle, le Tableau 2 peut être interprété comme l'indicateur d'une représentation des compétences linguistiques comme des compétences n'étant pas en soi génératrices de bénéfice.

[2] Toutes les traductions de l'enquête sont de moi, LVH.

De fait, le rôle joué par les langues étrangères dans l'économie de l'entreprise est peu visible, et on ne trouve au Danemark aucune étude réalisée dans ce domaine[3]. L'enquête n'était pas conçue pour éclairer cet aspect-là, mais elle fournit cependant une série de repères qui suggèrent que, du point de vue de la stratégie de communication internationale, la gestion des ressources linguistiques n'est pas optimale dans les entreprises danoises. En effet, même si les entreprises déclarent avoir des compétences linguistiques diversifiées, elles sont loin de les mobiliser dans la communication internationale.

## 2. Pratiques et expériences en contexte international

En ce qui concerne l'utilisation des langues étrangères sur les marchés internationaux, près de 60% des entreprises interrogées (59,7% des PME et 57,4% des GE) déclarent utiliser exclusivement l'anglais dans leur communication avec leurs partenaires hors du Danemark (Tableau 3 ci-dessous).

Seulement 8,7% des PME et 4,9% des GE déclarent utiliser exclusivement la langue de leur partenaire commercial, tandis que 26,2% des PME et 34,4% des GE pratiquent une alternance entre l'anglais et la langue du pays en question. On pourrait additionner les deux dernières catégories, mais cela ne modifie pas de manière décisive l'image dessinée par ce tableau, à savoir qu'une minorité d'entreprises utilise d'autres langues que l'anglais dans leurs relations internationales.

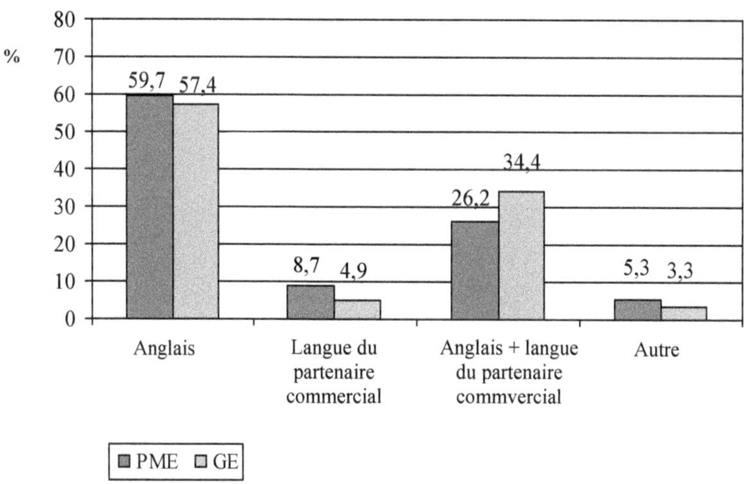


Tableau 3: Quelle est la langue principalement utilisée dans les relations avec vos partenaires les plus importants?

[3] Les résultats des recherches pionnières menées à l'Université de Genève dans le cadre du projet LEAP permettront de mieux connaître cet aspect précis de "l'économie des langues". Pour plus de détails sur ce projet, voir Grin/Sfreddo/Vaillancourt (2007).

Quand on demande aux entreprises pourquoi elles n'ont pas recours à la langue de leur partenaire, elles répondent que ce n'est pas nécessaire, parce que leurs interlocuteurs internationaux connaissent bien l'anglais. Sur la base de ces réponses, on serait tenté de conclure que tout va pour le mieux dans le meilleur des mondes des entreprises et que l'anglais est tout simplement devenu *la* langue qui marche dans les affaires internationales. Qu'on se détrompe!

Dans la section de l'enquête consacrée aux "Pratiques et expériences avec les langues étrangères dans l'entreprise", on trouve deux questions qui, à un niveau général, concernent des situations de communication vécues comme problématiques et qui permettent de se faire une idée de l'écart entre la pratique actuelle des entreprises et les conditions requises pour réussir la communication dans une langue étrangère (ce qui a été défini plus haut comme le *besoin objectif*):

a) Avez-vous fait l'expérience qu'un manque de compétences linguistiques constitue une barrière pour les activités internationales de l'entreprise?[4]
b) Est-ce que l'entreprise a fait l'expérience de problèmes de communication qui peuvent être attribués à un manque de compétences linguistiques chez votre partenaire commercial?

Les réponses se répartissent ainsi:

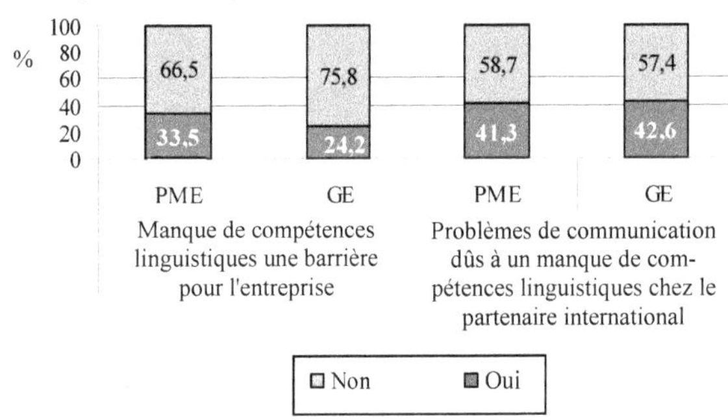


Tableau 4: Expérience de barrières linguistiques

Dans les deux cas, les réponses affirmatives expriment la perception subjective d'une situation où une sorte de "bruit" ou de "brouillage" a perturbé la communication. Ce qui diffère dans les deux questions, c'est la localisation de la source de ce bruit: dans le premier cas, elle se situe dans l'entreprise danoise, dans le deuxième cas chez le partenaire international.

Les résultats indiquent que la perception de barrières linguistiques – ou de problèmes de communication liés à un manque de compétences linguistiques – se renforce lorsque la formulation de la question situe la source du brouillage *ailleurs* que dans l'entreprise.

[4] Les difficultés se manifestent de diverses manières: l'entreprise a tantôt perdu des marchés, tantôt renoncé à promouvoir ses activités sur un marché donné, tantôt – et surtout – elles éprouvent de sérieuses difficultés dans des situations de négociation.

Dans les commentaires, qui accompagnent cette réponse, les répondants expliquent que le problème est parfois dû à des différences culturelles. Mais le plus fréquemment, les commentaires constituent des variations sur le thème: "À l'étranger, ils ne maîtrisent pas suffisamment l'anglais". Ci-dessous quelques exemples où le répondant a d'abord indiqué le(s) pays où il a connu des difficultés, ensuite l'origine des problèmes:

- "France: manque de compétences linguistiques".
- "France, Pologne, Espagne: les partenaires commerciaux ne connaissent pas toujours l'anglais"
- "Pays francophones: marchés perdus".
- "Russie: Mauvaises compétences en anglais en Russie. A crée de l'incertitude au sujet de la base d'un accord sur un marché important".
- "Espagne, Italie, et à un degré moindre la France: Difficile de vendre si pas suffisamment de compétences linguistiques."
- "Turquie, Finlande, Allemagne: Manque de compétences en anglais chez les acheteurs".
- "Allemagne: Problème de compréhension".

Ces commentaires indiquent que la communication internationale constitue un défi de taille pour les entreprises mais, aussi, que les enterprises n'ont peut-être pas pris la mesure de ce défi. En effet, on repère une tendance à placer la responsabilité de la communication manquée sur les défaillances linguistiques de l'autre, c'est-à-dire sur le manque de compétences en anglais hors du Danemark!

On touche ici à une différence d'attitude par rapport à ce que donnent à lire des enquêtes plus anciennes sur les langues étrangères dans les entreprises danoises. Par exemple, en 1992, le rapport sur l'enquête FLAIR (projet piloté par M. Stephen Hagen) cite un répondant danois qui constate que l'entreprise ne parvient plus à écouler son produit sur le marché français depuis le départ du seul collègue francophone (Grinsted 1992). Ici, le répondant considère que les compétences linguistiques présentes dans l'entreprise danoise jouent un rôle décisif pour la réussite de la communication alors que quinze ans après, on repère une tendance à considérer que l'anglais a définitivement acquis le statut de langue de commerce sur les marchés internationaux et que l'adoption de la langue du client n'est plus une nécessité (apparemment ni en termes de courtoisie ni comme possible stratégie de différenciation).

Si on pousse ce raisonnement jusqu'au bout, on pourra dire que les entreprises danoises sont confrontées à des problèmes parce que les Espagnols parlent espagnol, les Français le français, etc. L'attitude des entreprises danoises peut alors être considérée comme une expression d'"anglocentrisme" dans le sens défini par Robert Phillipson:

> The term of *anglocentricity* has been coined by analogy with ethnocentricity, which refers to the practice of judging other cultures by the standards of one's own. There is a sense in which we are inescapably committed to the ethnocentricity of our own world view, however much insight and understanding we have of other cultures [...]. Anglocentricity takes the forms and functions of English, and the promise of what English represents or can lead to, as the norm by which all language activity or use should be measured. It simultaneously devalues other languages, either explicitly or implicitly. (Phillipson 2000 [1992]: 47-48)

Taxer l'attitude des entreprises danoises d'"anglocentriste" est une manière de dire que les entreprises, en faisant de l'anglais la norme de toute pratique linguistique, dévaluent simultanément l'importance des autres langues étrangères. Cette affirmation se voit étayée par les réponses données à la question qui priait les répondants de classer, par ordre de priorité, les compétences qui leur semblaient les plus importantes pour leur entreprise dans les relations internationales, ce qui a donné le résultat suivant (1 = le plus important, 7 = le moins important):

1) Savoir technique sur le produit à vendre.
2) Sens des affaires.
3) Qualifications linguistiques en anglais.
4) Compréhension interculturelle.
5) Sens du marketing.
6) Compétences sociales.
7) Connaissance de la langue du pays concerné.

Tableau 5: Quelles sont, selon vous, les compétences les plus importantes pour votre entreprise dans les relations internationales?

On voit ici que, malgré la constatation de compétences insuffisantes en anglais à l'étranger, les entreprises considèrent que la connaissance d'une langue étrangère autre que l'anglais est la compétence la moins utile dans le commerce international.

De même, en dépit des barrières linguistiques rencontrées, les entreprises danoises estiment ne pas avoir un besoin accru d'employés ayant une formation en langues étrangères: parmi les 31,5% des entreprises ayant déclaré être confrontées à des barrières linguistiques, près d'un tiers estime ne pas avoir besoin de compétences linguistiques supplémentaires.

Les tableaux 4 et 5 ont livré des éléments importants pour répondre à l'interrogation fondamentale de la présente étude. En effet, il me paraît fondé de soutenir que les langues étrangères autres que l'anglais ne sont pas considérées, par les enterprises danoises interrogées dans le cadre de cette enquête, comme un facteur susceptible de faire la différence entre la réussite et l'échec dans les relations internationales, c'est-à-dire comme un avantage concurrentiel. Ce qui explique, entre autres, pourquoi le facteur linguistique pèse de si peu de poids dans les pratiques de recrutement (cf. Tableau 2).

Cependant, étant donné que plus de 40% des enterprises interrogées se heurtent à des barrières linguistiques, il me paraît également fondé d'avancer qu'entre les besoins objectifs des entreprises danoises (les conditions requises pour réussir la communication dans une langue étrangère) et les besoins subjectifs (la perception qu'ont les entreprises interrogées de leur besoin futur en langues étrangères), il existe un *besoin non reconnu* de compétences linguistiques. Un besoin non reconnu par les entreprises – et pas davantage par les responsables nationaux de la politique linguistique et éducative.

En effet, l'anglo-centrisme fait l'objet d'un consensus social observable à plusieurs niveaux de la vie publique où des acteurs puissants défendent l'idée que l'anglais suffit à "relever les défis de la mondialisation" – pour reprendre les termes galvaudés du débat public. Ci-dessous quelques exemples en guise de conclusion.

## 3. En guise de conclusion: le *tout-anglais* pour "relever les défis de la mondialisation"!

Depuis une dizaine d'années, le terme "globalisation" (ou mondialisation) est un des mots les plus fréquemment utilisés dans le débat public danois où il est, le plus souvent, accompagné de celui de "défis". Ce dernier terme couvre des phénomènes légèrement inquiétants comme les délocalisations, les pertes d'emplois, la montée en puissance des pays comme la Chine, l'Inde, la Russie et le Brésil, et la menace que cela représente pour la compétitivité européenne. Et puis, il y a l'aspect linguistique de la mondialisation présentée comme une réalité principalement anglophone, ce qui débouche sur un discours qui reconnaît à l'anglais le statut de *lingua franca* dans tous les domaines considérés comme essentiels pour le renforcement de la compétitivité nationale, c'est-à-dire le monde des entreprises, le système de l'éducation et les institutions de savoir.

Ce parti-pris du *tout-anglais* est particulièrement visible dans le rapport publié par le gouvernement danois en 2006 sous le titre *Progrès, innovation, sécurité. Stratégie pour le Danemark dans l'économie globale* (mieux connu sous le nom de *Rapport de la globalisation*). Un des objectifs déclarés de ce rapport visant à faire du Danemark un des pays les plus compétitifs du monde, est l'adaptation du système de l'éducation aux besoins des entreprises. Les priorités du gouvernement sont donc la lecture/l'écriture du danois, les mathématiques, les sciences et – en vue d'assurer la perspective globale de l'enseignement – l'anglais:

> [...] des compétences linguistiques ainsi que des connaissances sur des cultures et sociétés étrangères sont essentielles pour une participation active dans la société marquée par la mondialisation. Il s'agit de compétences fondamentales dont les bases doivent être posées avant l'entrée au lycée. C'est pourquoi l'enseignement de l'école fondamentale [de 6 à 15 ans] doit avoir une perspective globale. L'enseignement de l'anglais doit être renforcé. (*Fremgang, fornyelse og tryghed* 2006: 21)

On remarque le lien de causalité établi entre les deux dernières phrases: la perspective globale est renforcée par le biais de l'anglais bien que, à plusieurs reprises, la nécessité de donner aux jeunes une bonne compréhension d'autre*s* langue*s* et culture*s* est soulignée. Seulement, quand on en vient aux recommandations concrètes, le pluriel des déclarations d'intentions [langue*s* et culture*s*] est systématiquement remplacé par le singulier qui égale "anglais". À titre d'exemple quelques recommandations pour les écoles (c'est moi qui souligne dans tous les exemples):

1) Il faut encore renforcer le niveau en anglais aux lycées et dans les écoles techniques (ibid. 49).
2) Il faut proposer plus de matières et plus de cours importants en anglais (ibid. 49).
3) Il faut obliger les écoles à utiliser du matérial en anglais dans les différentes matières (ibid. 50).
4) Les écoles techniques et les lycées doivent, plus qu'aujourd'hui, établir des accords avec des écoles dans d'autres pays et faire venir davantage de professeurs invités ayant des langues utiles, notamment l'anglais (ibid. 50).
5) Stratégie pour l'internationalisation: [...] toile ['web'] en anglais (ibid. 50).

Aucune autre langue que l'anglais n'est mentionnée dans le rapport qui synthétise assez fidèlement le discours sur les langues tenu par chefs d'entreprises et décideurs politiques depuis, au moins, le début du XXIe siècle.[5]

Les effets sociaux du discours anglocentriste sont patents. L'anglocentrisme est allé de pair avec un intérêt décroissant pour toutes les autres langues étrangères dans le système de l'éducation.[6]

Une étude récente (Lauridsen 2008) a démontré, chiffres à l'appui, que le nombre d'élèves qui renoncent à étudier une deuxième langue étrangère (après l'anglais qui est obligatoirement la première langue étrangère) dans l'enseignement secondaire est en hausse et, de fait, on n'a jamais vu aussi peu d'étudiants se diriger vers les filières langues dans l'enseignement supérieur. On voit difficilement comment cela pourrait changer étant donné que la récente réforme des lycées entrée en vigueur en 2005 a réduit la proportion d'élèves ayant plus de deux langues étrangères dans leur programme du baccalauréat de 41 à 6%. La base de recrutement pour les filières langues de l'enseignement supérieur s'est donc singulièrement rétrécie depuis 2005.

Reste à se demander si la stratégie détaillée dans le *Rapport sur la globalisation* nous a engagés sur la bonne voie? Est-ce que la liquidation de la diversité linguistique au profit du seul anglais est le bon choix pour améliorer la compétitivité des entreprises danoises? Et est-ce que celles-ci optent pour la meilleure stratégie possible en misant sur l'anglais à un moment où les contacts entre agents économiques sont plus intenses que jamais? La réponse n'est pas aisée. Mais la tendance générale qui se dégage de l'enquête – où l'usage de l'anglais a crée des problèmes pour plus de 40% des entreprises danoises interrogées – laisse penser que le maintien d'un enseignement efficace et approfondi d'un certain nombre de langues étrangères *autres que l'anglais* est tout sauf un luxe superflu pour la société danoise!

Pour en arriver là, à un enseignement ouvert à la diversité linguistique, il faudrait opérer un véritable retour en arrière, ce qui présuppose toutefois un profond changement d'attitude envers les langues. Et c'est bien là que réside, à mon sens, un des plus grands défis que pose la mondialisation à la société danoise: dans la question de savoir comment et par où il faut commencer pour en finir avec l'attitude du *tout-anglais* – non seulement dans le monde des entreprises mais dans la société toute entière.

## 4. Ouvrages cités

*Fremgang, fornyelse og tryghed. Strategi for Danmark i den globale økonomi.* April 2006. København: Regeringen.

Grin, F./Sfreddo, C./Vaillancourt, F. (2007): *Langues étrangères dans l'activité professionnelle* (*LEAP*). Genève: Université de Genève. www.unige.ch/eti/recherches/groupes/elf/recherche-activite/projets-en-cours/LEAP/RappInt-PoPo-v4.pdf.

5 Certes, des points de vue opposés se font également entendre, mais comme le plus souvent ils viennent du côté des institutions vouées à la défense de la langue danoise, des associations des professeurs des langues étrangères, des traducteurs et des enseignants de langues, on leur accorde moins de crédit que lorsqu'ils viennent du côté du patronat par exemple.

6 À l'exception notable du chinois proposé dans un nombre croissant d'établissements.

Grinsted, A. (1992): *Foreign language analysis in industrial regions of Europe*. Kolding, Det erhvervssproglige Forskningsinstitut, Handelshøjskole Syd.

Lauridsen, E. (2008): *Andet fremmedsprog i folkeskolen. Del 1: Hvad siger tallene?* Aarhus: Institut for Sprog, Litteratur og Kultur, Aarhus Universitet.

Phillipson, R. (2000) [1992]: *Linguistic imperialism*. 5th impr. Oxford: Oxford University Press.

Vandermeeren, S. (2003): German language needs in Danish companies. In: *Hermes. Journal of linguistics – Revue de linguistique – Tidsskrift for Sprogforskning – Zeitschrift für Lingvistik*, 31-2003, 13-29.

Martin Stegu

# Language needs in business: myths and realities. Considérations générales et autrichiennes


## Abstract

Das Beharren auf dem Ideal von Mehrsprachigkeit, sowohl innerhalb als auch außerhalb Europas, wird bisweilen als nicht mehr zeitgemäße und teilweise auch kostspielige Utopie angesehen, die meist von etwas realitätsfremden "SprachenliebhaberInnen" vertreten wird. Letztere stürzen sich dann mit umso mehr Enthusiasmus auf Stimmen "aus der Wirtschaft", die behaupten, dass Mehrsprachigkeit letzten Endes keine Mehrkosten verursacht, sondern größere Marktchancen und damit auch größere Gewinne verspricht. Bei den zu diesem Zweck immer wieder durchgeführten Umfragen zum Sprachenbedarf ist aber zu beachten, dass diese keinen direkten Zugang zu realen Notwendigkeiten, sondern nur zu Meinungen und Behauptungen zu diesen ermöglichen. Dies soll weder den Wert von Bedarfsanalysen noch von – ganz allgemein – "Sprachen für die Wirtschaft" in Frage stellen. In diesem Beitrag geht es nur darum, "Mythen" (= Stereotype und Vorurteile) und "Wirklichkeit" im Zusammenhang mit Nutzen und Kosten von Sprachen genauer auseinanderzuhalten. Der ökonomisch-betriebswirtschaftliche Diskurs allein kann die Notwendigkeit von Mehrsprachigkeit jedenfalls weder zur Gänze begründen noch widerlegen. Dies sollte jedem/jeder bewusst sein, dem/der Mehrsprachigkeit weiterhin ein großes Anliegen ist.


## 1. Introduction

When we look at the the topic of language needs, we have to ask ourselves whether such needs can be directly and empirically "proved", or whether we only have access to them via beliefs, attitudes, 'awarenesses' about such needs. Even if we happen to differentiate between "real" and "imagined needs", one should not neglect that these phenomena always overlap and are not easily delimitable from each other, neither practically nor theoretically.

In general, the "world of business" or – more concretely – business people have rather positive attitudes towards the learning of (foreign) languages; therefore they are particularly interesting for language politicians, because they represent a very important potential lobby group for multilingualism.

As the "economic discourse" is seen by many people, consciously or inconsciously, as the actual world's leading "episteme" – using here a term from Foucault (see, for example, Foucault 1969) –, the whole question of European and worldwide multilingualism will become particularly interesting, if we concentrate upon the part ('foreign', second) languages play in the business world. In this contribution, on one hand, we would like to underline the importance of economic and business arguments for questions of multilingualism and language competences, but, on the other hand, we argue that they cannot totally replace more general reflections and that they don't have an *a priori* privileged status in the overall discussion.

As at the Lisbon EFNIL conference, I had the honour to represent Austria, I would like to present briefly the language situation in my country, but already keeping in mind our general "myths vs. realities perspective".

## 2. Language situation in Austria

The main official language of Austria is German (89% of the population; Archan/ Holzer 2006: 18). As German is generally considered to be a pluricentric language, it will not come as a surprise that the standard German spoken and written in Austria is not identical with the standards of Germany, Switzerland etc. Between German speaking countries, though, you will not find clear cut language frontiers, but rather dialect continua, which will also influence the standard varieties of the countries concerned.

There are only a few traces of the multilingual reality of the former Austro-Hungarian monarchy, which are the so called "autochthonous" minority languages Slovene (Carinthia, Southern Austria); Croatian (the Burgenland variety, Eastern Austria), Hungarian (Burgenland), Czech and Slovak (Vienna) and Romanes. Especially in the urban agglomerations you find immigrant minorities with their languages (Turkish, Serbian/Croatian/Bosnian, etc.).

The main foreign language taught at the primary and secondary level (and even in the kindergartens) is of course English (approximately 98%), the other languages are, in the elementary schools, French 1.7%, Italian 1.8%, Spanish 0.1%, Slovene 0.5%, Croatian 3%, Hungarian 0.1%, and, in the secondary schools (grammar schools, "Gymnasien", etc.), French 29.0%, Italian 9.6% (especially in Carinthia and Tyrol), Spanish 5.1%, Russian: 1,5% (Archan/Holzer 2006: 21ss.).

Even a superficial analysis of these data will show us that the languages of the autochthonous minorites play a (modest) role almost exclusively at the primary level, apart from a few pilot and/or prestige projects (cf. the bilingual Gymnasien in Klagenfurt/ Carinthia and Oberwart/Burgenland), and that the immigrant languages are practically non-existant in the normal school curricula.

As we have already mentioned, we find Italian as language subject in many secondary schools in Carinthia, an Austrian federal province which has a border with Italy. The same "Bundesland" also has a border with Slovenia, but Slovenian is much less widespread in Carinthian schools than Italian – although it is also one of the two indigenous languages of Carinthia, and Italian is not. The number of schools with Czech, Slovak and Hungarian in the regions bordering on the corresponding countries is not very large either. Since the fall of the Iron Curtain, the situation has certainly improved in some respects, but it has never been possible to register a considerable 'run' to the (Middle and) East European languages, neither on the part of private learners, nor – still less – on the part of the school system with its offer of compulsory and optional language courses.

Although the myth of the Austro-Hungarian monarchy has always been present up to a certain degree in the Austrian population and the historical and geographical proximity of Austria to 'Eastern' countries has always been underlined – even and particulary in times, where the frontiers were still rather closed –, there were only ever a restricted number of people who developed a specific know-how in commercial and other kinds of contacts with those countries. The average Austrian had become more and more "West oriented", and this orientation has remained decisive also for the selection (and institutional) offer of foreign languages. Even the growing interest in (formerly rather cheap) holidays at the beautiful coasts of (Ex-)Yugoslavia was not able to overturn the general beliefs and prejudices about the especially high degree of difficulty (and the low degree of estethic attractiveness) of Slavic and other languages of the geographic region in question.

If we have a look at the tertiary university level, we have to distinguish language studies on one hand and other subjects with complementary language teaching on the other. For our context the second case is much more relevant.

In Austrian universities there had been a long tradition of complementary, optional language courses, called "für Hörer aller Fakultäten", which were free, but often held in didactically problematic large groups, especially for languages like Spanish and Italian.

As these courses were not part of the core curricula, most universities stopped this offer, with one remarkable exception, my own university, the WU/Wirtschaftsuniversität Wien (www.wu.ac.at). But in some other universities they founded so called language centers, which are no longer free of charge (or were not integrated in the normal tuition fees) and guaranteed a better quality management and smaller groups than in those mass courses mentioned before. (By the way, there is a scaling of the course fees so that they are still much less expensive for students than for external learners.)

The only non language curriculum category with a compulsory language programme is Business Administration and Economics. As an example, I just want to explain the system in the WU, where we have two main branches of study: Business Administration and International Business Administration. Business Administration has one compulsory language, most of the students choose English, but it is also possible to choose another language; International Business Administration in the bachelor system has two languages (the possible languages will be enumerated below). In the former Diplom- or Magistersystem it was even possible to study three or more languages, one as a so called "Langsprache" ("long language"= in the first and second part of the study), and the others either as "short languages", one in the first and one in the second part, or as optional subjects.

It is interesting enough to see that the Bologna System has not always brought along advantages, so for instance the language offer has suffered from the Bologna restructuring, at least in my university. In the former Magisterstudium there were many electives, and many students chose languages, and so they were given the opportunity to attend at least beginner courses in a third, fourth or fifth language. In the Business Administration programme now there are no more free electives, because the study programme has been filled up with marketing, economics, statistics, etc., which makes it very difficult to integrate totally curriculum independent language courses into the students' timetables.

In addition to this, the new master programmes are also not very language friendly because they were only planned by marketing, finance, etc. professors who were not supposed to integrate a preexisting language policy. This constellation has brought about the result of what I would call an "*implicit* language policy", which nobody has planned as such, but which sometimes has more consequences than an *explicit* one.

Which are the languages which can be chosen by our business students? English, French, Italian, Spanish, Russian, Czech, in a cooperation project with the Institute of Sinology of the University of Vienna, also Chinese, as "ordinary" language subjects; there are some other languages where you can attend courses for beginners in order to reach a "survival level" (e.g. Japanese, Arabic, Portuguese, Bosnian-Serbian-Croatian and many others). In the Diplom-/Magisterstudium the ordinary programme started with A2/B1 level and led to a B2/C1 level (of the Common European Reference Framework for Languages, Trim 2001), with a special focus upon economic language and communication.

There are also other universities, faculties, universities for applied sciences (Fachhochschulen), and some of them may have a broader or more specific language offer (I am thinking here of the FH Eisenstadt in the Burgenland which is specialized in the languages of Central and Eastern Europe), but in general, the canon of the languages offered is more or less identical. We have English, and French, Italian, Spanish and Russian, plus the one or other language.

## 3. Language needs and language needs analyses

In order to steer or to reorientate language learning offers and choices, from time to time educational and/or economic institutions conduct so called language needs analyses (cf. Vandermeeren 1998, Archan/Dornmayr 2006, but also the ELAN study, see bibliography). Normally in such analyses the actual language use in mainly export oriented and multinational companies is described, and the managers are asked whether the language competences seem to them to be sufficient or should be intensified and/or diversified. The results of such surveys are supposed to adjust and correct only tradition or intuition based beliefs about the importance of certain languages, and no one would deny the usefulness of such surveys which can deliver some concrete data about language use and language needs; but one should never forget that we can only get direct access to the beliefs of managers, stakeholders etc. *about* language needs, and not to language needs *as such*. The success of export sales is based upon so many different factors that I personally have doubts about the seriousness of claiming that the failure of a certain export project was *exclusively* caused by insufficient language competence.

I think that the whole "language needs and language needs analyses approach" still merits more fundamental, 'epistemological' reflection. The 'ideal' situation would of course be that the selling company speaks the language of its client perfectly (or maybe also that the client has a perfect competence of the language of the selling company). In a multinational company the ideal, utopian situation would be that every employee speaks all the languages of his/her colleagues at a C2 level (see above). The second best solution for both scenarios would be the perfect mastery of a *lingua franca*, for example English (cf. Seidlhofer 2004, Jenkins 2007). Here the question will arise whether a *lingua franca* can, by definition, be "perfectly mastered" and whether there are not still potential intercultural problems to be solved.

Of course, the "perfect mastery" of foreign languages (whether *linguae francae* or not) is such a utopian and unrealistic goal that nobody would discuss it seriously in the context of language needs (apart from language specialists, such as language teachers, translators, etc.). That shows us that language competences, i.e. the diversity of languages learnt and the levels of competence reached in each of them, within the language needs discussion will always have to do with some compromise, because we all know that it is impossible to know *all* the languages spoken by potential communication (and commercial) partners and that it is even less possible to know all these languages "perfectly".

In business contexts, on the other hand, "quality", "excellency" are frequently used words, and there will always be an at least implicit comparison and potential parallelism between the excellency of the sold product and the excellency of the communication processes which lead to the act of sale – of communication processes which, as we know, often happen in foreign languages.

Discussions about language needs in business in a possible didactic perspective oscillate in a sort of dialectic tension between realism – a certain minimum standard of competences in order to guarantee the communicative actability of commercial projects – and the goal of excellency even in foreign language aspects. It seems evident that in the case of two equally good products the communicative aspects (= very often the foreign language competences) may become a decisive criterion. Sometimes these communicative and foreign language competences may become even more important than the "objective quality" of a product.

In non business contexts the "perfect mastery" of a foreign language for most language didacticians is no longer a realistic didactic goal; for many supporters of the maintenance of European and world wide plurlingualism, the only way of saving this idea is to give up the absolute ideal of nearnativeness in the (foreign, second, third, etc.) languages concerned. There are many reasonable arguments for this claim; but everyone who has to do with business should know that in competitive constellations, the "quality" of language competence will be suddenly assigned a much larger importance than in the generally admitted *doxa* of foreign language didacticians. (We will come back to the role of "language awareness" in the next part, but we can still affirm that the "norm awareness" of business people and of foreign language didacticians do not [not yet?] absolutely coincide.)

Even if we attribute to the findings of language needs analyses a relatively high part of "realism", we still have to accept another form of compromise: It is impossible for schools and universities to always adapt immediately to permanently changing market demands. The offer of languages in official educational establishments will always be somehow conservative. This insight, however, should not justify the maintenance of certain "language canons" (for example "English, Latin, French" and nothing more) *per saecula saeculorum*.

As we wanted to show in this chapter the possibilities and limits of language needs analyses, we would like to discuss in the following paragraphs the role of "language needs awareness" and some other problems in the context of "economic and business arguments for the learning of languages".

## 4. Langues 'étrangères' et économie: quelques points de discussion

### 4.1 Language (needs) awareness

Nous avons déjà mentionné qu'on ne devrait pas identifier les résultats d'analyses de besoins linguistiques avec les besoins 'réels', mais seulement avec les croyances que les personnes interrogées se font de ces besoins. Il s'agit là d'un phénomène de "language awareness" ("conscience linguistique"; cf. James/Garret 1992), à savoir de "language needs awareness" (en suivant l'exemple de termes comme "language learning awareness"). Comme dans mon approche, l'"awareness" peut être également explicite et verbalisée et peut ainsi mener vers des réflexions (pré-)théoriques, nous pourrons y voir aussi une forme de "linguistique populaire" ("folk linguistics").

Sans trop vouloir entrer dans les détails de ces approches (voir Stegu 2008a), je voudrais juste souligner trois aspects:

a) Comme à notre avis il n'existe de ligne de démarcation nette et objective ni entre "expert theories" et "folk theories" ni entre "experts" et "non-experts" (en allemand: "Laien"; voir Stegu 2007), il faudra se rendre compte que tout le domaine de la politique linguistique ainsi que tous les propos ayant trait aux besoins linguistiques se trouvent toujours sur un continuum entre réflexion "scientifique" et réflexion "populaire".

b) La linguistique appliquée, dans sa passion pour une ouverture vers le monde si réel de l'économie et du business, ne devrait pas prendre les opinions de représentants de ce dernier naïvement pour des faits objectifs (ni pour de pures fictions, d'ailleurs). De toute manière, elle devrait étudier plus intensément l'origine et la genèse de ces croyances, convictions, attitudes, "awarenesses" pour pouvoir leur attribuer le statut qu'ils méritent.

c) La plupart des linguistes ont une attitude positive vis-à-vis du plurilinguisme et seront toujours heureux d'être confrontés à des opinions provenant du monde économique qui favorisent également l'utilité, voire la nécessité du plurilinguisme pour les activités économiques et commerciales. Mais il ne faut pas oublier non plus quelles personnes, dans la plupart des entreprises interrogées, sont choisies pour répondre à des questionnaires portant sur des problèmes linguistiques: "Ah, c'est encore quelque chose pour Mme XY; elle s'intéresse aux langues […]!" Qu'il s'agisse d'opinions *pour* ou *contre* un renforcement du plurilinguisme, j'insiste une dernière fois sur le fait que nous avons affaire à des opinions subjectives qui ne décrivent "la réalité" que d'une façon indirecte.

### 4.2 Besoins réels vs. motivations personnelles

Dans les théories de la motivation, on distingue entre motifs extrinsèques et motifs intrinsèques (Dörnyei 2001, Stegu 2008b). Quand quelqu'un est un grand amateur d'opéras italiens et commence à apprendre la langue de ces livrets, il sera guidé par une motivation intrinsèque; quand une personne apprend qu'elle passera les cinq prochaines années de sa vie professionnelle dans une filiale de son entreprise à Rome, c'est plutôt une motivation extrinsèque qui la poussera à apprendre cette langue. La motivation est particulièrement forte, quand on arrive à synthétiser les motifs extrinsèques et intrinsèques: "J'ai toujours aimé l'Italie, c'est pourquoi j'ai posé ma candidature pour le poste à Rome. J'en profiterai aussi pour pouvoir enfin perfectionner mes connaissances de la langue italienne, un projet que j'ai déjà depuis longtemps."

La situation est bien sûr différente quand un élève doit "choisir" une langue à l'école. J'ai mis "choisir" entre guillemets, parce que a) souvent les alternatives sont très limitées et b) ce sont d'abord surtout les parents qui décident quelles langues seront plus utiles pour leurs enfants. Mais même après, quand l'étudiant en management international ("International Business Administration", voir ci-dessus) pourra choisir deux ou trois langues parmi l'anglais, le français, l'espagnol, l'italien, le russe et le tchèque, sa décision reposera sur un "mix" de motivations extrinsèques et intrinsèques, de besoins (supposés!) réels et motivations personnelles. Dans la plupart des cas, l'étudiant ne saura pas dans quel contexte international il travaillera un jour, et même s'il a l'intention de s'installer bientôt en Corée du Sud, il verra probablement que le coréen n'est pas une langue offerte par son école de commerce.

Il choisira donc des langues qu'il considère comme importantes, peut-être pour un plan de carrière relativement concret, peut-être parce qu'elles sont "généralement" considérées comme importantes. Il aura certainement une confiance de base que les langues offertes par son école ou par son université sont importantes soit à l'échelle mondiale soit pour la situation spécifique de son pays. Cette importance, nous nous en doutons, est encore construite et déterminée par le discours et ne se base pas exclusivement sur des 'vérités objectives'. Cependant l'importance créée par le discours ne reste pas réduite à celui-ci, le discours peut aussi créer des faits réels; l'importance de l'anglais comme langue internationale par excellence est certainement au moins partiellement le résultat d'une construction discursive: puisque tout le monde a parlé et reparlé du rôle dominant de l'anglais, la langue est devenue 'réellement' importante.

Le choix de l'anglais par un étudiant en économie et en gestion est devenu entretemps un fait incontournable; le choix des autres langues – quand l'étudiant ne se décide pas à se contenter d'une seule langue – est plus intéressant.

Depuis quelques années, on peut observer une vague d'enthousiasme mondiale pour l'espagnol. C'est une langue qui unit, comme l'anglais, le Vieux et le Nouveau Monde, et ne présente pas non plus de difficultés phonétiques et/ou grammaticales insurmontables. Comme on peut très bien l'observer auprès des étudiants de la WU de Vienne, beaucoup d'étudiants qui choisissent cette langue ressentent une forte motivation intrinsèque, une forte sympathie pour la culture hispanophone, très souvent aussi pour celle de l'Amérique latine. En même temps, ils sont convaincus que le choix de cette langue est aussi 'économiquement' bien fondé.

Dans le cas de l'italien, les étudiants ont également un rapport émotionnel assez fort avec le pays, sa langue et sa culture; ils choisissent cette langue surtout pour des raisons d'intérêt personnel – comme les motifs professionnels comptent beaucoup moins dans le choix ce cette langue, on peut dire qu'ils choisissent l'anglais pour leur travail et l'italien pour le plaisir (cf. Polagnoli 2004, Richterová 2005).

Ce qui surprend, par contre, c'est qu'au moins pour l'économie autrichienne l'italien est toujours beaucoup plus important que l'espagnol, étant donné que l'Italie est – après l'Allemagne – le deuxième partenaire commercial de l'Autriche. Cela signifie que l'importance de l'espagnol pour un futur manager autrichien 'moyen' est plutôt un mythe qu'un fait réel.

Juste une petite remarque concernant le rôle du français pour nos étudiants: La langue française a été longtemps la deuxième langue étrangère 'automatiquement' apprise après l'anglais. Dans les écoles (secondaires) cette position est encore incontestée, mais dans les universités et les autres institutions de formation (écoles de langues etc.), c'est l'espagnol qui est en train de dépasser le français (ou l'a déjà dépassé). Pour les étudiants qui continuent à apprendre le français au niveau tertiaire, il y a seulement une minorité qui fait preuve de la même passion et du même degré d'identification que les étudiants ayant choisi soit l'espagnol soit l'italien. La plupart de ces étudiants continuent à apprendre le français pour la seule raison qu'ils le maîtrisent déjà, grâce aux connaissances acquises au lycée quelques années auparavant. (Alors que les étudiants parlant l'espagnol et l'italien voyagent très souvent dans les pays où ces langues sont parlées, j'ai rencontré très souvent des étudiants qui se présentent aux examens finaux de français sans avoir jamais mis le pied dans un pays francophone! Les autorités culturelles françaises ont certainement encore des tâches de marketing très intéressantes devant elles ...)

### 4.3 Utilités directes et indirectes

Il est impossible de prévoir quelles seront exactement les langues dont un étudiant de gestion aura "besoin" dans sa future activité professionnelle. Et même s'il nous paraît également impossible de donner une classification exacte et objective allant de langues économiquement *très* importantes à des langues *peu* importantes, chacun devra faire un choix entre au moins trois pôles: l'importance 'absolue' et mondiale d'une langue, l'importance régionale/locale d'une langue et l'importance (= la préférence) personnelle.

Dans ces réflexions, il ne faudra pas oublier que l'apprentissage d'une langue peut avoir aussi un effet indirect: Quand on apprend p.ex. l'italien, cet apprentissage ne sera pas inutile, même si on ne va jamais rencontrer de partenaire commercial italophone ou même si on ne va passer aucun séjour touristique en Italie. Chaque nouvelle langue élargit l'horizon interculturel et facilite ainsi le contact avec de nouveaux partenaires commerciaux étrangers ainsi que, très concrètement, l'apprentissage d'autres langues supplémentaires.

### 4.4 Quels niveaux pour quelles compétences?

En parlant de besoins linguistiques, on ne devrait pas dire qu'on a besoin "de l'anglais" en tant que tel ni "du français" ou "de l'espagnol", sans préciser de quel "anglais" etc., et de quels niveaux de langues et de quelles compétences partielles on est en train de parler. En outre, dans toutes les réflexions et discussions autour de ce sujet, nous observerons une scission quasi-automatique entre deux catégories fondamentales: entre l'anglais d'un côté et toutes les autres langues de l'autre.

Pour compléter cette vue panoramique, je voudrais juste évoquer encore quelques questions, sans toutefois vouloir ou pouvoir y donner des réponses définitives.

Quel anglais: l'anglais de la Grande-Bretagne ou des Etats-Unis ou d'une autre communauté anglophone? L'apprenant étranger doit-il se décider pour une seule variété anglophone reconnue? Pour un anglais (quasi-)parfait et (quasi-)natif? Ou bien pour l'anglais ('un' anglais?) comme *lingua franca*, avec de considérables éléments (substrats) de la langue de départ?

Lorsqu'un individu apprenant l'anglais *plus* au moins une autre langue 'étrangère': le niveau de l'anglais devrait-il être forcément meilleur que le niveau de l'autre langue (selon la formule: "Les négociations se font en anglais, le *small talk* dans la langue locale.")?

Quelles sont les compétences partielles qui sont particulièrement demandées: les compétences langagières, grammaticales, lexicales etc. (vs. les compétences pragmatiques et interculturelles); les compétences orales, écrites, productrices, réceptrices; *small talk* vs. langues de spécialité, etc.? (Ici encore, il ne suffit pas seulement de poser des questions à différents groupes de managers, mais de développer des designs de recherche plus sophistiqués qui, il est vrai, n'entraineront pas de résultats 'objectifs', mais au moins des résultats 'moins subjectifs'.)

Et – si on ne peut pas partir de l'idéal d'une perfection quasi-native – quels sont les niveaux réalistes à atteindre (voir les niveaux A1-C2 du Conseil de l'Europe)?

### 4.5 Besoins linguistiques et contradictions discursives

Sauf dans les rencontres de linguistes ou de représentants officiels d'organisations comme l'Union européenne et le Conseil de l'Europe, les discours portant sur l'importance des langues contiennent potentiellement des contradictions. Cela vaut aussi pour le monde de l'économie et du business qui est *a priori* très "glottophile". Mais il y a également une co-présence de voix qui ne cessent de prétendre qu'en principe l'anglais suffit comme seule langue de communication (et d'apprentissage). Ou bien, pour revenir à la situation de mon université, où personne ne dira officiellement et publiquement que "les langues ne sont pas importantes", mais quand il s'agit de prévoir des cours de langues dans les curricula, d'un seul coup toutes les autres matières deviennent plus importantes et il ne reste presque plus de place pour les langues ...

Même si on est d'avis que *tous* les discours sont potentiellement contradictoires, des analyses détaillées des discours portant sur les langues et sur le plurilinguisme pourraient vérifier si ces derniers sont peut-être soit plus contradictoires soit moins contradictoires que d'autres types de discours, ce qui nous donnerait une image intéressante sur le rôle effectivement attribué aux langues étrangères et à leur importance dans la société.

## 5. En guise de conclusion: raisonnements économiques vs. raisonnements culturels, politiques, philosophiques et éthiques

Quand on a l'intention de prêcher l'idée du plurilinguisme, on tend à chercher des arguments provenant d'autres domaines qui devraient et pourraient soutenir cette idée de base. Comme de nos jours le discours économique et "business" jouit d'un très haut prestige, certaines personnes veulent en quelque sorte remplacer les arguments traditionnels par des arguments économiques. Même si on essaie de mesurer la force économique de langues ou de compétences langagières (voir Grin 1996), je ne trouve pas justifié qu'on commence à considérer les arguments économiques comme les seuls arguments valables.

Bon nombre de linguistes, lesquels sont souvent très critiques vis-à-vis de l'influence que le 'pouvoir' peut avoir sur notre langue et sur nos processus communicatifs (voir Fairclough 1992), se méfient de la force totalisatrice du discours économique. Il faut relativiser ce dernier, surtout quand on veut l'analyser avec une certaine distance – ce qui n'exclut pas qu'on le prenne au sérieux, bien au contraire.

Pour défendre l'idée du plurilinguisme, il faut choisir une vue globale qui synthétise des réflexions culturelles, philosophiques, éthiques, politiques *et* économiques. En voulant se baser uniquement sur des arguments économiques, on adopte peut-être une attitude actuellement à la mode, mais qui ne peut pas tenir compte de la complexité du phénomène en question.

## 6. Bibliographie

Archan, S./Dornmayr, H. (2006): *Fremdsprachenbedarf und -kompetenzen. Unternehmensbefragung zu Ausbildungsqualität und Weiterbildungsbedarf.* Wien: ibw.

Archan, S./Holzer, C. (2006): *Sprachenmonitor. Zahlen, Daten und Fakten zur Fremdsprachensituation in Österreich.* Wien: ibw.

Dörnyei, Z. (2001): *Motivational strategies in the language classroom.* Cambridge: Cambridge University Press.

ELAN: *Effects on the European Economy of Shortages of Foreign Language Skills in Enterprise*, cf. http://www.cilt.org.uk/research/projects/employment/elan_finalreport.pdf (consulted on 7/4/2009).

Fairclough, N. (ed.) (1992): *Critical language awareness.* London: Longman.

Foucault, M. (1969): *L'Archéologie du savoir.* Paris: Gallimard.

Grin, F. (ed.) (1996): *Economic approaches to language and language planning* (Special issue). International Journal of the Sociology of Language, 121.

James, C./Garrett, P. (eds.) (1992): *Language Awareness in the Classroom.* London: Longman.

Jenkins, J. (2007): *English as a lingua franca.* Oxford: Oxford University Press.

Polagnoli, L. (2004): *Neue Marketingstrategien als Antwort auf verändernde Marktbedingungen: eine Analyse für das Fach Italienisch am Institut für Romanische Sprachen der Wirtschaftsuniversität Wien.* Wien: Wirtschaftsuniversität Wien (unpublished diploma thesis).

Richterová, L. (2005): *Mit welchen Sprachen zum Erfolg? Eine empirische Studie zur Wahl der Fremdsprachen an der Wirtschaftsuniversität Wien.* Wien: Wirtschaftsuniversität Wien (unpublished diploma thesis).

Seidlhofer, B. (2004): Research perspectives on teaching English as a lingua franca. In: *Annual Review of Applied Linguistics* 24, 209-239.

Stegu, M. (2007): Der/die 'ideale' Fachsprachenlehrende im Spannungsfeld 'ExpertIn – Laie'. In: Engberg, J./Grove Ditlevsen, M./Kastberg, P./Stegu, M. (eds): *New directions in LSP teaching*. Bern: Lang, 17-39.

Stegu, M. (2008a): Linguistique populaire, language awareness, linguistique appliquée: interrelations et transitions. Dans: Achard-Bayle, G./Paveau, M.-A. (coord.): *Pratiques 139-140*: "Linguistique populaire?". Metz: CRESEF, 81-92.

Stegu, M. (2008b): Warum welche Sprachen lernen? Möglichkeiten und Grenzen wirtschaftlicher und sprachwissenschaftlicher Argumentation. In: Tritscher-Archan, S. (Hg.): *Fremdsprachen für die Wirtschaft. Analysen, Zahlen, Fakten*. Wien: ibw, 117-129.

Trim, J. (ed.) (2001): *The Common European Framework of Reference for Languages. A guide for users.* Strasbourg: Council of Europe.

Vandermeeren, S. (1998): *Fremdsprachen in europäischen Unternehmen. Untersuchungen zu Bestand und Bedarf im Geschäftsalltag mit Empfehlungen für Sprachenpolitik und Sprachunterricht.* Waldsteinberg: Heidrun Popp Verlag.

Pirkko Nuolijärvi

# Language in business and commerce in Finland

This article deals with the language options available to Finnish firms and in particular with the extent to which the Finnish language is used in company operations. Finnish firms have become increasingly international in recent decades. Many major companies have become more and more clearly multinational, and many small and medium-sized firms have increased their foreign ties and joined international networks. While many practices have changed, nearly all firms have made decisions regarding the status of their own language in internal interaction and the kind of language skills needed for external operations. Other languages and proficiency in them are required for international operations. It is, however, noteworthy that Finnish and Swedish are still used in business operations. The development of the two principal languages of Finland in various sectors is also essential for businesses. Moreover, firms that enjoy public support have obligations toward Finnish society and Finnish citizens.

## 1. The internationalisation of Finnish firms

The internationalisation[1] of Finnish firms began relatively late, in fact not until the 1980s. Since then the pace has increased. At present the degree to which major firms of Finnish origin have internationalised is high, and approaches that of Sweden, where the process began much earlier than in Finland. As its pace has accelerated, internationalisation has also taken on new forms. Direct foreign investment, mainly company acquisitions, has continued to increase, while internationalisation based on agreements – international networking – has expanded alongside it.

Direct foreign investment, however, remains the most import form of internationalisation alongside exports. The foreign subsidiaries of Finnish firms have nearly 400,000 employees. This figure has tripled in ten years. Approximately one-fifth of the employees of the entire corporate sector and two-fifths of those employed in industry work abroad.[2] Technology (metal products, mechanical engineering, and electronics) is the largest sector, and here the number of foreign personnel after the merger of Nokia and Siemens in 2007 exceeded the number of personnel in Finland. By 2008 the group comprising the thirty largest firms accounted for more than two-thirds of the personnel in foreign units, while at the beginning of the 1990s this figure was still below 40%.[3] Large companies have moved into new markets the most rapidly, while at the same time seeking new forms of internationalisation such as international production networks, strategic alliances, and partnerships.

---

1 Unless stated otherwise, the source for the review of corporate internationalisation in chapter 1 is Kotiranta/Lundan/Ylä-Anttila (2008).

2 Most employees are local. More precise figures on the number of Finnish-speakers in foreign units is not available.

3 Pajarinen/Ylä-Anttila (2008).

The international economist Richard Baldwin uses the term 'second unbundling' to describe the present situation. No longer does internationalisation or the increasing division of labour between countries or regions necessarily take place on the level of sectors, but on that of functions or tasks. According to a survey made by Statistics Finland,[4] the relocation of (core) functions of production abroad is most frequent in high-tech industrial companies.

The internationalisation of the Finnish economy and Finnish business can be roughly divided into three periods. However, Finnish business had already expanded its operations abroad before these three periods, mainly to Sweden. The first significant investment was the establishment in 1903 of a subsidiary in Sweden by the Strengberg tobacco company of Pietarsaari, Finland. Geographical proximity was of course the reason, although a common cultural background and language, Swedish, which was the principal language of business at the time, also had an impact. Before 1945, 19 Finnish firms had invested in Sweden. The main sectors were tobacco, sweets, porcelain, and timber.[5]

The first major export-driven period occurred from 1940 to 1970. Efforts were made to retain strict Finnish ownership of Finnish firms, and only a few Finnish firms had production units abroad. The first steps in the process of internationalisation were associate membership in EFTA in 1961 and the conclusion of a free trade agreement with the EEC in 1973. Still, the volume of direct investment abroad at the beginning of the 1980s remained relatively small by international standards – only 2% of GNP. The second phase of internationalisation occurred at the beginning of the 1980s when investment abroad increased rapidly. The present type of internationalisation began at the end of the 1990s. Barriers to the free movement of capital and restrictions on foreign ownership were removed in 1992; in 1993 the average world level in foreign investment (as a percentage of GNP) was achieved and eventually accession to the European Union in 1995 and to the monetary union in 2000 made Finland part of the international economy.

Some 60% of the international moves by Finnish companies are to the EU area. The largest countries outside the EU are India, China, and Russia and a large volume of core business operations is being relocated in China, in particular. Finnish firms are mainly attracted abroad by lower labour costs, though strategic reasons are also important. The aim in relocating production may also be to move closer to the actual market area.

Internationalisation can also be divided into two groups according to whether domestic operations are transferred entirely abroad or whether the company has expanded outside of Finland. With respect to language options, all modes of internationalisation in any case signify a new kind of linguistic environment and call for consideration of language choices. The linguistic landscape has changed in all companies, and in them the environment confronted by the Finnish language is altogether different than it was 20 years ago.[6]

---

4 Ali-Yrkkö/Rikama (2008).

5 For investment in Sweden, see Fellman (2006).

6 See also Leppänen/Nikula (2008).

## 2. Legislation and business operations

Legislation governing the language of business operations is rare. The Language Act,[7] which applies to the national languages, concerns the rights of speakers of Finnish and Swedish in official contexts, and not private business operations. However, there are a few points in the Language Act that require firms to provide service in national languages. The first of these concerns the obligation of state and municipal enterprises and companies to provide service in Finnish and Swedish.

> Section 24 – Linguistic services of a public enterprise and a State and municipal company
>
> (1) A public enterprise and a service-producing company in which the State or one or more bilingual municipalities or municipalities using different languages exert authority shall provide services and information in Finnish and Swedish to the extent and manner required by the nature of the activity and its substantive connections and which in view of the totality cannot be deemed unreasonable from the point of view of the company. What is provided in this Act regarding authorities applies to a State company that attends to a function of an authority. (www.finlex.fi/english)

The following section of the Language Act stipulates how a private service provider of a public administrative function offers services in both languages.

> Section 25 – The obligation of a private individual to provide linguistic services
>
> If a public administrative task has been assigned by or under law to a private individual, the provisions of this Act on an authority apply to the said private individual in attending to this task. If the recipient of the task is determined on the basis of a decision or other action of an authority or on the basis of an agreement between an authority and the recipient, the authority shall ensure that linguistic services are provided in accordance with this Act in the performance of the task. This shall also be ensured when an authority assigns other than a public administrative task to a private individual, if the maintenance of the level of service required by this Act so demands. (www.finlex.fi/english)

Although most international companies do not perform tasks of the kind mentioned above, service companies that internationalise may increasingly carry out public functions in the future. In recent years statutory municipal services have also been increasingly outsourced to private companies. The more operations are transferred to the private sector for implementation, the more companies performing public administrative functions in Finland will be required under the Language Act to offer service in Finnish (and in Swedish).

In addition, the Language Act includes a provision requiring the labels to be provided with a product in unilingual and bilingual municipalities.

> Section 34 – Information to be provided on consumer goods
>
> When the law requires that a product to be sold is labelled in accordance with commercial practice with a name, a description of the product, instructions or a warning, the text on a product to be sold in a unilingual municipality shall be at least in the language of this municipality and the text on a product to be sold in a bilingual municipality shall be at least in Finnish and Swedish. In providing the information here referred to, Finnish and Swedish shall be dealt with on an equal basis. (www.finlex.fi/english)

---

[7] Language Act 423/2003.

In accordance with the minimum requirements of the Language Act, a Finnish-speaking user of services in a bilingual municipality is entitled to receive service in Finnish (likewise, Swedish-speakers in Swedish). Moreover, the buyer of a product must be able to obtain a description of the product and the instructions for using it or a warning in Finnish. Since Finnish is the majority language in Finland, a Finnish-language text is more than likely found on most products. Problems may arise from the kind of Finnish used in labels and instructions. There are many examples where native speakers of Finnish could make no sense of the instructions for using a product because the labels were not in clear, understandable Finnish. This shows that not all companies focus sufficient attention on the clarity of the language used.

The Language Act is general legislation regulating the activity of officials. Its impact is also apparent in other legislation – that is in legislation concerning company operations. Apart from the Language Act, for example the Government decree on the safety of machinery stipulates the use of Finnish (and of Swedish). According to this decree, information, warnings and instructions regarding machinery to be marketed or used in Finland must always be in Finnish and Swedish.[8]

In general, there are no provisions in company legislation regarding language. Membership of the European Union and the status of Finnish as an official language of the Union have, however, also affected legislation concerning companies. The impact of membership of the European Union on consideration of the Finnish language in legislation is apparent for example in the provision of the Consumer Protection Act[9] on the language of commercial contracts; this provision stipulates that commercial contracts or loan agreements must be drafted according to the buyers' choice, in either the language of their place of residence or of their country of citizenship if the country in question is an EEA country and the language chosen an official language of the European Union or either Norwegian or Icelandic (§6).

An act that explicitly requires use of Finnish and Swedish, the official languages of Finland, is the Act on foreign insurance companies. This legislation requires an official translation of documents into Finnish and Swedish (§71).[10] However, it would appear to require inclusion of a Finnish translation only when stipulated by the Insurance Supervisory Authority. No information is available on how this provision is implemented in practice.

Hence, there is on the whole very little legislation regulating the use of language or the choice of languages. To a great extent, the operations of companies are governed by the language of the customers to whom they are marketing their products and what this practical need means with respect to the launching or products or to other activity directed towards customers. Companies operating in Finland or selling products on the Finnish market naturally use Finnish for practical reasons because according to the familiar saying, you can buy in any language but sell only in the language of the customer.

---

8 Government decree on the safety of machinery 12.6.2008/400.
9 Consumer Protection Act 11.12.1997/1162.
10 Amendment to the Act on foreign insurance companies 18.7.2008/525.

## 3. The use of Finnish and other languages in written and spoken business communication

In general, companies do not have a public language policy (with the exception of the Finnish company Partek, which has clearly decided that the languages of the group are Finnish, Swedish, and English); in addition, local languages are used in material for the countries in question.[11] Here descriptions of the language practices are mainly based on information in the possession of representatives of the Confederation of Finnish Industries, corporate managing directors and communication directors,[12] and on information acquired in various studies on the experiences of employees.[13]

Numerous Finnish multinational companies such as Nokia, Kone, Metso and Tieto have adopted English as their corporate language or common working language during the process of internationalisation. Although no actual language policy has been stated other than with an announcement of a general nature concerning the corporate language, the practice is to write all official texts in English and to provide all spoken information to owners and the international public in English. English is used increasingly at the headquarters of multinational companies located in Finland for official records, memoranda, internal reporting and other internal communication.[14] If matters are expected to take on an international dimension at some stage, the texts concerned are in general written first in English and then if necessary in other languages as well (more exact information on the other languages are used in such situations is not available). The use of English ensures that basic information concerning the company is available throughout the company, in all parts of the world, with the same content and at the same time. Documents of significance solely to Finnish employees and the Finnish markets are mainly written in Finnish. On the other hand, spoken communication is still often in Finnish: among Finnish employees and in meetings in units in Finland, Finnish (or Swedish) remains the primary language. If there are many employees with different language backgrounds from other countries at the workplace English is used as the common language.[15]

Some 20 communication directors, communication officers or persons in similar positions were surveyed at the beginning of 2008 regarding the extent to which Finnish and other languages are used in their own work on the one hand and throughout the company or group on the other.[16] Replies were received from firms representing different sectors and of various sizes; large, multinational communication consultancies, publishing houses and from small news agencies, advertising and public relations companies, larger paper and chemical companies, travel companies and insurance companies. The survey also included Kone Corporation, which is one of Finland's most in-

---

[11] Lindblad (2001).
[12] The information was obtained from the Confederation of Finnish Industries and from a report by Helena Kangasharju.
[13] The information is based mainly on a 2008 article by Tiina Virkkula and on sources cited therein.
[14] Piekkari (2007).
[15] Sajavaara (2008).
[16] The survey was made by Helena Kangasharju, Professor of Finnish Language and Communication at the Helsinki School of Economics (Kangasharju 2008).

ternational companies. The estimates of the interviewees regarding the percentages of Finnish used in their own work or throughout the company or the use of Finnish by a unit operating in Finland were compiled in table 1. The figures are estimates given by the respondents.

| **Company** | **Sector** | **Interviewee's work: estimated % in Finnish** | **Entire company: estimated % in Finnish** |
|---|---|---|---|
| AstraZenica | pharmaceuticals | 90 | 80 |
| Dazzle Oy | consulting | 90 | 95 |
| Forma Publishing | publishing | 90 | 80 |
| Hill & Knowlton Finland | communication consulting | 60 | 30 |
| Kauppalehti | communications | 70 | 85 |
| Kemira GrowHow | chemical industry | 80 | 50 for all Kemira |
| Kone Corporation | manufacturing | 60-70 | 50 |
| Kreab | corporate communications | 80 | 60 Suomi, 10 for all Kreab |
| Luovat Sanat | communications | 99 | 99 |
| SanomaWsoy, investor relations | communications; investments | 60 | 35 |
| StoraEnso, financial communication | forest industry | 60-70 | 80-90 Helsinki |
| STT | news agency | 90 | 85 |
| PR Agency Taivas Relations | communications | 90 | 50 |
| Sulake Corporation | virtual company | **25** | **25** |
| Talentum | media | 95 | 95 |
| Tallink Group AS | travel | 85 | 85 |
| Tapiola Group | insurance | 90 | 95 |

Table 1: The use of Finnish in certain companies 2008 (the smallest percentage for Finnish is in bold)

The overall impression is that Finnish is still used to a great extent in many companies operating in Finland, even when operations extend to international arenas. The percentage of Finnish used in the work of a unit is reduced when information is provided or other contact maintained in multiple languages or in English; on average, 20% of the personnel's working time may involve use of a language other than Finnish. An exception is the Sulake Corporation, whose operations aim to unite young people of the world into the same virtual community through the use of animation, mobile games, and advertising. In fact, there are 15 different nationalities employed in its Helsinki unit and there the use of Finnish was the lowest of all the companies surveyed. Nevertheless, Sulake Corporation's Habbo Hotel and IrcGalleria operate in Finnish (and similarly in other languages). Another company that stands out from the others is the communications consultancy Hill & Knowlton Finland, whose English-language history and international present explain why the percentage of Finnish used throughout the company is low. These circumstances also affect the languages used by individual employees working in Finland.

Representatives of the companies that took part in the survey state that in large multinational companies texts concerning the entire group are often written first in English and then translated into other languages such as Finnish. However, the extent to which Finnish is used could vary greatly between units. Written communication such as email is mainly in English while conversations with one's closest colleagues are in Finnish.

Finnish is used most in publishing companies and communication consultancies operating in Finland. Here the percentage of Finnish is high in the work of both individual communication professionals and throughout the companies.

English has an important role in international corporate operations, and the managers and office employees of many Finnish companies use English daily. English-language emails are common in the work of all groups of personnel. Acquisition of language proficiency is essential in keeping competent professionals from becoming excluded due to deficient language skills.

The decision by a company to adopt English as its corporate language does not in itself make English the common language, for its use is not problem-free for all employees. Not everyone knows English as well as is generally assumed. Low proficiency in English and other languages also causes financial losses to companies.

In 2006, Education and Culture of the European Commission published a report[17] on the significance of skills in different languages and intercultural communication, the use of language professionals in companies, and on plans to improve language proficiency. The inquiry included nearly 2000 small and medium-sized enterprises in 29 European countries and some 30 major companies with headquarters in France. One tenth of the participating companies estimated that they had lost contracts because of deficient language skills. According to the replies from the companies, the situation could be improved by hiring native speakers of the languages, by using translators and interpreters, and by providing language training to employees. The representatives of the small countries were clearly more aware of cultural differences and the need for language skills while those of large countries assumed that others would learn their language.

Multilingualism can increase the innovative capacity of companies when global operating principles and solutions are adapted to local conditions that is, when the native languages of employees in subsidiaries operating in others countries are taken into account.[18] The employees of companies notice through their own experiences that par-

---

[17] Hagen et al. (2006).
[18] Piekkari (2007).

ticularly in competitive situations negotiators have an advantage when they know the native language of the customer.[19] It is possible to buy in English, but to sell knowledge of the customer's language is required.

## 4. Teaching of Finnish, language revision and translations services in companies

Nowadays, companies recruit speakers of Finnish and of other languages as well. Both groups need Finnish teaching. Native speakers, frequently highly trained employees, may even have a great need to take part for example in courses to maintain their language skills, in writing, and to improve their oral interaction skills. The significance of communication and interaction skills and the ability to write good text have been brought to the fore in many interviews in recent years. It is natural that corporate management seeks to recruit employees who possess the requisite basic skills for working life, such as mastery of their own language. Other language speakers need instruction in Finnish and Finnish culture so that it will be easier to take their place in Finnish society and working life.

Since more and more jobs involve text production and when nowadays all employees, right up to the top manager, write their own texts, language fluency is necessary for both the company itself and for communication directed at the customer.[20] All employee groups need training appropriate specifically for their own work and tailored to it. This is the most motivating kind of training and is an efficient means of both familiarizing staff with various work-related aspects and of teaching them to speak and write about work-related matters. Employees from other countries do not always find appropriate courses at the right time outside the company, so that teaching in Finnish as a second language must be arranged in the company itself, and is in the best interests of the company. For example in many building companies it is important that instructions concerning the flow of work are clear and understandable so that accidents and all kinds of lack of clarity related to the flow of work are avoided. Since company employees come increasing from many countries and language areas, instructions and working regulations should also be in the employee's own language unless it is possible to provide an interpreter.[21] For employees who are speakers of different languages and who come from elsewhere, the use of Finnish alone may be an on-the-job problem that cannot be resolved solely by increasing the use of English; greater use of other languages and more diverse language skills on various levels of operations are required.[22]

Knowledge of Finnish is the key to the employment and integration of immigrants. The Act on the Integration of Immigrants and the Reception of Asylum[23] seekers stipulates that employment offices and municipalities can arrange for example instruction in Finnish and Swedish as measures and services to promote and support integration (§7).

---

[19] For the language experiences and skills of company employees see Virkkula (2008).
[20] For the potential of customers to understand complex texts see for example Tiililä (2007).
[21] Sajavaara (2007).
[22] Nowadays employees in the building sector come from many different countries and hence companies should have speakers of Finnish and Estonian, Finnish and Russian, and Finnish and Polish.
[23] Act on the Integration of Immigrants and Reception of Asylum Seekers 493/1999.

Integration means that immigrants are supported in the acquisition of the basic information and skills needed to function in society. Proficiency in Finnish is one of the most important skills with respect to employment. In general, companies employing immigrants would like to have courses on the ABCs of Finnish society because their own efforts are not always sufficient for assisting immigrants to adapt. Companies would like to have these courses offered to those who have already been hired directly by them as well and not only for those taking part in integration programmes or for refugees. Apart from language skills, guidance for example regarding matters related to employment contracts, working hours, leave, pay and culture would also be needed.[24]

In virtually every sector, skills in Finnish are emphasized, skills that graduates with an English-language BBA from a university of applied science do not in general possess. For example in the pharmaceutical industry, "errors resulting from deficiencies in language skills cannot be tolerated in customer service and quality control".

Nowadays, there are already companies that support multiculturalism at the workplace and offer training to employees of different language backgrounds. One of these is Itella (formerly the Finnish Postal Service), whose successful efforts are apparent in a continuous rise in the number of employees with foreign backgrounds and improvements in their career development. For example, Itella offers its employees training in Finnish and other languages and also training for 'culturally aware supervisors'. At the beginning of 2007, Itella started a multicultural working group with the aim of supporting and promoting multiculturalism and diversity throughout the company. At that time a total of 15 Itella employees, hailing from eight different countries, began to study Finnish. Efforts to promote multiculturalism and familiarisation with diversity are thus a part of Itella's operations. "We would like to further integrate our employees with immigrant backgrounds into Finnish society," explains HR manager Wilberforce Essandor on Itella's website.[25]

Translating and the use of translating services is an essential element of business operations and an important factor in interaction. Many companies have their own translation units, in which translators familiar with the sector in question are employed. Many companies also continue to use the same translation agency or translator, making cooperation with the translator close, despite the outsourcing. If in contrast, the translation services have to be purchased from various translators and contacts with translators are therefore more haphazard, it is not always possible to be certain whether the translators have sufficient experience with texts from the sector in question and whether they have an opportunity to adequately familiarise themselves with the vocabulary and key concepts.[26]

---

[24] Hopes of this kind were expressed when the Kluuvi employment office in Helsinki, which specialises in service to job applicants with a higher education, sent a survey in summer 2008 to some 500 employers, of whom more than one hundred responded. They also interviewed representatives of seven different sectors. See Liiten (2008).

[25] Itella (2008).

[26] Sajavaara (2008).

No data on how companies arrange language revision for texts in Finnish or other languages are available. Although some companies do have professionals in Finnish who both write and revise texts in Finnish no more detailed information on how this work is arranged in companies is available.

## 5. Company names, professional titles and professional terminology

When foreign investors began to invest in Finland during the 19th century, many companies were established that remain well-known Finnish brands to this day. In recent decades, they have invested in the region and established units for example in Estonia and Russia. Such companies include Stockmann[27] and Karl Fazer Oy. They took their founders' surnames, which have been retained as the company name and have become their trademarks.

Although Finnish remains the most frequent language when company names are chosen, English has gained ground. Finnish and English are also combined in the same name (*Poutapilvi Web Design Ab*, *Riento Import*, *Kauneushoitola PS-Beauty*, *Ohjelmatoimisto Bluewest Oy*, *Suomen Hot Food Oy*). The growing importance of English is apparent in the fact that in mixed-language names, English is generally used in those parts of the name where comprehension of meaning is essential. Finnish is also combined with names in other languages, for example in the following: *Biltema Suomi Myynti Oy*, *Hoitola La Perle*, *Viestintätoimisto Signal Oy*. Since the 1980s, one typical trend has been to devise names for companies that are not really in any language (for example *Nordea*, *Destia*, *Itella*, *Sonera*, *Sportuna*, *Vecorex*).[28]

Internationalisation is also apparent to some extent in job advertisements.[29] In the four Sunday editions of the newspaper *Helsingin Sanomat* of February 2008, there were 692 advertisements under the headings 'Job Openings' and 'Vacant Posts'. This figure includes advertisements that were of at least two columns; hence small, one-column advertisements were excluded (all of them were in Finnish). Advertisements that were entirely in Finnish accounted for 85% (588) of all advertisements and advertisements in English for 8.4% (58). Advertisements in Finnish, in which all or some of the job titles were in English, accounted for 5.9% (41). Advertisements in Swedish accounted for 0.7% (5). The 'Vacant Posts' were all in Finnish.

On the basis of this sample, the percentage of Finnish advertisements is rather constant: 82-85% in all publications. Most of the English-language advertisements belong to multinational listed companies such as Atria, Eaton, Finnair, Ruukki, American Express, and Securitas Systems, in which English is the corporate language and which announce job openings at the same time in different countries with the same advertisement. Of the public institutions in the survey, the Helsinki School of Economics (HSE) and the Ministry for Foreign Affairs advertised in English. Nevertheless, English-language advertisements still account for less than 10% of all advertisements. The

27 For a history of the company see Damstén (1961).
28 For the history of Finnish company names and related legislation and present names see Sjöblom (2006).
29 Nuolijärvi (2008).

percentage of advertisements in Swedish is small, which is explained by the fact that Swedish-language advertisements in Finland are most often published in the Swedish-language press.

In the Finnish-language advertisements the most popular English title is *Manager* with various meanings (21 different titles in four Sunday editions). *Analyst*, *Controller*, *Assistant* and *Engineer* appeared more than once. The most extraordinary included titles such as *Head of Equity*, *Senior Salkunhoitaja* and *Jack & Jones supplymyyjä*. Finnish and English are therefore also combined in the same title. Sometimes the use of English-language titles causes problems for those preparing the advertisements. The result is clumsy when the name cannot be declined without some difficulty: *Etsimme nuorekkaaseen dynaamiseen joukkoomme: Business Manager* [*We are looking for a 'Business Manager' to join our team*].[30]

Most of the language proficiency requirements in company job advertisements focus on English, and describe the language skill sought with the words *fluent*, *excellent*, *very good*, *solid*, *and good*. Often Finnish is used alongside English. The demanding skills required in Finnish are described with the following expressions: *fluency in spoken and written Finnish and English*, *good skills in written and spoken expression*, *communicates fluently in Finnish and English*. Companies require proficiency in other languages, including Swedish, much less often.[31]

Within companies and their sectors, a special vocabulary that is not part of the general language is naturally used. The terms and expressions needed in each sector are developed in various terminology working groups and there are numerous special vocabularies. Loan words are naturally adopted in special fields, and words of Finnish origin are often used alongside the foreign word (*benchmarking*, *benchmarkkeeraus*, *esikuva-analyysi*, *vertaisanalyysi*). Loan words from English are often used even when a good Finnish equivalent is available because the foreign word is regarded as more precise than the Finnish word, for example *implementointi* = *täytäntöönpano*, *sopimuksen scope* = *sopimuksen soveltamisala*.[32] Hence all sectors have a constant need to develop their own vocabulary and to specify terms.

## 6. Multilingualism is an advantage in business

Although English is part of everyday life in companies that are international or are at present undergoing the process, all companies need adequate proficiency in written and spoken Finnish. The aim ought to be bilingual or multilingual speakers who maintain their national identity and who have the skill needed to communicate with non-natives.[33] Thus corporate internationalisation obviously requires more than the use of English[34] and also spoken and written proficiency in either Finnish or Swedish but preferably in both. The more proficient in languages the personnel of companies, the

[30] For material collected at the beginning of the 21st century see Laaksonen (2003).
[31] For material from 2006 and 2008 see Salo (2006) and Nuolijärvi (2008).
[32] Sajavaara (2008).
[33] For more details see Virkkula (2008).
[34] For discussion relevant to this see Paatola (2008) and Söderlundh/Melander (2008).

better and the more reliable they are in running the operations of a company and in contributing to its success. Proficiency in Finnish and Swedish is the essential foundation of language skill and also an important element in the operations of international companies.

It would be important for large multinational companies to draw up clear language strategies that state where both written and spoken Finnish and/or Swedish are used alongside other languages in everyday operations. Companies should consider a high degree of proficiency in Finnish a merit and reward those who possess it. In companies where there are employees of different language backgrounds, written and spoken proficiency in Finnish should be maintained by arranging tailor-made training for texts relevant to the sector in question and for interaction situations. In such cases it is best to offer an opportunity to study Finnish on the job so that is possible to master the professional language of the sector in question in a real working environment. It is in the interest of companies to ensure that professionals handle translation services and language revision. Government should promote the integration and employment of immigrants by ensuring that professionally skilled teachers give statutory instruction in Finnish and that the teaching itself is of a high quality and also effective. Hence, there will also be a workforce with proficiency in Finnish available to private companies. The maintenance of proficiency in Finnish would also be promoted by support from government to those companies that see to the arrangement of instruction in Finnish and Swedish and to the maintenance of both Finnish and Swedish in their operations.

## 7. Sources

Ali-Yrkkö, J./Rikama, S. (2008): Intia ja vanha EU vetävät palveluja, Kiina ja uusi EU teollisuutta [India and the old EU lead in services, China and the new EU industry]. In: *Tieto & Trendit 2/2008*, 12-17.

Asetus maahanmuuttajien kotouttamisesta ja turvapaikanhakijoiden vastaanotosta [Decree on the Integration of Immigrants and the Reception of Asylum Seekers] 22.4.1999/511. (Read 30.11.2008).

Damstén, B. (1961): *Stockmann sadan vuoden aikana* [Stockmann in the course of a century]. Helsinki: Tilgman.

Fellman, S. (2006): Utvidgad hemmamarknad eller språngbräda till Europa? Tidiga finska företagsetableringar i Sverige. – Svenskt i Finland – finskt i Sverige [An expanded domestic market or a springboard to Europe? Early establishments of Finnish companies in Sweden. – Swedish in Finland – Finnish in Sweden]. In: Aunesluoma. J./Fellman, S. (ed.): *Från olika till jämlika: Finlands och Sveriges ekonomier på 1900-talet* [From unequal to equal: The economies of Finland and Sweden in the 1900s]. (Svenskt i Finland – finskt i Sverige. Utg. för samtliga vol. är Nils Erik Villstrand, 3). (= Skrifter utgivna av Svenska litteratursällskapet i Finland 0039-6842; nr. 682:3. III). Helsinki/Stockholm: The Society of Swedish Literature in Finland & Atlantis, 283–324.

Hagen, S. et al. (2006): *Effects on the European Economy of Shortages of Foreign Language Skills in Enterprise*. Brussels: European Commission. http://ec.europa.eu/education/policies/lang/doc/elan_en.pdf (Read 28.9.2008).

Itella (2008): www.itella.com/group/vastuullisuus/sosiaalinen/monikulttuurisuus.html (Read 28.9.2008).

Kielilaki/Språklag [Language Act] 423/2003. www.finlex.fi (Read 12.9.2008).

Kirjanpitolaki [Accounting Act] 30.12.1997/1336. www.finlex.fi (Read 1.12.2008).

Kotiranta, A./Lundan, S./Ylä-Anttila, P. (2008): *Yritysten kansainvälistymisen vaikutukset kotimaan talouteen ja työllisyyteen – katsaus kirjallisuuteen* [The impact of corporate internationalization on the Finnish economy and industry – a literature survey]. (= Keskusteluaiheita, Discussion Papers 1154). Helsinki: ETLA, Elinkeinoelämän tutkimuslaitos, The Research Institute of the Finnish Economy.

Kuluttajansuojalaki [Consumer Protection Act] 11.12.1997/1162. (Read 1.12.2008).

Laaksonen, M. (2002): *Englanninkieliset ilmoitukset työpaikkailmoituksen osana.* Pro gradututkielma. Helsingin yliopiston suomen kielen ja kotimaisen kirjallisuuden laitos [English-language advertisements as part of a job advertisement]. University of Helsinki, Department of Finnish Language and Literature: Master's thesis.

Laaksonen, M. (2003): Etsimme Sinua, Development Manager [We're looking for you, Development Manager]. In: *Kielikello* 2/2003, 18–21.

Laki ulkomaisista vakuutusyhtiöistä annetun lain muuttamisesta [Amendment to the Act on foreign insurance companies] 18.7.2008/525. (Read 1.12.2008).

Leppänen, S./Nikula, T. (2008): Johdanto [Introduction]. In: Leppänen, S./Nikula, T./Kääntä, L. (toim.): *Kolmas kotimainen. Lähikuvia englannin käytöstä Suomessa* [The third domestic language. A close-up view of the use of English in Finland]. (= Tietolipas 224). Helsinki: Finnish Literature Society, 9–40.

Liiten, M. (2008): Työnantajat: Maahanmuuttajille opetettava suomalaisyhteiskunnan aakkoset [Employers: Immigrants must be taught the ABS of Finnish society]. In: *Helsingin Sanomat* 29.10.2008.

Lindblad, R. (2001): *Om språken inom Partekkoncernen. Esitelmä* [Languages in the Partek Corporation. Presentation]. Nordmål forum [Nordic Language Forum], Parainen, Finland. 16.-18.11.2001.

Ljung, U. (2008): *Språknormer inom den finländska arbetsmarknaden – hur tryggas den svenska servicen inom den privata arbetsmarknaden genom språkliga rättigheter? Pro gradu-tutkielma* [Language norms in the labour market of Finland – how to secure service in Swedish within the private labour market through language rights]. Åbo Akademi University, Department of Law in the Faculty of Economics and Social Sciences: Master's thesis.

Nuolijärvi, P. (2008): *Helsingin Sanomien työpaikkailmoitusten kieli, ilmoituksissa käytetyt ammattinimikkeet ja kielitaitovaatimusten esittäminen* [The language of job advertisements in *Helsingin Sanomat*, the professional titles used in the advertisements, and the presentation of language proficiency requirements]. Käsikirjoite/Manuscript.

Paatola, U. (2008): English Invading Finnish and Swedish Companies – Domain Loss or Domain Sharing? In: *Multiethnica* 31 (Meddelande från Centrum för multietnisk forskning. Uppsala universitet [Publications from the Centre for Multiethnic Research, the University of Uppsala]), 25–28.

Pajarinen, M./Ylä-Anttila, P. (2008): *Large corporations in the Finnish economy.* (= ETLA Discussion Paper 1138). Helsinki: ETLA, The Research Institute of the Finnish Economy.

Piekkari, R. (2007): Yhteisestä bisneskielestä voi olla niin hyötyä kuin haittaakin [A common business language can be both an advantage and a disadvantage]. In: *Helsingin Sanomat* 23.8.2007.

Salo, M. (2006): *Havaintoja Helsingin Sanomien työpaikkailmoitusten kielitaitovaatimuksista* [Observations on the language proficiency requirements of job advertisements in *Helsingin Sanomat*]. www.jyu.fi/hum/laitokset/solki/tutkimus/projektit/kiepo/Havaintoja.pdf (Read 15.9.2008).

Sjöblom, P. (2006): *Toiminimen toimenkuva. Suomalaisen yritysnimistön rakenne ja funktiot* [The job description of the structure and functions of the names of Finnish companies]. (= Transactions of the Finnish Literature Society 1064). Helsinki: Finnish Literature Society.

Söderlundh, H./Melander, B. (2008): Language beyond English – A Reply to Ulla Paatola. In: *Multiethnica* 31 (Meddelande från Centrum för multietnisk forskning. Uppsala universitet [Publications from the Centre for Multiethnic Research, the University of Uppsala]), 29–30.

Tiililä, U. (2007): *Tekstit viraston työssä. Tutkimus etuuspäätösten kielestä ja konteksteista* [Texts in government office work. A study of the language and contexts of decisions on benefits]. (= Transactions of the Finnish Literature Society 1108). Helsinki: Finnish Literature Society.

Virkkula, T. (2008): Työntekijän kokemuksia englannista yritysmaailman yhteisenä kielenä [Experiences of an employee on English as a common language in the business world]. In: Leppänen, S./Nikula, T./Kääntä, L. (toim.) *Kolmas kotimainen. Lähikuvia englannin käytöstä Suomessa* [The third domestic language. A close-up view of the use of English in Finland]. (= Tietolipas 224). Helsinki: Suomalaisen Kirjallisuuden Seura, 382–420.

## 8. Expert opinions

Kangasharju, H. (2008): *Suomen kielen käyttö yrityksissä. Puheenvuoro suomen kielen toimintaohjelmaa valmistelevan ryhmän tapaamisessa Kotimaisten kielten tutkimuskeskuksessa* [The use of Finnish in companies. Views expressed at a meeting of the group preparing an action programme for Finnish at the Research Institute for the Languages of Finland]. 5.2.2008.

Piekkari, R. (2007): *Monikansallisten yritysten kielimaailma. Puheenvuoro suomen kielen toimintaohjelmaa valmistelevan ryhmän tapaamisessa Kotimaisten kielten tutkimuskeskuksessa* [The language world of multinational companies. Views expressed at a meeting of the group preparing an action programme for Finnish at the Research Institute for the Languages of Finland]. 27.9.2007.

Sajavaara, A. (2008): *Suomen ja englannin kielen käyttö yrityksissä. Puheenvuoro suomen kielen toimintaohjelmaa valmistelevan ryhmän tapaamisessa Kotimaisten kielten tutkimuskeskuksessa* [The use of Finnish and English in companies. Views expressed at a meeting of the group preparing an action programme for Finnish. At the Research Institute for the Languages of Finland]. 13.3.2008.

Guy Berg

# Active multilingualism in Luxembourg
# The use of languages in a stable polyglossic economy

**Abstract: Aktiv Méisproochegkeet zu Lëtzebuerg. De Sproochegebrauch an enger stabiler polyglosser Economie**

Mat senge ronn 480.000 Awunner gehéiert d'Groussherzogtum Lëtzebuerg zu deene klengsten nationalen Economien an Europa an ass déi Economie mat dem héichsten Undeel un Auslänner (43%). Donieft ginn ca. 40% vun allen Aarbechtsplazen am Land vu Frontalieren besat, déi Dag fir Dag aus Frankräich, der Belsch an Däitschland an d'Land erapendelen.

Déi lëtzebuergesch Economie gëtt charakteriséiert vun enger aktiver Méisproochegkeet an engem komplexe sozialen Ëmfeld.

D'Basis vun dëser sproochlecher Diversitéit läit an der traditioneller an institutionaliséierter Triglossie, déi tëschent Lëtzebuergesch, Franséisch an Däitsch besteet, an déi ënnert anerem och an der Schoul enseignéiert gëtt.

Déi wirtschaftlech a sproochlech Diversitéit vum Land ass net d'Resultat vun der moderner Globaliséierung, mee geet zeréck op politesch Entwécklungen am 19. Joerhonnert, wéi déi héréditéiert territorial Méisproochegkeet ersat gouf duerch eng gewollten institutionell Méisproochegkeet. Duerno hunn italienesch, an nach méi spéit portugisesch Immigranten weider Sproochen an d'Land bruecht.

Déi jonk national Economie wor vun Ufank un op auslännescht Kapital ugewisen, a laang Joerzéngten iwwer huet déi dominant Sidérurgie si an en enke monolithesche Corselet gedréckt. An der Zäit nom Zweete Weltkrich konnt d'Economie sech méi a méi diversifiéieren, absëns duerch d'Installatioun vun US-amerikaneschen Entreprisen an duerch den Opbau vun der Banken- a Finanzplaz Lëtzebuerg.

Wéinst der geographescher Lag vum Land op der Intersectioun tëschent dem germaneschen an dem romanesche Kulturraum an domat tëschent zwee enorme Wirtschaftsraim gëtt eng aktiv Méisproochegkeet vu quasi allen Acteuren als Viraussetzung fir all Zort vun Activitéite betruecht.

Nieft den dräi traditionelle Sprooche vum Land huet och Englesch a bestëmmte Secteuren, wéi dem Finanzsecteur, eng dominant Positioun. Am Eenzelhandel domineiert Franséisch, en Ëmstand, dee vun der autochtoner Populatioun ëmmer erëm kritiséiert gëtt.

Eng offiziell Sproochereguléierung gëtt et zu Lëtzebuerg net, grad esou wéineg wéi speziell Richtlinnen iwwert de Gebrauch vun de Sproochen oder aner legal Dispositiounen. Och d'Sproochegesetz aus dem Joer 1984 mecht do keng Exceptioun; mat him gëtt déi traditionell a gewuessen Triglossie vum Land confirméiert.

D'Erfarung huet gewisen datt d'Feele vu legalen Dispositiounen a Moossnamen der wirtschaftlecher Diversifizéierung zegutt kënnt an d'Economie stäerkt. Grad esou ass op sproochlechem Plang erwisen datt dës laang an intensiv Sproochekontakt-Situatioun net dozou féiert, datt eng vun de concernéierte Sproochen eliminéiert gëtt, mee datt si am Géigendeel vu groussem Notzen ass fir déi nach jonk Nationalsprooch Lëtzebuergesch.

The sociolinguistic and economic realities of Luxembourg can be roughly described in a few key statistics: some 480,000 people of all nationalities are living on a territory of 2,586 square km. The capital, Luxembourg City, accounts for some 86,000 inhabitants, and is the country's greatest agglomeration. Luxembourg is one of Europe's smallest economies and the one with the highest percentage of foreigners (43%). The most important group of foreigners is that of Portuguese immigrants, with 17.7%. The country's labour market is characterised by an extremely high number of cross-border workers (120,000), coming in day by day from France, Belgium and Germany. These cross-border workers hold 40% of all jobs. The large employers are – apart from the financial institutions – groups with Luxembourgish roots, such as the steel group *ArcelorMittal*, the air-carrier *Cargolux*, the media groups *RTL* and *SES Astra*, together with American firms like *Good Year* and *DuPont de Nemours*, as well as various retail groups from Luxembourg, France, Belgium and Germany.

Luxembourg's economic diversity is strongly encouraged by the government, and is accompanied by an active multilingualism embedded in a complex social context. The basis of this linguistic diversity is founded on the traditional, stable and institutionalised triglossia that exists between Luxembourgish, French and German. Within this triglossic situation, Luxembourgish functions as the national language, and is spoken by the native Luxembourgers in everyday life as the common language for all purposes. It is complemented in most public areas by French and German as the written languages. In economic affairs, this triglossia is becoming broadened out further by the use of English and, to a certain extent, Portuguese.

Children become familiarised with Luxembourgish not only at home, but also through early-schooling programmes. Socialisation comes later, in primary school, where they learn to read and write in German. Education in French starts with the second year of primary school. Luxembourgish is also taught, but in a less formal manner. English can be added as a fourth language, but only at secondary level. Furthermore, most secondary schools also offer Italian, Spanish, and sometimes Russian.

This collective and institutionalised multilingualism, actively promoted by school education, may be considered as one of the reasons for the stability and constancy of Luxembourgish society, which is a society unconfronted by xenophobia, social conflicts and social exclusion, despite the high percentage of foreigners. Multilingualism may also be considered as one of the reasons for the rapid and dynamic growth of the country's economy. The economic and linguistic diversity of the country is, indeed, not a result of modern globalisation, but goes back to political developments in the early nineteenth century.

It was at the beginning of post-Napoleonic Europe at the Vienna Congress of 1815 that the Duchy of Luxembourg was reinvented as a 'Grand Duchy'. Its territory consisted of the possessions of the medieval Duchy, but without various eastern parts that were ceded to Prussia. The traditional division of Luxembourg into a French-speaking part in the west (the so-called *quartier wallon*) and a German- or Germanic-speaking part in the east (the so-called *quartier allemand*) was inherited by the new Grand Duchy. Administration was carried out in both these languages, but Luxembourgish itself did not figure at all in official life.

Throughout the whole of the nineteenth century, Luxembourg worked hard to build up its political and economic independency. The young economy, with its dominating agricultural sector, was highly dependent on foreign money. The first banking institutions were established with money that came in from Germany and Belgium, while the first railways were owned by French companies.

Luxembourg, the capital city, was a military fortress held by the Prussians, while at the same time the rest of the Grand Duchy was linked to the Kingdom of the Netherlands, held in personal union by its king, who was also the Grand Duke of Luxembourg. The basis of the modern parliamentarian monarchy was founded in 1848, when the country received its first Constitution. The languages used in Parliament were French and German – as opposed to the Luxembourgish and French of today.

The partitioning of the country in 1839 made Luxembourg lose all its French-speaking territories. These were ceded to Belgium, leaving the remaining territories to correspond more or less to the former *quartier allemand*. From that moment on, the Grand Duchy was diglossic, with Luxembourgish and German as its languages. The country, however, did persist with its traditional trilingualism, although the use of French was no longer a necessity, but rather the expression of a deliberate political choice. In a word, territorial multilingualism came to be replaced by institutional multilingualism. The Education Act, which was passed in 1912, contributed to the further fostering of trilingual and triglossic education in primary and secondary schools.

Growing political independency led to growing economic diversification, dominated by a flourishing and prosperous steel industry. The constant increase of production generated strong internal migrations to the steel-mills in the south of the Grand Duchy, followed by waves of immigration from Italy, and later on from Portugal. Linguistic integration took place, and is still taking place, in Luxembourgish and French.

The early twentieth century is marked by the country's joining up with international structures, such as UEBL, the trading union with Belgium, and BENELUX, the economic union with Belgium and the Netherlands.

Following the Second World War, Luxembourg became one of the founder-members of the United Nations and of the European Economic Community, the latter of which in 1952 established its head-quarters in Luxembourg City. Although the European Commission later left Luxembourg for Brussels, Luxembourg has remained the seat of powerful European institutions, among which are the European Court of Justice, the European Court of Auditors, the Secretariat-General of the European Parliament, the European Investment Bank, and the European Statistics Office. All these institutions offer some 8,000 jobs, which are held by nationals from all the 27 member-states of the European Union.

The growing international dimension of the tiny national economy is fully backed up by the Government, and has led to the establishment of international groups and of electronic service-providers such as *Google*, *Yahoo*, *Apple* and *Amazon*, for which Luxembourg is head-quarters to their European business. The targeted consolidation of Luxembourg as a financial centre with more than 80,000 jobs has completed this development.

From a sociolinguistic point of view, Luxembourg appears to be an open-minded and cosmopolitical economy, characterised by intense international business links, contact with which is not bound by any official language regulation, but free to operate in the language or languages of its choice.

Because of the country's geographical position at the intersection of Germanic and Romance cultures, and thus between two enormous retail markets, active multilingualism is considered by almost all economic operators to be a precondition for any activity.

Traditional triglossia still dominates in the national administration. Most official bodies can be seen as protected sectors, inasmuch as jobs there depend on the ability to speak and write the three languages, Luxembourgish, French and German.

A general differentiation between the oral and written use of language is helpful for understanding the linguistic particularities of the country. Native Luxembourgers use only Luxembourgish for oral communication, as this is their mother tongue. The last three decades have additionally seen the development of a strong tendency to use Luxembourgish also in written communication, instead of French or German. Government bodies, retail-banking institutions, insurance companies, and other service-providers use French or German as their written languages, as well as sometimes Luxembourgish, depending on the wishes of the customer, whereas oral communication normally takes place in Luxembourgish.

The preference of the big economic operators is for French and English, the internationally used languages, since the tiny home-market is very largely dependent on export business. Small and medium enterprises by contrast, whose customers are often local residents, prefer the traditional languages of the country.

Actually, language-choice in a precise economic language contact environment depends to a large extent on the type of contact and interaction inside the enterprise or institution, as well as between these and their customers. If the owner of the enterprise is a native Luxembourger, French, Belgian, or Portuguese, then internal correspondence and correspondence with his customers will be in French. The oral languages will most likely be French and Luxembourgish. If the owner is German, internal correspondence and correspondence with customers will probably be in German. Spoken languages will be German, Luxembourgish and French.

In hotels, restaurants and pubs, the most commonly used language is French. French, German, and Belgian supermarket retailers in Luxembourg behave as though the country is simply French-German bilingual. Product information in shops is in French, or in French and German. This is true also of advertising.

Commercial advertising in national TV-broadcasting is carried out almost exclusively in Luxembourgish, sometimes in French, in national radio-broadcasting only in Luxembourgish. Newspaper advertising is done in all three languages, occasionally also in English. Advertising by posted leaflet is done usually in French and German.

Active multilingualism is considered by all economic operators as a precondition for any activity. Multilingualism is one of the reasons why foreign operators establish themselves in Luxembourg. In this border region between Romance and Germanic cultures, the knowledge of both French and German is a vital necessity to many economic operators, who must be able to satisfy their French-speaking as well as their German-speaking customers.

The need to know three or more languages is clearly reflected in newspaper job advertisements. These advertisements are published in French, German, Luxembourgish, or English. The language chosen for the advertisement provides a tacit preselection of possible applicants. Job descriptions normally ask for knowledge of the three languages of the country, plus English. More unusual language-profiles, such as Dutch, Danish, Italian and others, also appear.

This linguistic diversity has proven itself to be rather uncomplicated in everyday life. However, in retail sectors such as supermarkets, shops and restaurants, the dominant position of French currently comes in for criticism, as many native Luxembourgers are annoyed at not being able to order a product in their mother tongue, but instead being forced to order in French.

Despite some criticism, the government has never seen any need for language-regulation in economic affairs. No official language-regulation exists, nor are there any guidelines as to language-use, or any compulsory legislation. There are no prescriptions or codes of conduct concerning the use of one or more languages, neither for the internal management of an enterprise, nor for any external contacts with other economic operators, or with customers.

The Languages Act, which dates from 1984, simply confirms the country's traditional triglossia. It defines Luxembourgish as the national language of the Luxembourgers and enshrines the use of French and German in State administration. Language-use in affairs of the economy is not, however, affected by this Act.

In conclusion, I would say that this government reluctance in language matters does not come about by omission, but rather by purpose. The country's economic prosperity is partially due to this common and unregulated active multilingualism, which gives all economic operators the possibility of flexible, diversified and cross-border development.

The experience of the last two centuries has shown that the absence of any language-guiding measures fosters economic development and diversification and supports the welfare of the whole economy. There is evidence also that this intense and long-term situation of language contact does not lead necessarily to the exclusion of any of the languages concerned. The Luxembourgish triglossia model proves instead to be highly beneficial to Luxembourgish, which is the young national language of the Grand Duchy. Today Luxembourgish is as vital and productive as it was never before – despite, or rather thanks, to the multilingualism that surrounds it.

Walery Pisarek

# Language use in business and commerce in Poland

**Summary / Streszczenie: Użycie języka w biznesie i handlu w Polsce**

W Polsce używanie w wewnętrznej komunikacji języka innego niż polski zależy głównie od zasięgu działania firmy. Języka innego niż polski używa się równie często w firmach przemysłu ciężkiego, bankowości, handlu, marketingu, a nawet na wyższych szczeblach zarządzania w mediach masowych. W firmach działających na terytorium Polski, ale mających swoją centralę za granicą w którymś z krajów nieanglomownych, częstym zjawiskiem jest używanie w komunikacji wewnętrznej trzech języków: angielskiego, polskiego i języka "centrali", którym najczęściej jest język niemiecki, znacznie rzadziej francuski i hiszpański.

Języka innego niż polski używa się w biznesie i handlu z następującą motywacją: są rynki lokalne, do których obsługi nadają się języki lokalne (jak język polski), i jest rynek globalny, na którym się mówi po angielsku (albo co najmniej według wzorów angielskich).

W Polsce zakres obligatoryjnego używania języka polskiego określa ustawa o języku polskim. Od 1 maja 2004 r. obowiązek jego używania ograniczony został do komunikowania się firmy z konsumentem (B2C). Powszechny obowiązek używania języka polskiego w komunikacji B2C dotyczy informacji o właściwościach towarów i usług w ofertach, na opakowaniach i w reklamie. Kontrolę używania języka polskiego w tym zakresie sprawuje Urząd Ochrony Konkurencji i Konsumentów, Inspekcja Handlowa oraz rzecznik konsumentów.

## 1. Historical background

The problem of using a language other than Polish in commerce and industry appeared in Poland only in the beginning of the 90s of the last century. Until that time, the Polish language was used exclusively in both these fields within the territory of the Republic of Poland, except for international trade or – to present it more broadly – for any contacts with foreign countries. And in the foreign trade and economic cooperation with foreign countries, the languages of Poland's foreign trade partners of that time (the Soviet Union, the German Democratic Republic and Czechoslovakia, among others) were used (aside from the English language) as auxiliary languages as well as the languages of marketing and advertising abroad.

After World War II the most important economic partner of Poland was the Soviet Union with the Russian language. The significance and position of the Russian language in the international cooperation of Poland at that time used to be much larger than it would appear from the Soviet Union's share in the foreign trade of Poland, because Russian was the working language of the Comecon whose members, apart from Poland, included other Central-European countries, among them the most important – after the Soviet Union – economic partners of Poland: Czechoslovakia and the GDR. This situation has changed diametrically after 1990: due to the aspirations of Poland – liberated from the Soviet hegemony – Germany, France and Italy moved to the top of the list of Poland's economic partners (see the table below).

The table shows that in the beginning of the 90s, Germany took the role of the first partner of Poland in the foreign trade from the Soviet Union. One would be mistaken to think, however, that since 1990 the German language has replaced Russian. It did not happen because at the same time the English language had already dominated the international commercial contacts of Western European companies. This applies also to such flagship German economic entities as the Deutsche Bank.

| Specification | First partner | Share (in %) | Second partner | Share (in %) | Third partner | Share (in %) |
|---|---|---|---|---|---|---|
| 1938 Imports | Germany | 14,5 | USA | 12,2 | UK | 11,4 |
| 1938 Exports | UK | 18,2 | Germany | 14,5 | Sweden | 6,0 |
| 1950 Imports | USSR | 28,8 | Czechoslovakia | 13,2 | GDR | 11,5 |
| 1950 Exports | USSR | 24,3 | GDR | 13,9 | Czechoslovakia | 9,2 |
| 1960 Imports | USSR | 31,2 | GDR | 12,5 | Czechoslovakia | 8,5 |
| 1960 Exports | USSR | 29,4 | GDR | 9,4 | Czechoslovakia | 8,5 |
| 1970 Imports | USSR | 37,7 | GDR | 11,1 | Czechoslovakia | 8,6 |
| 1970 Exports | USSR | 35,3 | GDR | 9,3 | Czechoslovakia | 7,5 |
| 1980 Imports | USSR | 33,1 | FRG | 6,7 | GDR | 6,6 |
| 1980 Exports | USSR | 31,2 | FRG | 8,1 | Czechoslovakia | 6,9 |
| 1992 Imports | Germany | 23,9 | Russian Fed. | 8,5 | Italy | 6,9 |
| 1992 Exports | Germany | 31,4 | Netherlands | 6,0 | Italy | 5,6 |
| 1995 Imports | Germany | 26,6 | Italy | 8,5 | Russian Fed. | 6,7 |
| 1995 Exports | Germany | 38,3 | Netherlands | 5,6 | Russian Fed. | 5,6 |
| 2000 Imports | Germany | 23,9 | Russian Fed. | 9,4 | Italy | 8,3 |
| 2000 Exports | Germany | 34,9 | Italy | 6,3 | France | 5,2 |
| 2005 Imports | Germany | 24,7 | Russian Fed. | 8,9 | Italy | 7,1 |
| 2005 Exports | Germany | 28,2 | France | 6,2 | Italy | 6,1 |
| 2007 Imports | Germany | 24,1 | Russian Fed. | 8,7 | China | 7,1 |
| 2007 Exports | Germany | 25,9 | Italy | 6,6 | France | 6,1 |

Table 1: Structure of the foreign trade turnover of Poland by main trading partners in 1950-2005 (in %). Source: Yearbook of Foreign Trade Statistics 2008. Central Statistical Office. Warsaw 2008.

On the threshold of the 90s, almost all of Polish industry, commerce, media and banks were in the hands of the state or the local governments. And since 1945, the "decree on the state language and the working language of government and self-government administrative authorities" was formally binding. In accordance with this decree, all "government and self-government authorities and offices", including companies in the business and commerce sector, should have worked using the Polish language. Meanwhile, since the beginning of the 90s, the process of privatization and reprivatization of the whole economy has begun in Poland. The state sold individual factories and companies to private buyers. As the purchasers of those objects were usually Western European or American entities, agreements of sale were drawn up also in a foreign language and sometimes **only** in a foreign language, which was obviously at odds with the spirit and the letter of the decree on the state language.

The Supreme Chamber of Control became interested in this issue. In 1996, a report concerning the use of Polish as the state language in operations of entities controlled in 1992-1996 was prepared by this institution. Inspections revealed glaring examples of documents (in the majority of cases, this concerned the agreements of sale) being drawn up by the state offices exclusively in foreign languages. A suspicion arose that an exclusively foreign form of at least some of the agreements made it possible to conceal certain terms of those agreements, unfavourable to the Polish party. The findings of these inspections contributed, to a considerable degree, to the passing of the Act on the Polish language in 1999.

## 2. Current state of affairs

Today the use of a language other than Polish in internal communication does not depend on the sector of economy or the size of the company but chiefly on the scope of operation and the ownership relations (they decide which foreign language is used). Languages other than Polish are equally often used in heavy industry, banking, trade, marketing, even in mass media companies. Although the use of a language other than Polish occurs much more frequently in large rather than small companies, it results from the fact that large supranational as well as international companies are seldom Polish firms, while they are often parts of large international concerns. Practical reasons usually determine the use of a foreign language within the company: if non-Polish speaking representatives of foreign shareholders sit on the supervisory board and its Polish members know a given foreign language, the talks are held in this foreign language, most often in English, even if the company has its registered headquarters in a non-English speaking country.

In companies operating within the territory of Poland, but having their headquarters abroad, in one of the non-English speaking countries, it frequently occurs that three languages are used in the internal communication: English, Polish and the language of the "central office", usually German, less often: French and Spanish.

In Poland, no research is conducted on the perceptions and attitudes of the employees or trade unions regarding the issue of language use within companies. At least in the media, there is no evidence of internal conflicts, between the employees (and trade unions, as their advocates) and the management of the company, concerning the language.

On the one hand, an atmosphere of kind social approval for the spontaneous use of foreign names in commerce and services in the borderland can be noticed and advertisements written solely in English or German are administratively tolerated, on the other – there are citizens' complaints to the Ministry of Culture or Polish Language Council about foreign-language job offers printed in journals and magazines, even about using foreign-language names of positions (like *corporate dealer*, *operation manager*, *project manager*, *account manager*, etc.) in Polish-language recruitment advertisements.[1]

---

1 However, psychological research confirms social credibility and a higher social prestige of foreign-language texts (English, French, German) in comparison with Polish ones. It applies also to the phenomenon of an informal and formal higher hierarchy (rating), in the academic environment, of a

The main job requirements, specified in recruitment advertisements, may be taken for a reliable indication of the position of individual foreign languages in commerce and business in Poland. Tens or even hundreds of such advertisements are published in special supplements or sections in the leading national dailies. Those advertisements are roughly divided by editorial teams according to sectors of economy and social life. From such editorial practices, one can easily conclude that the saturation of particular sectors with advertisements seeking employees with a knowledge of foreign languages is very diverse and ranges from zero (there is no requirement to know a foreign language in the offers of the public administration sector!) to 95% (almost every job offer in the management staff sector requires the knowledge of at least one foreign language).

The analysis of job offers indicates that the choice of a foreign language used in individual companies depends not that much on the sorts of products or services but rather on the registered headquarters of the main shareholder, in the sense that the majority of offers requiring knowledge of the German language come from German firms. For every 100 offers requiring the knowledge of any foreign language, 68 require the knowledge of the English language and 19 – the knowledge of German. The requirement to know a language other than English, German and Polish appears very seldom in job offers.

I am not familiar with any spectacular examples where the success or failure of a company in Poland was determined by its internal use of a language. However, the success of certain Polish companies (especially abroad, e.g. in Germany) is attributed to their names, suggesting their non-Polishness (e.g. *Gino Rossi*, *Simple*, *Monari*, *Tatuum*, *Diverse*). On the other hand, one can come across suggestions that one of the factors contributing to the failure of a new magazine was its foreign-language name (e.g. *Glamour*, *Marie Claire*, *Votre Beauté*).

## 3. Legal conditions

The use of the Polish language in public activities and legal transactions on the territory of the Republic of Poland is regulated by the Act on the Polish language of October 7th, 1999. According to this Act, until May 1st 2004, i.e. until the moment of Poland's accession to the European Union: the Polish language should have been "used in legal transactions made on the territory of the Republic of Poland when at least one of the parties thereto is a Polish entity". That should have applied "in particular to names of goods or services, offers, advertisements, manuals, information on qualities of goods or services, terms of guarantee, invoices, bills and receipts". These regulations were changed, in regard to their content and application, on May 1st, 2004: since then the obligation to use the Polish language has been limited to the business-to-consumer (B2C) communication. As far as the internal communication is concerned (as well as the "B2B" communication), the Polish language should still be used by Polish entities entrusted with public tasks and controlled by the state, local governments, and territorial agencies of public administration.

text published in a language other than Polish. The appeal of foreign languages is used in marketing and advertising, especially in the naming of Polish companies, proper names of products as well as in advertising catchphrases (compare the slogan "Japan Beauty", created by a Polish company to be used in a promotion of a Japanese automobile, *Suzuki Liana*, in Poland).

The obligation to use the Polish language "applies in particular to warnings and information for consumers [...], manuals and information on qualities of goods and services". Information on qualities of goods and services should be expressed in Polish also in advertisements.

The control of the Polish language use is exercised by the Office for Competition and Consumer Protection, Commercial Inspectorate and the consumer ombudsman. In April 2004, the Supreme Chamber of Control published its report "on the results of control of the realization of the Act on the Polish language", based on its own research from the years 2001-2003. This research concerned also the question of the Polish language use in descriptions of goods and services. The following conclusions from this research were included in the report:

> 1. [...] From the beginning of 2001 to the middle of 2003, the Commercial Inspectorate carried out [...] 39082 (55.3% inspections in total) inspections concerning the observance of the Act on the Polish language. The inspections revealed 2260 cases of infringement of the Act on the Polish language, consisting in, among other things, a lack of Polish-language names and descriptions of products and a lack of translation of manuals and maintenance instructions into Polish. [...] In 1552 cases, motions for punishment for the offence under article 15 of the Act on the Polish language were filed. As a result of these motions, 1296 persons were punished, including 1254 punished with a fine.

Furthermore:

> 2. Provincial inspectors of the Commercial Inspectorate issued, upon the requests of customs authorities, 169 opinions in cases concerning the introduction of products without the required Polish-language labels into the Polish customs territory.

The Supreme Chamber of Control assessed negatively the observance of the Act on the Polish language by the majority of large format retail centers in which substantial, intensifying irregularities in the Polish language use in business trade were revealed.

Control testing revealed substantial irregularities related to the non-compliance with the Act on the Polish language in 40 out of 48 large format retail centers controlled (83,3%).

The revealed irregularities consisted mainly in a lack of translation into Polish of certain information contained in the original text, including: the name of foodstuff type, method of preparation or use, storage conditions, notices preceding the minimum shelf-life or best before date, all ingredients occurring in the foodstuff, qualities of the product, warning notices. Presenting the Polish-language version of the text as secondary to the foreign-language text by using a smaller font has also been found.

And finally the Supreme Chamber of Control concluded:

> The results of the control indicate that the Polish language does not have an equal position with foreign languages in business trade. The aim of the Act, described by the legislator as the protection of the Polish language status as the state language and a national cultural asset has not been fully achieved.

Every two years the Polish Language Council prepares a "report on the state of the protection of the Polish language". These reports – presented to the Polish Parliament – take into account, among other things, the adherence to the provisions of the Act on the Polish language in the scope of the Polish language use in commerce with consumer participation. While the research conducted for these reports does not indicate distinct changes for the better as far as Polish descriptions and instructions on products in retail trade are concerned, it is hard to say how the situation would look if there were no relevant regulations at all.

It is extremely difficult to obtain credible and representative data about the reach and scope of the use of languages other than Polish for internal communication in individual companies. However, it is obvious that many companies in Poland wouldn't be able to operate, if they had to restrict themselves to Polish in their internal communication.

As the research conducted recently in Poland proves, in the internal communication and the non-consumer (B2B) communication, languages other than Polish are used by the Polish business people with the following self justification: there are local markets, for the handling of which local languages (like the Polish language) are suitable and there is the global market in which English is spoken (or at least English language patterns are used).

Guðrún Kvaran

# The Icelandic language in business and commerce in Iceland


## Abstract

Í greininni verður fjallað um stöðu íslenskrar tungu í verslun og viðskiptum bæði innanlands og erlendis. Sagt verður frá væntanlegri málstefnu sem lögð verður fyrir Alþingi í nóvember og tekur m.a. á íslensku í viðskiptalífinu. Síðan verður þeim átta spurningum, sem fyrirlesararnir voru beðnir um að taka tillit til, svarað út frá íslenskum veruleika í dag. M.a. verður rætt um innanhúss samskipti innan fyrirtækja sem starfa á Íslandi en eiga einnig viðskipti við útlönd. Komið verður að auglýsingum í fjölmiðlum, námskeiðum fyrir erlenda starfsmenn á Íslandi og fleira sem viðkemur samskiptum Íslendinga og erlendra starfsmanna. Að lokum verður rætt um það hvað mikilvægast er fyrir íslenska tungu ef hún á ekki að verða undir á viðskiptasviðinu.


## 1. Introduction

In my paper I have the intention to describe the status of the Icelandic language in business and commerce in Iceland. The main task of the Icelandic Language Council has for over a year been to write a draft of the first official Icelandic language policy. This was requested by the minister of education who has for her part already accepted the proposals suggested by the council about aims and actions. The language policy was presented publicly on November 16th, the official Icelandic language day, and was proposed for parliamentary resolution the following week (Íslenska til alls 2008). Eleven areas of the national life, that the Language Council considered most important to study, were selected, one of them being language in business and commerce, which will be my topic in this paper.

## 2. The eight leading questions

When I offered to give a talk last summer no one suspected what was to come in the Icelandic financial- and business world. The state of Icelandic companies was good, both in the domestic and the international markets, a far cry from what it is today. But although many things have taken a turn for the worse, the status of the Icelandic language is the same as before, and that is our only concern here. I will answer as far as possible the eight leading questions sent by the organizers of this convention, which they requested were to be considered in the report. I will describe the situation like it was before the bank-crisis. I consider the problems temporary, already there is rebuilding going on, and the status of the Icelandic language will be the same, whether the companies are small or large. The following is based, among other things, on the studies performed for the language policy by the Language Council.

### 2.1 The first question

The first leading question was whether companies in Iceland use a different language than the official national language for internal communications. The Icelandic economy became in a relatively short time much more internationalized than it had been before. Many Icelandic companies set up workstations outside of Iceland with non-

Icelandic employees, and in addition the number of foreign employees of companies in Iceland – specialists and non-specialists alike – increased dramatically. Foreign investors own shares in Icelandic companies and sit on their boards of directors. Therefore there has been an increase of other languages than Icelandic, primarily English, being used as the language for communication in business and commerce within Iceland.

In some areas, for example the construction industry, until recently a part of the workers did not use Icelandic at work, but other languages instead, sometimes one among themselves (for example Polish) but another one (usually English) for communicating with their Icelandic superiors. In commerce and service foreign workers increased greatly the past few years and very often they had to work and communicate with Icelandic customers in English because they were not sufficiently proficient in Icelandic. Now, amidst an economic depression, the situation has changed already. Foreign workers, e.g. in the construction industry, mostly Polish, are now returning home, because less work is available, and it may be expected that in these areas the primary language will again be Icelandic, with some foreign languages mixed in.

About six months ago a survey was made on behalf of the Icelandic Language Council on what language was used for communications in the countries' largest companies (Karlsson/Jónsdóttir 2008). These were banks, export companies, companies in the production industry and service industry. On an European scale the companies are small, but rather large on the Icelandic scale. All the companies were domestic, since few international companies have established themselves in Iceland, with the exception of foreign shop franchisees run by Icelanders. 51 companies were contacted and replies came back from 50. In 31 of the companies e-mail was written exclusively in Icelandic, in 4 of them it was almost only in English, but about equally Icelandic and English in 7 companies. Meetings were mostly conducted in Icelandic in 26 of the companies, exclusively in Icelandic in 21, but only in one company exclusively in English.

Protocols were exclusively written in Icelandic in 24 companies, mostly in Icelandic in 19, only in English in 4, but equally in Icelandic and English in 3. The results were different when the homepage was concerned. 28 companies had their homepage both in Icelandic and in English, but only 12 exclusively in Icelandic. 4 companies had an exclusively English homepage. The survey also revealed that although Icelandic was still the primary language of communication in most of the companies, English was usually or often used if there was one foreigner in the group. Language use can therefore vary according to the various departments of the companies. More and more Icelandic companies that have branches in other countries, conduct the meetings of their stockholders in English, even though the meetings are most often held in Iceland, and the majority of those attending is Icelandic. Yearly reports of many Icelandic companies and various documents regarding their operations are also exclusively in English, even though the companies are in majority ownership of Icelanders.

## 2.2 The second question

The second question deals with the perceptions and attitudes of the employees and of interlocutors regarding the issue of language used within companies. The answer is that the general public in Iceland, including Icelandic employees of most companies, want to use Icelandic as the language for communication for as long as possible, but admit that it may be necessary to use a foreign language if someone present is foreign and has to be able to participate in discussions and decisions. Most often English is used, but also Danish, when the person concerned is from a Nordic country. It is well known that people from the Nordic countries can quite well communicate in Scandinavian, that is in Danish, Norwegian and Swedish, or a mix of the three languages. Trade unions do not interfere in language use in the workplaces, but in several cases foreign workers are offered courses in Icelandic for a minimal fee or for free. The trade unions support foreign workers in learning the language, but also the ministry of education and often the company that employs the worker, for example hospitals, nurseries and retirement homes and the larger companies. This is done with that in mind that the foreign workers can more easily adapt to the Icelandic society if they are able to express themselves and participate in workplace discussions and communicating with their wards. Issues of security are also considered.

## 2.3 The third and fourth question

The third question is about whether there are in the country companies that use languages other than the national language in contacts with customers, in marketing, and in advertising. The fourth question asks about the perceptions and attitudes of customers and the general public on the use of languages other than the official language of the country in advertising, commercials, job opportunities, or the like. As these questions are closely related I will answer them both at once. No company known to me uses another language than Icelandic in customer communications or marketing domestically, and such a move would undoubtedly meet with very great general disapproval. The state radio is a medium that is extensively used for advertising. It has established it's own language policy. It says e.g.: “Advertisements shall be in flawless Icelandic and presented with a good pronunciation. Given a special reason the radio director can however allow singing or talking in a foreign language in advertisements“.

The state television adheres to the same policy. The law on monitoring illegal business practices and market transparency from 2005 states that advertisements meant to appeal to Icelandic consumers shall be in Icelandic. The same applies for general terms of service providers and guarantee statements in writing. The mass media themselves demand the law to be followed in advertising, and advertisements are seldom seen in newspapers in other languages than in Icelandic. Advertisements that are only published in foreign languages are primarily notices for general meetings in companies operating in part abroad and on the other hand some work-advertisements. In such cases both Icelandic and a foreign language are used, mostly English, for stockholders meetings but usually Polish in the case of work-advertisements. Work-advertisements in foreign languages are regarded differently if an Icelandic advertisement is published as well.

## 2.4 The fifth question

The fifth question concerns the language or languages which are typically used by companies in international business and commerce. It is easily answered. English is the dominant language in international business, although both Scandinavian and German are used in business directed to the Nordic countries or Germany. It must be said, however, that English is fast pushing the Scandinavian languages aside, though it is still mandatory in Iceland to learn Danish in primary and high school. Younger people prefer using English for communicating with the Nordic nations, on the grounds that those who can use their native language in all sorts of business, negotiations and debates, have the advantage over those forced to use a foreign language. It is well known that one can say what one wants in ones native language, but only what one knows how to express in a foreign language. German and French are not any more both mandatory subjects in Iceland, as they were for decades, and have been to some extent replaced by Spanish, Italian, Russian and Japanese. Many have been concerned about English becoming for Icelanders the main language of communication with foreign countries, since the increased use of English carries with it the danger that Icelandic starts declining and even vanish completely from certain areas of the business world. Such a loss of domain would be irreplaceable. They believe that the status of the Icelandic language would weaken, if it were not any longer useable in all areas of the Icelandic society and Icelanders could no longer count on being able to work and do business in their native language in their own country. That would entail a distinct loss of quality of life for Icelanders. Furthermore the growth of Icelandic specialist vocabulary would stop for the lost areas and Icelandic language use and the extant specialist vocabulary could be lost. Therefore it could prove very difficult to regain lost domains. My remarks should however not be taken to imply that we should eradicate English or other languages from business and commerce in Iceland. The use of English or other languages is indispensable in international communications. The goal is rather to insure the co-habitation of Icelandic and English in an environment where Icelandic is the main language of communication, that is to insure that Icelandic is on an equal footing with English in business and within companies domestically, that an Icelandic vocabulary develops normally in business and commerce and that increased foreign communication is not at the expense of the Icelandic language in Iceland.

## 2.5 The sixth question

The sixth question on whether the choice and use of language is regarded as factors contributing to the success or failure of business and commerce in Iceland is easy to answer. Customers and the general public domestically regard more positively companies that use Icelandic as the language for communication. An Icelandic company that would start using English or another foreign language to communicate with Icelanders would not enjoy respect or popularity. It would most probably be forced to change its policy if it did not want to go under. Business abroad is a quite different matter. It is perfectly clear of course that abroad one has to use a foreign language. Icelandic is not useable in international business, since so few people abroad are capable of using it in writing or orally.

## 2.6 The seventh and eight question

The questions seven and eight regarding specific laws or other official regulations drawn up by the government or other political institutions for the use of languages by and within companies in my country I have already answered. The laws that have to do with language and business mainly deal with language in advertising, but also states that general conditions of service providers, and guarantee statements in writing, must be in Icelandic. In other respects the choice of language is not legislated, neither regarding business domestically nor Icelandic business abroad.

## 3. Conclusion

This is the situation as it has been until now. Following the financial crisis no one knows what is to come next. Many people have lost much and for the foreseeable future business abroad will be low. But although much has been lost the nation still has one thing in common: the language. The Icelandic Language Council will therefore continue undaunted to fight for the use of Icelandic in all areas of society, including in business and commerce. The language policy that is being developed and I mentioned at the start of my presentation has the suggestion that Icelandic companies should be encouraged and supported as possible in forming a clear language policy for themselves with the aim of insuring the status of the Icelandic language in the economic life. Forming a policy on language use should be a natural part of all policy-making in Icelandic companies. As I said before the aim cannot be to eliminate the use of foreign languages in an international working environment, but foreign languages cannot replace Icelandic, rather the Icelandic language must retain its place among other languages.

If the goals of the Icelandic Language Council should to be reached it is important that there will be a positive discussion in the community and within companies about the benefits of Icelandic as the primary language in the Icelandic economic life and the qualities of life that entails for Icelanders. The responsibility for this lies with the nation itself. If Icelanders are to be able to purchase goods and services in Iceland in Icelandic and work in Iceland using the Icelandic language, laws and regulations will not be sufficient if the nation does not side with the Icelandic language. As the situation is today I have no concern that this will not be the case.

## 4. References

Karlson, Þorlákur/Jónsdóttir, Dagný (2008): *Tungumál og málfar í viðskiptalífi og stjórnsýslu.* Written for The Icelandic Language Council. Unpublished.

*Íslenska til alls.* Tillögur Íslenskrar málnefndar að íslenskri málstefnu. Menntamálaráðuneyti 2008. [The Icelandic Language Councils draft of an Icelandic language policy.]

Corina Cilianu-Lascu / Marius Sala

# Les langues de la communication professionnelle dans les entreprises de Roumanie: enjeux, réalités, perspectives

## 1. Introduction: enjeux économiques, politiques et culturels

À l'époque actuelle, les mutations intervenues dans le monde du travail imposent la maîtrise de la langue, et plus spécifiquement des codes de la communication professionnelle, qui apparaît comme un facteur déterminant pour accéder à l'emploi et à la performance dans la carrière. Nous partons de l'idée que toute situation de travail est une *situation de communication* et *d'échange* extrêmement complexe dont les éléments contribuent chacun à la réussite ou à l'échec de l'activité.

Tout cela implique une stratégie de communication multilingue conçue par l'étude de référence ELAN: ("Incidences du manque de compétences linguistiques des entreprises sur l'économie européenne") comme "l'adoption planifiée d'une gamme de techniques visant à permettre une communication effective avec les clients et les fournisseurs à l'étranger" (ELAN 2005) et dans le pays d'origine, dans la communication interne et externe.

Il faut aussi réfléchir à l'articulation des compétences langagières aux compétences professionnelles afin d'intégrer d'une manière cohérente les compétences communicatives dans le cadre des savoir-faire profesionnels. Dans une société où "quand faire, c'est dire" (Mourlhon-Dallies 2007), il faut prendre en compte tous les aspects des *échanges formels et informels* dans le cadre de l'exercice de la profession car le plan du dire et celui du faire s'interpénètrent au sein même des compétences professionnelles.

La communication professionnelle comporte des étapes de nature différente, cognitive, affective et conative qui orientent la hiérarchie des effets de la communication sur les résultats du travail en séquences successives selon la théorie des approches séquentielles (Lavidge/Steiner, in Décaudin 1995: 32) dont le modèle englobe: connaissance → attitude → comportements (*learn – feel – do*).

D'où la nécessité d'une modélisation des mutations récentes du monde du travail

- à partir de données fiables d'une analyse de terrain
- à l'aide des disciplines qui modélisent l'activité de travail: sociolinguistique, sociologie du travail, sciences de la communication, analyse des discours et des actions, analyse du travail.

Nous avons essayé de mettre à profit les idées du groupe de recherche "Langage et travail" tout aussi bien que celles du modèle global de "l'agir communicationnel" de l'école de Genève.

Les caractéristiques de la communication professionnelle sont l'apanage des cultures professionnelles, elles mêmes composantes de la culture d'entreprise. Les rapports entre les cultures d'entreprise différentes en contact dans les sociétés nouvellement créées dans le contexte des changements économiques internationaux déterminent le choix des langues de la communication professionnelle au sein de ces sociétés.

La Roumanie s'est inscrite dans un contexte économico-social et politique national en plein changement après 1989, et son ouverture internationale grâce à l'adhésion à l'Union Européenne suppose des échanges économiques et culturels accrus, des investissements étrangers, la rencontre de cultures d'entreprise différentes. Ce sont des enjeux importants qui sont en étroite relation avec la qualité des compétences langagières de spécialité.

Une étude diachronique donnerait une image des changements du niveau des compétences linguistiques en langues étrangères et de l'attitude des Roumains concernant l'apprentissage des langues: après un fort engouement après 1989 quand tout le monde voulait apprendre plusieurs langues étrangères et, par conséquent, il y avait un nombre très grand de cours de langues dans les curricula scolaires et universitaires, actuellement nous constatons une démotivation alarmante et une réduction drastique des cours de langues, ce qui est contraire aux besoins réels des professionnels des entreprises. En même temps, notre expérience dans le cadre d'un MBA de gestion des entreprises nous a donné la possibilité de constater aussi, surtout avec le changement des générations d'élèves, un fort accroissement du nombre des professionnels connaissant l'anglais au détriment de ceux qui connaissent le français et une baisse continue du niveau des compétences de communication en langues étrangères.

## 2. Objectifs et contenus de l'enquête de terrain

Pour connaître concrètement les réalités roumaines, nous avons conçu un questionnaire et reccueilli des informations auprès de 190 entreprises:

127 entreprises multinationales,

31 PME nationales,

26 PME locales.

Cette démarche vise plusieurs objectifs:

- analyser la place que ces entreprises réservent aux compétences linguistiques et interculturelles dans leurs stratégies de communication;
- recenser les différences qui les séparent, entre autres les différences entre les sociétés de trois régions de Roumanie prises en compte;
- étudier les rapports entre l'emploi du roumain et des langues étrangères dans l'exercice de la profession;
- recenser les options pour les langues internationales et pour d'autres langues selon la culture d'entreprise (valeurs partagées, attitudes, comportements au travail) et l'origine du personnel.

Nous avons proposé notre questionnaire à des représentants de différentes entreprises de trois zones régionales de Roumanie: la région de Bucarest, la Transylvanie (Cluj et Sibiu), le Dobroudja (Constanța).

Nous avons interviewé deux catégories de professionnels:

- les responsables des stands des entreprises présentes à deux salons pour l'emploi (octobre 2008);
- des jeunes professionnels des entreprises: les élèves d'un MBA de gestion des entreprises ayant des antennes dans les régions envisagées et les étudiants d'un master de communication des affaires en milieu multiculturel.

Notre questionnaire est orienté sur 3 axes d'intérêt:

- la (les) langue(s) employée(s) dans la communication professionnelle;
- la politique de l'entreprise quant aux compétences langagières;
- l'attitude des salariés.

Les questions portent sur tous les aspects de la communication d'entreprise selon le schéma ci-dessous (cf. Demont et al. 2001: 12):

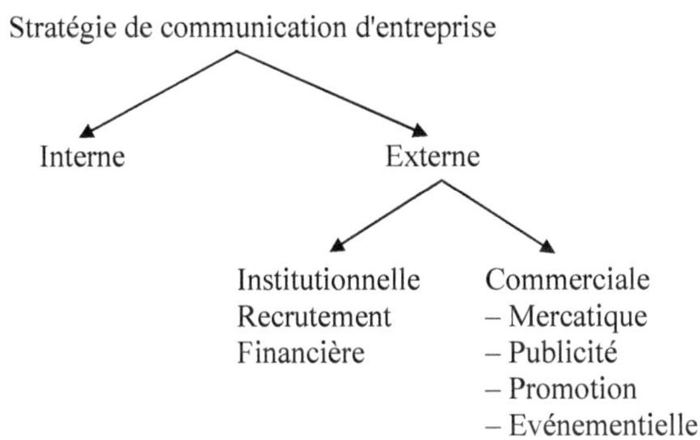


En fait, l'utilisation des langues dépend directement de tous les facteurs de la situation de communication: interlocuteurs, message, canal. Pour l'instant, nous nous sommes arrêtés surtout sur la communication interne écrite et/ou orale tout en considérant les types de rapports entre les interlocuteurs et le contenu de la communication (relations hiérarchiques, aspects socio-professionnels):

- formelle
  a) au niveau des relations entre la direction et l'encadrement,
  b) verticale (entre la hiérarchie et les subordonnées),
  c) horizontale (transversale) (entre les départements),
- informelle.

Il y a seulement deux questions qui portent sur des éléments de communication externe, la première concerne la politique de l'entreprise quant aux compétences langagières des candidats lors du recrutement, la deuxième, les langues utilisées dans la communication commerciale et les départements qui utilisent les langues étrangères avec les partenaires externes.

## 3. Traitement des données de l'enquête

Les résultats de l'enquête ont été traités séparément selon les types de sociétés (internationales, nationales, locales) et les catégories de questions.

### 3.1 Types de sociétés

Une analyse ultérieure, plus détaillée, traitera les informations fournies par l'enquête concernant les langues de la communication professionnelle selon le secteur d'activité, le statut juridique et le type de capital social, roumain ou étranger.

Vu les caractéristiques des personnes interviewées, notre corpus comprend beaucoup plus de sociétés internationales, un nombre assez proche de sociétés nationales et locales et très peu d'institutions administratives:

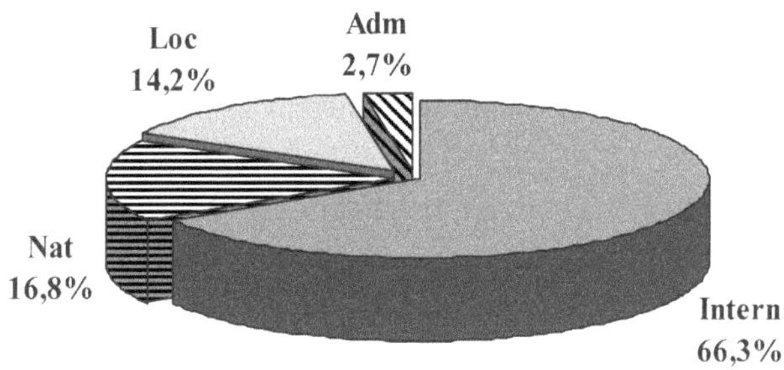


## 3.2 Les langues de travail

### 3.2.1 Les sociétés internationales

#### 3.2.1.1 La langue officielle

Le pourcentage des sociétés où l'anglais représente la ***langue officielle*** est plus important que l'ensemble des sociétés employant d'autres langues:

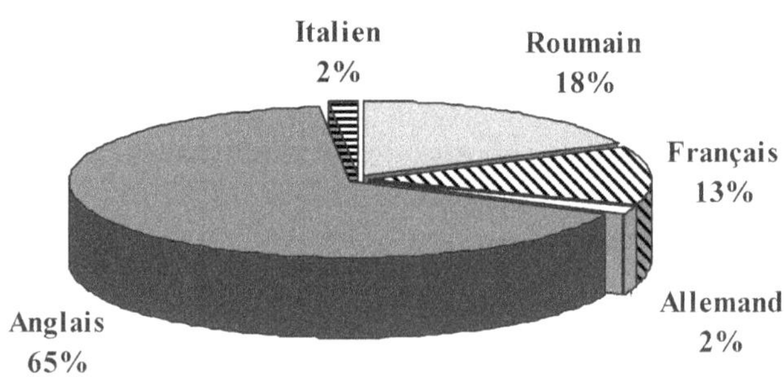


Certaines sociétés ont deux ou trois langues officielles, mais l'anglais reste la première langue dans 49% des cas, alors que la seconde langue est représentée par: le roumain (29%), le français (18%), l'allemand (4%):

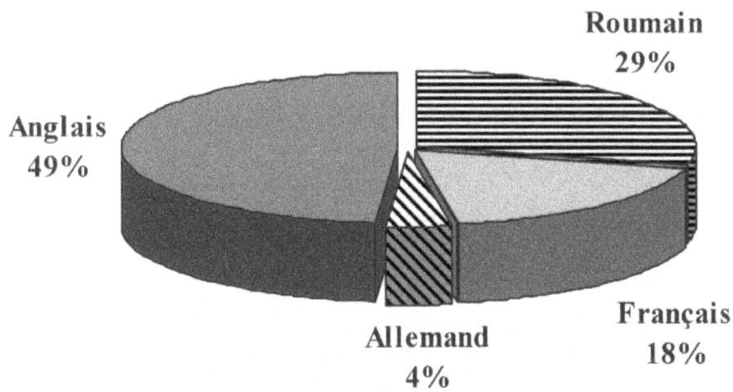


Dans d'autres cas, il y a des sociétés où la seconde langue est différente par apport aux situations ci-dessus:

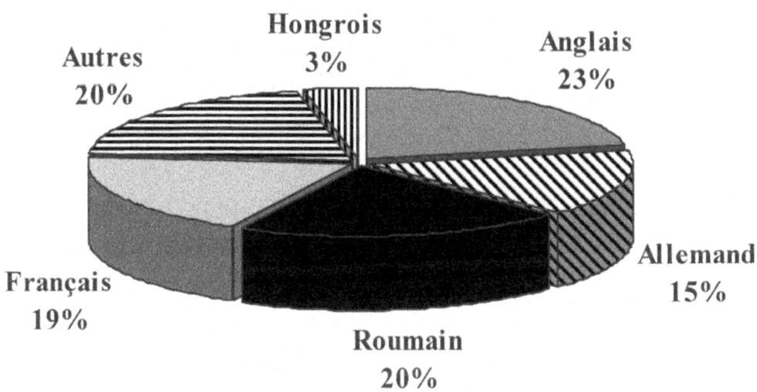


L'anglais s'impose comme langue officielle dans beaucoup de sociétés à capital français (*Alcatel*, *Lafarge*, *Sanofi*, etc.), étant donné leur statut d'entreprises multinationales. En même temps, il y a des sociétés grecques ou turques qui imposent leurs langues à côté de l'anglais comme langue officielle.

Il est intéressant à remarquer que, selon le capital social investi, d'autres langues sont utilisées dans un certain nombre de sociétés: d'une part, le turc, l'italien, l'espagnol, l'hébreu, le polonais, le japonais, avec un pourcentage assez important, et le bulgare, le grec, le russe, le hollandais et le norvégien, avec un pourcentage très faible:

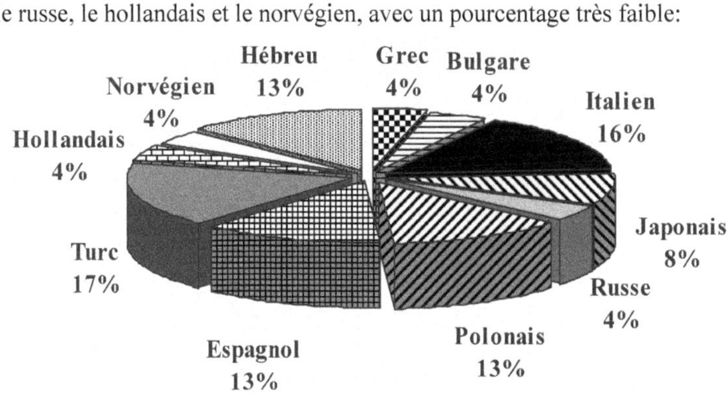

3.2.1.2 Les langues de le communication entre la direction et l'encadrement

Au niveau de la communication entre ***la direction et l'encadrement***, l'anglais est employé dans 40% des sociétés internationales le français et le roumain occupent la deuxième, respectivement la troisième place:

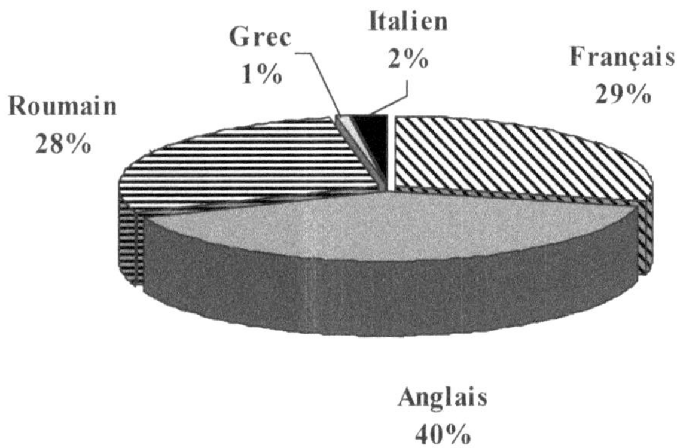


Dans beaucoup de sociétés, si pour la communication orale on emploie plusieurs langues, pour l'écrit, l'anglais est obligatoire. Selon l'origine du capital étranger investi, il y a des cas où, à ce niveau, les investisseurs principaux emploient leur langue.

3.2.1.3 Les langues de la communication transversale

La situation n'est pas la même, bien sûr, pour la ***communication transversale***, entre les différents départements de l'entreprise, où la plupart des salariés sont roumains:

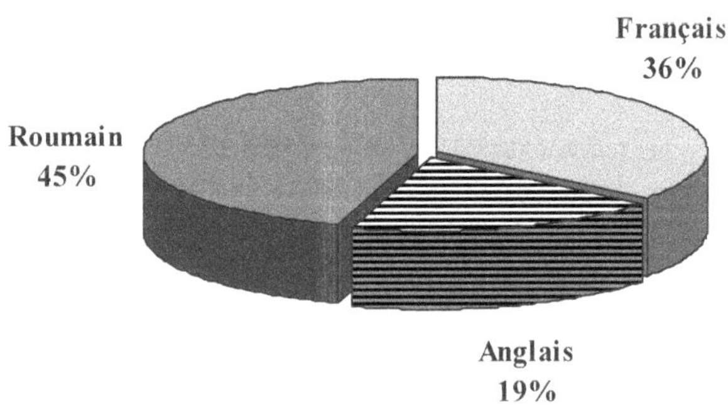


3.2.1.4 Les langues de la communication informelle

Pour ce qui est de la ***communication informelle***, il est normal que le roumain occupe la première place avec 70%, vu les circonstances de communication entre et avec les salariés roumains:

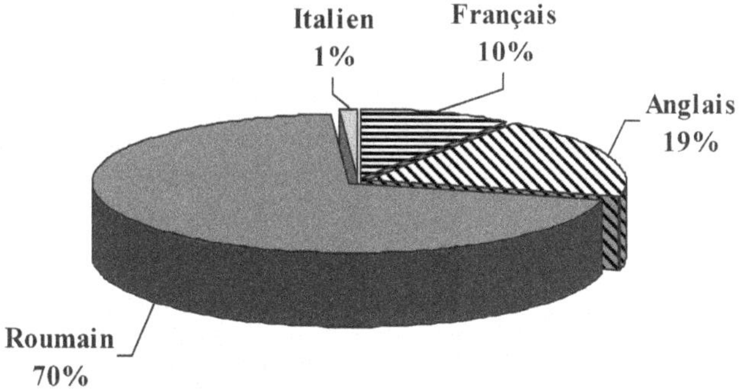


La communication informelle dans l'autres langues que le roumain dépend des cas concrets où les sociétés emploient des étrangers en Roumanie.

3.2.2 Les sociétés nationales

Dans toutes les sociétés nationales, le roumain est utilisé en tant que première langue de communication, alors que l'anglais est utilisé en tant que seconde langue dans 52% des sociétés interviewées, le français, 33%, l'allemand, 11%, et le hongrois, 4%.

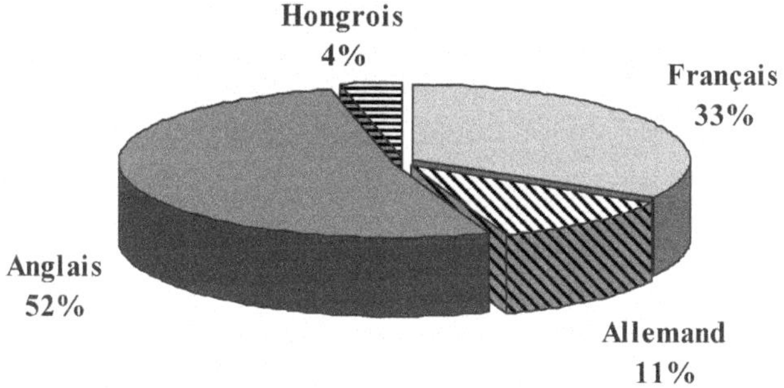


3.2.3 Les sociétés locales

Les langues de travail dans les sociétés locales sont les mêmes que celles des sociétés nationales, sans que les pourcentages soient les mêmes: le roumain représente la première langue dans toutes les sociétés, l'anglais, 60%, le français, 33%, l'allemand, 7%.

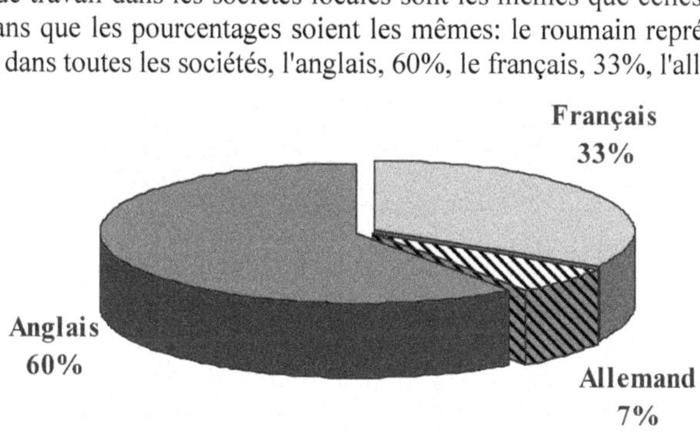

### 3.3 La politique des entreprises quant aux compétences en langues: sociétés internationales

Pour des raisons d'espace, nous ne ferons référence qu'à la politique des sociétés internationales concernant les compétences langagières, sans présenter la politique des sociétés nationales et locales.

#### 3.3.1 Le recrutement

*Le* ***recrutement*** de locuteurs natifs dotés de compétences langagières est une méthode de gestion linguistique très répandue: 95,1% des entreprises internationales de Roumanie y recourent.

La plupart des sociétés exigent des connaissances obligatoires d'une ou de deux langues internationales, tandis que dans 20%, la connaissance d'une ou de plusieurs langues représente un atout:

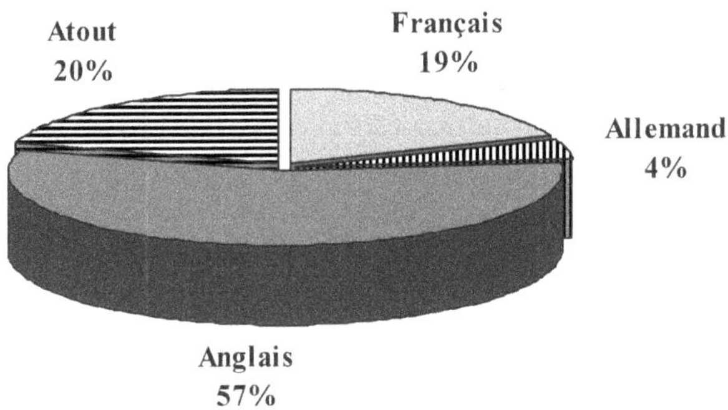


#### 3.3.2 La formation linguistique du personnel

Une forte proportion d'entreprises (57% de l'échantillon) propose une ***formation linguistique*** à leur personnel:

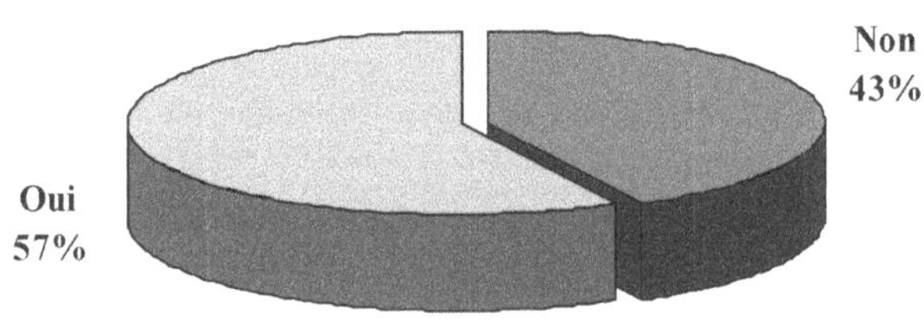


Cependant, petites et grandes entreprises préfèrent recruter des collaborateurs possédant déjà des compétences linguistiques, plutôt que d'investir dans la formation.

Pourtant une proportion importante de sociétés organise des cours de langues:

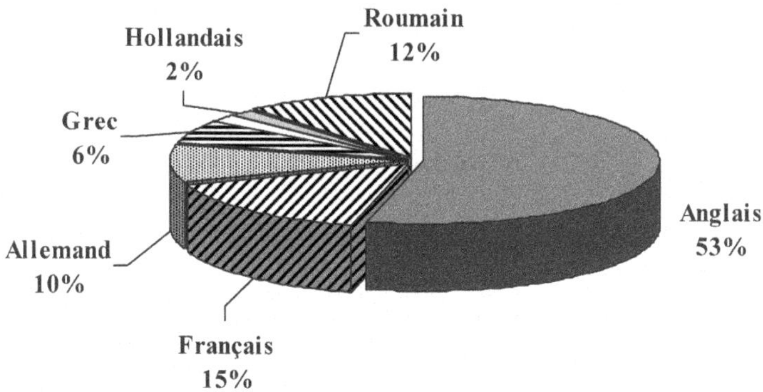


Il faut y ajouter aussi le turc pour deux des sociétés interviewées.

Il est intéressant à souligner que, selon la politique des entreprises et leurs propres options, beaucoup de professionnels étrangers qui travaillent en Roumanie apprennent le roumain. Il y a même une société française où tout le personnel n'emploie que le roumain au travail.

Les exigences des entreprises au recrutement quant à la connaissance des langues étrangères sont différentes, bien sûr, par rapport au type de poste à pourvoir. En même temps, les cours de langues sont organisés, selon les entreprises, tout le temps, périodiquement ou occasionnellement, et sont offerts à tout le personnel, mais le plus souvent, à ceux qui occupent des postes qui exigent la maîtrise de la communication en langues étrangères.

### 3.4 L'attitude des salariés

Dans leurs activités de commerce extérieur, les PME se heurtent à des barrières interculturelles et linguistiques.

Au moins 50% des personnes interrogées pensent avoir besoin de compétences linguistiques supplémentaires dans les années à venir, mais il n'y en a que très peu qui sont disposées vraiment à y investir de l'argent et des efforts. Plus de 5% des personnes interrogées disent avoir éprouvé des difficultés d'ordre interculturel.

Les réponses à la question sur le rôle que les compétences langagières jouent dans la performance des entreprises sont assez générales, ce qui indique que, pour l'instant, en Roumanie, la conscience de ces besoins n'est pas assez forte. Dans beaucoup de cas, les cours de langues ne sont pas assez efficaces à cause d'un effort très faible de ceux qui les fréquentent.

## 4. Conclusions

### 4.1 Les rèsultats de l'enquête

La collecte des données statistiques et l'étude des attitudes illustrent l'utilité des compétences linguistiques et l'application de celles-ci dans toutes les entreprises interrogées.

Les résultats de notre enquête sur les langues de la communication professionnelle nous conduisent à certaines conclusions générales:

- l'anglais est plus utilisé comme langue véhiculaire à l'intérieur des compagnies multinationales que dans les PME, vu son statut de “langue d'entreprise”;
- malgré tout, la demande de compétences dans d'autres langues que l'anglais est supérieure à la demande de compétences en anglais;
- pour des raisons d'efficacité, l'utilisation de l'anglais comme “langue d'entreprise” est souvent encouragée, voire imposée.

On ne peut toutefois pas dire avec précision dans quelle mesure le régime linguistique réel des entreprises concernées se conforme à ces politiques.

Nous avons constaté des différences nettes entre l'emploi des langues au niveau des relations entre la direction et l'encadrement, d'une part, et la communication transversale et informelle, d'autre part. Il est rare que la situation soit similaire au niveau de la communication externe et de la communication direction – encadrement. Pour celle-ci, le roumain est plus employé dans la communication orale, alors que l'anglais s'impose à l'écrit.

Dans beaucoup d'entreprises, les communications informelles favorisent un environnement multilingue.

Il nous reste à continuer le traitement des données de notre enquête auprès des sociétés nationales et locales sur les différents types de communication interne tout comme sur la politique de ces sociétés.

Tous les résultats de notre enquête relèvent de tendances qu'il faut relativiser par rapport:

- au degré de représentativité de notre échantillon national;
- au subjectivisme des personnes interviewées.

La réalité demande l'articulation des compétences en langues et des compétences professionnelles.

## 4.2 Perspectives

Les besoins en compétences linguistiques iront en augmentant et l'on prévoit une augmentation de la demande en compétences interculturelles. Ces prévisions

- impliquent la concertation et la responsabilité des facteurs de décision (Gouvernement, Parlement, Patronat) et du monde académique (Académie roumaine, universités, instituts de recherche, etc.) sur la qualité du roumain pour la circulation et l'utilisation de l'information spécialisée et sur l'enseignement/apprentissage des langues;
- répondent aux besoins accrus de la communication professionnelle unilingue ou multilingue pour la réussite de la collaboration internationale de la Roumanie;
- imposent le décloisonnement des barrières psychologiques et bureaucratiques entre les différents milieux concernés (entrepreneurial, administratif, académique);
- demandent une forte volonté de changement des mentalités et de stratégies d'enseignement/apprentissage des langues.

Les évolutions technologiques et la tertiarisation de l'activité de travail déterminent l'augmentation de la "part langagière du travail" de sorte que le "faire" revient de plus en plus à du "dire" (Mourlhon-Dallies 2007: 14).

Alors que la mondialisation touche tous les pays, les attitudes et les comportements ne sont pas les mêmes d'un pays à l'autre.

Une telle étude n'est importante que dans la mesure où elle ouvre de nouvelles perspectives d'***actions concertées*** en vue de ***l'amélioration des compétences langagières et interculturelles*** des salariés, qui ont un impact direct sur les performances économiques des entreprises. Pour cela, il faut savoir se servir des données empiriques de l'enquête sur le lieu même du travail pour établir des ***classes de besoins et de motivations*** qui se trouvent à la base ***des stratégies et des tactiques de l'enseignement/apprentissage des langues étrangères*** et, en général, de l'acquisition et de la maîtrise des compétences de communication professionnelle.

Cette analyse n'est que le début d'une recherche plus ample qui envisage, d'une part, une enquêtre plus approfondie des milieux professionnels concernés, d'autre part, le traitement plus nuancé des informations obtenues en vue des activités futures de formation du personnel des entreprises.

Les observations des situations et des conditions de travail à partir du ***caractère multicanal*** (voix, posture, enregistrements, lectue, rédaction, etc.) et ***multimodal*** (analyses audio-vidéo-linguistiques) définissent "la part langagière du travail" (Mourlhon-Dallies 2007: 14) et déterminent les contenus et les stratégies du processus de formation des cadres dans l'optique des "compétences d'interaction" (v. le CECRL).

Il est nécessaire aussi de prendre en compte les tendances révélées par l'enquête et ne pas se fier trop aux ***pourcentages relatifs*** de l'utilisation de telle ou telle langue ou à la politique de telle ou telle entreprise.

La complexité de cette problématique exige la mise en oeuvre de ***projets de recherche interdisciplinaires et transdisciplinaires***, les seuls capables de révéler l'enchevêtrement des interrelations.

Nous devons envisager les changements conceptuels des dernières années du côté du management transversal des compétences qui remplace la vision centrée sur l'individu, par la vision centrées sur les communautés collaboratives (v. Mourlhon-Dalies 2007: 24).

En dépit de tous les obstacles, les enjeux d'un tel défi nous obligent

- à persévérer dans notre détermination à contribuer, par la mise en oeuvre de ce type d'étude, à la réussite économique des entreprises de Roumanie;
- à trouver les moyens humains, financiers et technologiques par les partenariats multisectoriels (enseignement, administration, secteur privé des entreprises) et les partenariats multilingues.

La mise en commun des ressemblances et surtout des différences, des savoirs, des savoir-faire et des savoir-être n'est possible que par des ***échanges entre les différents***

***spécialistes*** d'un même pays ou de pays différents et par le ***réinvestissement de leurs expériences*** de recherche fondamentale et appliquée afin de diminuer les risques et d'accroître les opportunités. La réussite n'est possible que par l'ouverture d'esprit et par la collaboration des chercheurs et des professionnels des entreprises.

## 5. Bibliographie sélective

Cilianu-Lascu, C. (2004): *Communication d'entreprise: concepts, stratégies, techniques, pratiques*. Bucureşti: Editura InfoMega.

Boutet, J. (2002): La part langagière du travail. In: *Langage et Société* 98. Paris, pp. 17-42.

Bronckart, J.-P./Fillietaz, L. (2005): *L'analyse des actions et des discours en situation de travail. Concepts, méthodes et application*. Louvain-la-Neuve: Peeters.

CECRL = Cadre Européen Commun de Référence pour les Langues – Prendre, Enseigner, Évaluer (1998, 2001). Strasbourg: Conseil de l'Europe.

Décaudin, J.M. (1995): *La communication marketing. Concepts, techniques, stratégies*. Paris: Editions Economica, pp. 15-39.

Demont, L. et al. (2001): *Communication des entreprises: Stratégies et pratiques*. Paris: Nathan.

ELAN = *Incidences du manque de compétences linguistiques des entreprises sur l'économie européenne* (2005). Direction générale de l'Éducation et Culture de la Commission européenne.

Ferrari, M. de (2007): Langue et situations de travail: décloisonner pour mieux articuler. In: *Le français dans le monde*, juillet, pp. 46-57.

Gicquel, Y. (2008): *Communication des entreprises*. 3ème édition. Chambéry: Génie des Glaciers.

Mourlhon-Dallies, F. (2007): Quand faire, c'est dire: évolutions du travail, révolutions didactiques? In: *Le français dans le monde*, juillet, pp. 12-32.

Neuner, G. (1998): Le rôle de la compétence socioculturelle dans l'apprentissage et l'enseignement des langues. In: *Le Français dans le monde*, juin, pp. 97-156.

František Čermák

# Leading questions and answers on the situation in individual countries: Situation in Czechia

## Shrnutí v češtině

Neoficiální jazyky v České republice (ČR) užívají zvláště mezinárodní společnosti a vrcholní manažeři. Zaměstnanci cítící v případě němčiny někdy mocenské pozadí preferují angličtinu. Český trh bývá zpravidla osloven v češtině. Informace o vnímání cizího jazyka v reklamě apod. nejsou, takové reklamy ale jsou řídké, i když si zvláště mladí lidé uvědomují důležitost znalosti cizích jazyků. V mezinárodním obchodu se zásadně užívá angličtina, okrajově i němčina a angličtina. Volba jazyka se považuje za důležitou (viz data ELAN). V ČR nejsou zvláštní zákony či nařízení regulující užívání jazyka v obchodní oblasti.

1) *Are there companies in your country which use a language other than the official national language(s) for internal communication? Please explain with regard to features such as:*
   - *type of company (production industry, trade, service, banking, etc.)*
   - *large companies as opposed to small*
   - *international companies as opposed to national or local ones*
   - *whether another language is used alongside or instead of the national language(s)*
   - *whether another language is used within the whole company or only in special sectors.*

Yes, this occurs in all types of companies which are branches or subsidiaries of companies abroad (e.g. all banks are foreign now), joint ventures or companies with other forms of integration of foreign capital. It occurs most often in situations where foreign delegates or "expatriates" are actually working on the premises of the companies, as it is not typical for the majority of foreign employees to learn Czech beyond a symbolic, polite level. It also occurs when the companies do not have foreign delegates physically present, but are often visited by them and/or are in regular telephone and e-mail contact with them.

This occurs in companies of all sizes, but presents a greater problem in smaller companies with more limited financial resources to invest in foreign and/or Czech language training.

In cases of large companies, in particular the production industry, it is often the case that the foreign languages are used at the top- and middle management levels, and Czech is used at the level of production. At the higher management levels, if a foreign employee is present, a foreign language (often English or German) is used or interpreters are hired. Written correspondence which is intended for all top managers or which will eventually travel to the parent company tends to be written in a foreign language.

As concerns production, language problems loom on the horizon, because unemployment in the Czech Republic is becoming gradually lower and there is a shortage of skilled production workers. This means that it is necessary for the companies to import production workers from elsewhere (Poland, Vietnam, and other countries), and somehow provide for the communication needs of these new groups of workers.

2) *What is known about the perceptions and attitudes of the employees and of interlocutors such as trade unions etc. regarding the issue of language use within companies?*

A university research has shown that it depends very much on the communication dynamics of a given situation or company. And in the Czech Republic, this is related to the historical situation and can be interpreted as a problematic power issue which Czech employees may evaluate negatively. In German-owned companies, Czechs are at a disadvantage when speaking German. One solution to this has been to implement English as the official corporate language. However, Czechs, particularly older Czechs (over 40), are still at a disadvantage when speaking English to Germans or Austrians. These dynamics change, for example, in Japanese or Korean companies, where the foreign employees' level of English is much lower than that of German employees and the interaction with Czechs may thus be more even.

One is not aware of any current trade union activity regarding this issue.

3) *Are there companies that use languages other than the national language in contacts with (potential) customers, in marketing, and in advertising within the country (for the national rather than the international market)?*

The national market is primarily addressed in Czech. There are a few exceptions to this. For example, banks such as *Česká spořitelna* and *Komerční banka* have an "expat center" which is oriented toward people who live in the Czech Republic but do not speak Czech. Also, there are smaller companies in the service industry which cater to non-Czech speaking recent immigrants, particularly speakers of Russian, Ukrainian, Vietnamese and English. In this case, however, the company owners are also native speakers of those languages (and not of Czech).

There are also many advertisements which use (at least in part) languages other than Czech for stylistic or "artistic" reasons rather than for practical ones. There are several articles on this topic.

4) *What is known about the perceptions and attitudes of customers and the general public on the use of languages other than the official language of the country in advertising, commercials, job opportunities, or the like?*

No knowledge is available of specific research which has addressed these perceptions and attitudes, but the following observations have been made:

Customers – In the business world, there is an established understanding that the client can choose the language of the transaction, even if this means hiring interpreters. This appears to be accepted in the Czech context.

General Public – Other languages (mostly English and German) appear in advertising. It is common to see job advertisements (particularly for jobs in the companies described above) in other languages in daily newspapers such as Mladá Fronta Dnes or Lidové Noviny. It is especially teenagers as a target group on advertising that takes English here in friendly manner.

In terms of job opportunities, this is a highly generational issue. Among the younger generation, it appears to be generally accepted that foreign language knowledge increases one's employability.

5) *Which language or languages are typically used by companies in your country in international business and commerce? Are any differences based on the sorts of products or services provided or the target countries or regions?*

English (dominating), marginally also German, Russian. The similarity of West Slavic languages is often also utilized in contacts with Poland and Slovakia.

6) *Contributing to the success or failure of business and commerce in your country?*

Yes, see also ELAN report which is available.

7) *Are there specific laws or other official regulations drawn up by your government or other political institutions for the use of languages by and within companies in your country, concerning either the home market or the export markets or both?*

Basically no. The only one one is aware of concerns the fact that products sold in the home market must be labelled in Czech or in an "easily understandable language", as per EC regulation 112/79. An observation in the companies studied says that texts such as fire or health regulations posted in the companies are in Czech because this is required by law, but this law has not been examined in detail yet. One is also told in some companies that if native speakers of other languages (such as Vietnamese) are hired to work in production, manuals and other technical materials must be produced in those speakers' languages as well.

8) *What is known about the effect of such measures as those mentioned in Point 7 above?*

See above. This is a component of a research project which is only just beginning.

Janez Dular

# Gebrauch der Sprachen im europaweiten Geschäfts- und Handelsverkehr – Slowenien

**Raba jezikov v poslovanju in trgovanju po Evropi (Slovenija)**

Slovenska javnost je zaradi zgodovinskih izkušenj občutljiva na poskuse grobega vsiljevanja tujega jezika, posebno njena politično-gospodarska elita pa ima manj zadržkov glede vrivanja rabe tujih jezikov z »mehkimi« metodami, npr. z uveljavljanjem načela prostega pretoka oseb, blaga, kapitala in informacij v okviru Evropske zveze. To vrivanje se obravnava kot neizogibna »kolateralna škoda« v prizadevanju za družbeno in gospodarsko blaginjo. Taka usmeritev se že na široko uveljavlja v znanosti in visokem šolstvu, v tem referatu pa so predstavljena njena znamenja na treh področjih gospodarskega poslovanja in trgovanja: v notranjem sporazumevanju podjetij v tuji lasti, v sporazumevanje s potrošniki (strežba, označevanje izdelkov, navodila, reklame) ter v imenih firm in lokalov.

Die slowenische Öffentlichkeit reagierte in der Vergangenheit empfindlich auf Versuche eines groben politischen oder sogar militärischen Aufdrängens einer Fremdsprache auf das slowenischen Umfeld, achtet jedoch weniger auf heutige Fälle, bei denen der Gebrauch einer Fremdsprache durch "weiche" Methoden durchgesetzt wird, z.B. durch die Funktionsweise des offenen Arbeitsmarktes oder durch den Grundsatz der Freizügigkeit des Waren- und Informationsverkehrs. Die Politik begrüßt eine solche Liberalisierung und unterstützt sie als starke Anregung für die wirtschaftliche und gesellschaftliche Entwicklung, übersieht dabei aber absichtlich oder unabsichtlich oft das umstrittene Eindringen von Fremdsprachen als "Kollateralschaden". Sie wünscht keine Warnungen zu hören, auch nicht aus soziolinguistischen Kreisen: Dass nämlich die strittigen Phänomene eine Störung der gesellschaftlichen Verständigung darstellten, deren Fortführung oder gar Intensivierung zum fortschreitenden Hinausdrängen der Nationalsprache führen könnte. Derartige Phänomene sind heute auf drei Gebieten des Geschäfts- und Handelsverkehrs zu beobachten.

## 1. Gebiet

Gleich nach Sloweniens Unabhängigkeit und dem Wechsel der politischen Ordnung kamen viele ausländische Firmen auf den slowenischen Markt, wobei **Ausländer oft auch die Mehrheitseigentümer** slowenischer Unternehmen wurden. Dadurch wurde die Frage nach der **innerbetrieblichen Verständigung** aufgeworfen, da die neuen Geschäftsführer sowie andere Führungskräfte meistens nicht der slowenischen Sprache mächtig waren und in einigen Fällen auch nicht bereit waren, diese zu erlernen.

Laut dem "Gesetz über Wirtschaftsgesellschaften" hat eine Geschäftsführung sicherzustellen, dass die Verständigung mit den Mitarbeitern im Unternehmen in wichtigen Situationen in slowenischer Sprache erfolgt (bzw. in Gebieten mit italienischen und ungarischen Minderheiten auch in der italienischen oder ungarischen Sprache). Laut Gewerkschaften kommt es bei der Verständigung ausländischer Arbeitgeber mit den Arbeitnehmern gelegentlich zu Problemen, die bisher auf unterschiedlichste Weise gelöst wurden. So kam es schon vor sieben Jahren in Maribor zu einem heftigen Streit zwischen der Betriebsführung eines in fremdem Eigentum stehenden Unternehmens und der Gewerkschaft, weil die Betriebsleitung fremdsprachige Aufschriften an den Bürotüren anbringen ließ ("Rechnungsführung", "Vorstandsvorsitzender" u.Ä.). In einer anderen Fabrik mit einem österreichischen Geschäftsführer wurden einige Abteilungsleiter und Werkmeister in einen Deutschkurs geschickt und der Geschäftsführer verständigt sich nun mit ihnen auf Deutsch, wobei sie wiederum mit den Mitarbeitern auf Slowenisch kommunizieren. Zugleich hat jedoch auch der Geschäftsführer das Erlernen der slowenischen Sprache in Angriff genommen. In einer Fabrik mit einem französischen Vorstandsvorsitzenden erfolgt die Verständigung unter Zuhilfenahme eines Dolmetschers. Meistens fungieren die Sekretärinnen als Übersetzerinnen, sodass es aufgrund ihrer schlechten Übersetzungen gelegentlich zu Missverständnissen mit den Arbeitern kommt. Zudem berichten die Gewerkschaften aus einigen Unternehmen, dass die Arbeiter dort oft in Sitzungen einwilligen, die in der der Betriebsleitung entsprechenden Fremdsprache stattfinden, sofern sie diese Fremdsprache einigermaßen verstehen. Dies geschieht, da die Übersetzung aufgrund von Ungenauigkeiten und Verwirrungen oft die Inhalte vernebelt und darüber hinaus viel Zeit in Anspruch nimmt, die den Arbeitern dann bei der Verrichtung der dringenden alltäglichen Arbeit fehlt.

Laut Angaben der staatlichen Aufsichtsbehörden für diesen Bereich gibt es nur wenige Verletzungen von Gesetzesvorschriften, einige wurden jedoch von den Arbeitsinspektoren festgestellt. Im Jahr 2007 wurden nur zwei Verstöße gegen das "Gesetz über den öffentlichen Gebrauch der slowenischen Sprache" aufgedeckt, die sich auf Akten oder die interne Geschäftsführung in slowenischer Sprache bezogen. Im Jahr 2008 notierte die Aufsichtsbehörde vier derartige Verstöße (nur bis Ende Juli). In zwei Fällen wurde festgestellt, dass der Geschäftsführer seine E-Mail-Mitteilungen an die Angestellten hinsichtlich sich aus dem Arbeitsverhältnis ergebender Rechte und Pflichten nur in der Fremdsprache verfasste. Im dritten Fall stellte der Inspektor fest, dass in der slowenischen Niederlassung eines ausländischen Unternehmens die Fremdsprache als allgemeine Verständigungssprache gebraucht wurde, im vierten Fall schloss der Arbeitgeber die Urheberverträge mit einer Opernsängerin nur in der Fremdsprache ab.

## 2. Gebiet

**A)** Slowenien wurde verpflichtet, die Bestimmungen des Verbraucherschutzgesetzes und andere Vorschriften an die Anforderungen der Europäischen Union anzupassen. Diese sehen vor, dass die Verständigung des Unternehmens **mit den Verbrauchern, Werbemitteilungen und gesetzlich vorgeschriebene Informationen bei der Kennzeichnung von Leistungen oder Produkten** (z.B. auf der Verpackung) "in der slowenischen Sprache zu erfolgen hat, bzw. in der Sprache, die für die Konsumenten auf dem Gebiet der Republik Slowenien leicht verständlich ist". Davon habe ich schon im Rahmen der EFNIL-Konferenz in Riga (2007) referiert. In der Praxis konnte man vor kurzem eine entsprechende Auslegung antreffen, als in Portoroz das Luxushotel Kempinski eröffnet wurde, in dem viele Leute ohne Slowenischkenntnisse angestellt wurden. Da Portoroz in dem Gebiet Sloweniens liegt, in dem die italienische Minderheit lebt, gilt dort neben Slowenisch auch Italienisch als Amtssprache. An der Rezeption des Hotels Kempinski wird der ankommende Gast oftmal jedoch weder auf Slowenisch noch auf Italienisch angesprochen, sondern wie selbstverständlich auf Englisch.

Es gibt zahlreiche Fälle, in denen die Käufer Sprachfehler in den übersetzen Anweisungen importierter Produkte bemängeln oder sogar beteuern, dass **die Gebrauchsanweisungen** unverständlich seien. Oft fertigen die Importeure die "Übersetzungen" selbst "stümperhaft" an und rechtfertigen dies mit der Begründung, dass sich das Einschalten eines fachkundigen Übersetzers angesichts des kleinen Marktes nicht lohne. Angaben über die von den Aufsichtsbehörden getroffenen Maßnahmen liegen in solchen Fällen nicht vor, obwohl das Gesetz über den öffentlichen Gebrauch der slowenischen Sprache (§§ 31 und 32) hier eindeutig ist: Stellt die zuständige Aufsichtsbehörde fest, dass die Produkte keine entsprechende Kennzeichnung aufweisen, "kann durch Verordnung deren Vertrieb und Verkauf solange ausgesetzt werden, bis sie vom Hersteller oder Distributeur bzw. Verkäufer mit der entsprechenden Textbeschriftung versehen werden". Besonders häufig gibt es Gebrauchsanweisungen für **elektronische Geräte**, die in schlechtem Slowenisch abgefasst sind. Ähnlich verhält es sich mit der in Fernsehgeräten, Autoradios, Playern, Haushaltsgeräten und anderen Anlagen eingebauten Software, die nur selten mit **slowenischen Menüs** ausgestattet ist. (Da die slowenische Sprache problemlos auf den Bildschirmen von Mobiltelefonen eingesetzt wird, bedeutet dies, dass sie mit ein wenig mehr Sprachbewusstsein und Willen auch in den angeführten Fällen benutzt werden könnte.) Viele Händler gehen jedoch lieber das Risiko ein, gegen die Vorschriften zu verstoßen, zumal sie fast keinen Druck seitens der slowenischen Käufer verspüren – kaum einer beschwert sich darüber. Aus diesem Grund kofinanziert das Kulturministerium in diesem Jahr die Erstellung und Schaltung eines Fernsehspots zur Popularisierung der slowenischen Sprache **auf den Bildschirmen elektronischer Anlagen**, in dem der strittige Standpunkt problematisiert werden soll, dass der Gebrauch der slowenischen Sprache in der Elektronik nicht nötig sei, "da ja wir alle Englisch verstehen, nicht wahr?". Das Kulturministerium möchte damit die Hersteller und Importeure elektronischer Anlagen dazu anhalten, die eingebaute Software weiter zu entwickeln bzw. sie mit Slowenisch zu ergänzen, und die Käufer wiederum dazu anregen, von den Händlern ausdrücklich eine benutzerfreundliche Software mit Menüs auf Slowenisch zu verlangen.

**B)** Es ist schwer zu erklären, warum manche Slowenen selbst – Einzelpersonen und sogar einige Staatsbehörden – geben der Fremdsprache Vorrang vor dem Slowenischen. Sogar das "Amt für Kommunikation der Regierung der Republik Slowenien" führte slowenienweit eine breit angelegte **Werbeaktion** zur besseren Erkennbarkeit Sloweniens durch Versendung des Werbematerials mit einer englischen Variante des Logotyps (Schutzmarke) "I FEEL S***LOVE***NIA" an alle Staatsbehörden, öffentliche Einrichtungen und Familien durch, wobei eine slowenische Variante des Logotyps gar nicht erst angefertigt wurde. Ähnlich war der Fall bei der Einführung des Schengen-Regimes an den internationalen Flughäfen in Slowenien: bei den Aufschriften an der Grenzkontrolle findet man nur in Slowenien an der ersten Stelle Englisch und erst darunter heimische Sprache.

**Werbeplakate** für öffentliche Veranstaltungen oder neue **Gewerbemarken**, **Modelle** u.Ä. sind oft in englischer Sprache verfasst – auch wenn es sich um slowenische Veranstalter oder Eigentümer der Marken, Modelle etc. handelt. Als die Handelskammer Sloweniens in diesem Jahr eine Werbekampagne unter dem Titel KUPUJEM

SLOVENSKO ("ICH KAUFE SLOWENISCH") in Gang brachte und damit slowenische Konsumenten zum Kauf slowenischer Lebensmittel anregen wollte, hielten wir es im slowenischen Kulturministerium für notwendig, darauf aufmerksam zu machen, dass diese Kampagne bei der Benennung ihrer Gründe einseitig sei, da sie nur an den slowenischen Verbraucher gerichtet war, der durch den Kauf slowenischer Produkte zur Erhaltung der Arbeitsplätze in der heimischen Lebensmittelindustrie beitragen sollte. Die Aktion hat jedoch nicht die Hersteller selbst zu größerem Entgegenkommen gegenüber den slowenischen Käufern aufgerufen, z.B. beim Gebrauch der slowenischen Sprache in den Namen der Modelle, Marken, Unternehmen oder Ähnlichem. Nach Meinung slowenischer Unternehmen werden Erkennbarkeit und Attraktivität von Produktnamen besonders durch den Gebrauch fremder, in der slowenischen Schriftnorm nicht bestehender Buchstaben wie x, y, q und w erzielt oder durch fremdsprachige Buchstabenverknüpfungen, insbesondere im Englischen.

## 3. Gebiet

Das "Gesetz über Wirtschaftsgesellschaften" legt in § 20 fest, dass **der Firmenname** slowenisch sein muss, dem eine Übersetzung in die Fremdsprache beigefügt werden kann. Jedoch ist in demselben Paragraphen eine Bestimmung enthalten, die so viele Arten zulässiger fremdsprachiger Ausnahmen aufführt, dass unter ihnen fast jeder Antragsteller die Rechtsgrundlage für die Geltendmachung eines fremdsprachigen Namens findet (z.B. Ekopool, Job Smile, Proadventure, Dentallab, Dentex, Kotosafe, Sport Cars, Club of Wellness). Die Antragsteller behaupten dabei, dass der Gebrauch der slowenischen Sprache im Namen neuer Unternehmen die Erkennbarkeit und die Wettbewerbsfähigkeit des slowenischen Unternehmertums auf dem internationalen Markt beeinträchtige, obwohl wir wissen, dass eine ganze Reihe der größten und lebensfähigsten slowenischen Exportunternehmen slowenische Namen trägt (z.B. Iskra, Belinka, Krka, Gorenje, Lek, Lesnina usw.).

Das Gesetz über den Gebrauch der slowenischen Sprache (§ 18) schreibt den Gebrauch des Slowenischen auch bei **Namen von Gastgewerbelokalen, Geschäftslokalen und Gewerbelokalen** vor, jedoch wiederum mit zahlreichen Ausnahmen für einen zulässigen Gebrauch von Fremdwörtern. Diese Bestimmung wird in der Praxis zuhauf verletzt, jedoch reagieren die Aufsichtsbehörden überhaupt nicht darauf.

Unsere im Jahr 2007 angenommene Resolution über das nationale Programm für Sprachpolitik spricht bei einer der geplanten Maßnahmen genau über "die Geltendmachung der Sprachkultur als wichtigem Faktor der geschäftlichen Vorzüglichkeit". Um dieses Ziel zu erreichen wird es erforderlich sein, das Bewusstsein der Geschäftsleute zu steigern und sie entsprechend auszubilden; als Motivation wird die Berücksichtigung der Sprachkultur bei der Verleihung von Auszeichnungen und Preisen in der Wirtschaft geplant.

# THE LISBON RESOLUTION OF EFNIL ON LANGUAGE USE IN BUSINESS AND COMMERCE IN EUROPE

**approved by the EFNIL General Assembly of 14 November 2008**

**in 26 languages including the 23 official languages of the states of the European Union**

| | | | | | |
|---|---|---|---|---|---|
| bg | български | fr | français | nl | Nederlands |
| cs | čeština | ga | Gaeilge | no | norsk |
| da | dansk | is | íslensk | pl | polski |
| de | Deutsch | it | italiano | pt | português |
| el | ελληνικά | lv | latviešu valoda | ro | română |
| et | eesti keel | le | Lëtzebuergesch | sk | slovenčina |
| en | English | lt | lietuvių kalba | sl | slovenščina |
| es | español | hu | magyar | sv | svenska |
| fi | suomi | mt | Malti | | |

**bg**

# Лисабонска резолюция за използването на езика в бизнеса и търговията в Европа

*Одобрена от Общото събрание на ЕФНЕИ на 14 ноември*

1. Европейска федерация на националните езикови институции (ЕФНЕИ) признава, че езиковата компетентост и комуникативните умения все повече се превръщат в ключови фактори за бизнеса и търговията в Европа и света.

2. ЕФНЕИ насърчава по-голямото сътрудничество между Европейския съюз и страните-членки за развитието на политиките, които отговарят на това предизвикателство. Те би трябвало да включват като отправни точки:

   - да повиши разбирането за значението на езиците и езиковите умения като фактори за успех или провал в рамките на бизнес средата;
   - да поощри и финансира разработването на инструменти за езикова обработка и езиково обучение в бизнес средата;
   - да поощри и финансира разработването на специфични обучителни програми за ефективното използване на езиците в бизнеса, като особено благоприятства по-малко използваните езици.
   - да подпомогне научните изследвания, особено на факторите, които определят как езиците и езиковите умения съдействат на процеса за създаване на ценности.

3. Стъпките за реализирането на политиката и мерките би трябвало да отчетат значението на:

   - *националните езикови* умения като ключов фактор в бизнес комуникацията (а не само чуждоезиковите умения);
   - всички европейски езици като инструменти за локализация (а не само по-големите);
   - езиковата компетентост на мигриращите работници;
   - (чуждо)езиковата компетентост в съответната област, както и за практическото решаване на специфични задачи като съставни части на професионалното обучение и образование;
   - преводът (човешки и автоматичен) и терминологичната работа като необходимо помощно средство за предаване на местния колорит и приспособяването към чуждите пазари и техните клиенти.

4. ЕФНЕИ призовава Европейската комисия да създаде общоевропейска служба за информация и документация за компаниите и служителите на държавната администрация и да популяризира най-добрия опит.

5. Становището на ЕФНЕИ е, че въпросът за използването на езика в бизнеса не би трябвало да се гледа изключително от гледната точка на свободната търговия, а също и от перспективата на правата на клиентите и работниците, като по този начин вземе под внимание съображенията от социален характер като осигуряване на равни възможности за всички, опасността от социална дискриминация на по-малко образованите граждани и ефикасното разпространение на информацията. Следователно ЕНФЕИ призовава Европейския съюз да предложи повече възможности за регулация от страна на страните-членки в полза на техния език (езици), за да гарантира достатъчно социално равноправие.
6. ЕНФЕИ предлага своята експертна компетентост, за да подпомогне вземащите решения лица в развитието и мониторинга на политиките в тази област и да обезпечи съответното зачитанс на националните и регионалните условия и специфики.

**cs**

# Lisabonská rezoluce o užívání jazyka v podnicích a obchodu v Evropě

*Schválená Valným shromážděním EFNIL 14. listopadu 2008*

1. *Evropská federace národních institucí pro jazyk* (EFNIL) uznává, že jazyková kompetence a komunikační dovednosti jsou pro podniky a obchod v Evropě ve stále rostoucí míře klíčovými faktory.

2. EFNIL vyzývá k větší spolupráci mezi Evropskou unií a členskými státy při rozvíjení politiky, která je odpovědí na tuto výzvu. Ta by měla zahrnovat následující body:
   - zvyšovat uvědomování si důležitosti jazyků a jazykových dovedností jakožto faktorů vedoucích v podnikovém prostředí k úspěchu či selhání;
   - povzbuzovat a financovat rozvoj nástrojů pro zpracování jazyka a jazykové výuky v podnikovém prostředí;
   - povzbuzovat a financovat rozvoj specifických učebních programů pro efektivní užívání jazyka v obchodu a zvlášť přitom upřednostňovat méně užívané jazyky;
   - podporovat vědecký výzkum, zvláště těch faktorů, které rozhodují o tom, jak jazyky a jazykové dovednosti přispívají k procesu tvorby hodnot.

3. Kroky a opatření této politiky by měly věnovat náležitou pozornost významu toho, že:
   - dovedností v národních jazycích jsou klíčovými faktory v obchodní komunikaci (ale nejen dovednosti v cizích jazycích);
   - všechny evropské jazyky jsou nástroji lokalizace (a nejen ty větší);
   - jsou i jazyky cizích trhů vně Evropy a ty je důležité stimulovat a tak i vzájemnost, tj. to, že neevropský obchod by měl věnovat srovnatelnou pozornost i evropským jazykům;
   - je i jazyková kompetence migrujících pracovníků;
   - jazykové kompetence je i v oborových a pro daný účel specifických (cizích) jazycích jakožto nedílných součástech profesního výcviku a vzdělávání;
   - překlad (lidmi či stroji) a činnosti v terminologii jsou nepostradatelné pomůcky pro lokalizaci a přizpůsobování se cizím trhům a jejich zákazníkům.

4. EFNIL vyzývá Evropskou komisi k tomu, aby vybudovala celoevropský informační a dokumentační servis pro podniky i veřejnou administrativu a aby zde podporovala tu nejlepší praxi.

5. EFNIL je toho názoru, že otázka užívání jazyka v obchodu by se neměla posuzovat výlučně z hlediska volného obchodu, ale i perspektivy práv uživatelů a pracovníků, čímž by se poskytl prostor i sociálním ohledům jako jsou rovné příležitosti, nebezpečí sociální diskriminace vůči méně vzdělaným občanům a efektivnímu šíření informací. EFNIL proto vyzývá Evropskou unii, aby nabízela více příležitostí k regulování ze strany členských zemí ve prospěch svých vlastních jazyků, aby se tak zaručila dostatečná sociální rovnost.
6. EFNIL nabízí svou expertízu a pomoc tvůrcům politiky při rozvoji a monitorování politiky v této oblasti, aby se tak zajistilo, že národní a oblastní okolnosti a vnímavost se vezmou patřičným způsobem do úvahy.

**da**

# Lissabon-resolution om sprogbrugen i erhvervslivet i Europa

*Godkendt af EFNIL's Generalforsamling: 14. november 2008*

1. Den *europæiske sammenslutning af nationale sproginstitutioner* (EFNIL) konstaterer at sprogkundskaber og kommunikationsfærdigheder i stigende grad er vigtige faktorer for erhvervsliv og handel i Europa og resten af verden.

2. EFNIL opfordrer til større samarbejde mellem EU og medlemsstaterne om udviklingen af politikker der tager denne udfordring op. Disse bør omfatte følgende målsætninger:
   - at øge bevidstheden om betydningen af sprog og sproglige færdigheder som faktorer for succes eller fiasko i erhvervslivet;
   - at fremme og finansiere udviklingen af værktøjer til sprogbehandling og sprogindlæring i erhvervslivet;
   - at fremme og finansiere udviklingen af særlige uddannelsesprogrammer for effektiv anvendelse af sprog i erhvervslivet, og herved især at tilgodese mindre udbredte sprog;
   - at støtte videnskabelig forskning, specielt med henblik på de faktorer der bestemmer hvordan sprog og sprogfærdigheder bidrager til værdiskabelse.

3. Politiske tiltag og foranstaltninger bør tage behørigt hensyn til betydningen af:
   - *nationale sprogfærdigheder* som vigtige faktorer i virksomhedernes kommunikation (og ikke kun fremmedsprogsfærdigheder);
   - lokalisering af computerprogrammer, websider og andre produkter til alle europæiske sprog (og ikke kun til de store);
   - sprogene i udenlandske markeder uden for Europa, for at stimulere gensidighed således at ikke-europæiske virksomheder også bliver opmærksomme på europæiske sprog;
   - de sproglige kompetencer hos de indvandrere som arbejder i landet;
   - domæne- og opgavespecifikke (fremmed)sproglige kompetencer som integrerede dele af professionel undervisning og uddannelse;
   - oversættelse (både manuel og automatisk) og terminologiarbejde som en uundværlig støtte til lokalisering og tilpasning til de udenlandske markeder og deres kunder.

4. EFNIL opfordrer Kommissionen til at etablere en europæisk oplysnings- og dokumentationsservice for både virksomheder og den offentlige administration og til at fremme den bedste praksis.

5. Det er EFNIL's opfattelse at spørgsmålet om sproget i erhvervslivet ikke udelukkende bør betragtes ud fra et frihandelsperspektiv, men også bør ses i lyset af forbrugernes og arbejdstagernes rettigheder og således give mulighed for at inddrage sociale aspekter såsom lige muligheder for alle, faren for social diskriminering af borgere med begrænset uddannelse og effektiv spredning af information. Derfor opfordrer EFNIL EU til at give medlemsstaterne bedre muligheder for at vedtage reguleringer til fordel for deres eget (egne) sprog og derved sikre tilstrækkelig social lighed.
6. EFNIL tilbyder sin ekspertise til at bistå de politiske beslutningstagere ved udviklingen og overvågningen af politikker på dette område og til at sikre at der bliver taget behørigt hensyn til nationale og regionale sproglige forhold.

**de**

# Die Resolution von Lissabon zum Sprachgebrauch in der Wirtschaft in Europa

*Angenommen von der Generalversammlung von EFNIL am 14. November 2008*

1. Die *Europäische Föderation nationaler Sprachinstitutionen* (EFNIL) erkennt an, dass Sprachenkompetenz und kommunikative Fertigkeiten zunehmend Schlüsselfaktoren für Unternehmen und Handel in Europa und in der Welt werden.
2. EFNIL drängt auf engere Zusammenarbeit zwischen der Europäischen Union und ihren Mitgliedstaaten bei der Entwicklung von Vorgehensweisen, welche dieser Herausforderung begegnen. Hierzu sollten folgende Handlungsfelder gehören:
   - die Erkenntnis der Bedeutung von Sprachen und Sprachfertigkeiten als Faktoren für Erfolg und Misserfolg im beruflichen Umfeld zu verstärken;
   - die Entwicklung von Hilfsmitteln für Sprachverarbeitung und Sprachenlernen im Berufsleben anzuregen und zu finanzieren;
   - die Entwicklung von speziellen Lernprogrammen für die effektive Sprachverwendung im Beruf, speziell von weniger gebräuchlichen Sprachen, anzuregen und zu finanzieren;
   - die wissenschaftliche Erforschung besonders der Faktoren zu fördern, die den Beitrag von Sprachen und Sprachfertigkeiten zu Prozessen der Wertschöpfung bestimmen.
3. Sprachenpolitische Aktionen und Maßnahmen sollten besondere Aufmerksamkeit richten auf:
   - die Beherrschung der jeweiligen Nationalsprachen (und nicht nur von Fremdsprachen) als Schlüsselqualifikation für die berufliche Kommunikation;
   - alle europäischen Sprachen (nicht nur die größeren) als Mittel der Lokalisation (d.h. der geschäftlichen Ortsspezifik);
   - die Sprachen von außereuropäischen Märkten, verbunden mit der Anregung von Gegenseitigkeit, d.h. dass außereuropäische Geschäftspartner europäischen Sprachen eine entsprechende Aufmerksamkeit widmen;
   - die Sprachenkompetenz von Arbeitsmigranten;
   - die domänen- und aufgabenspezifischen (Fremd-)Sprachenkenntnisse als integrale Bestandteile beruflicher Aus- und Fortbildung;
   - Humanübersetzung, maschinelle Übersetzung und Terminologiearbeit als unabdingbare Hilfe zur Lokalisation und Anpassung an fremde Märkte und ihre Kunden.

4. EFNIL drängt die Europäische Kommission, einen europaweiten Informations- und Dokumentationsdienst einzurichten, der Firmen und der öffentlichen Verwaltung nützen wie auch der Förderung vorbildlicher Praxis dienen soll.
5. EFNIL ist der Auffassung, dass der Sprachgebrauch in der Wirtschaft nicht ausschließlich vom Gesichtspunkt des freien Handels, sondern auch unter der Perspektive von Verbraucherrecht und Arbeitnehmerrechten zu sehen ist und so soziale Aspekte wie Chancengleichheit, die Gefahr der Benachteiligung weniger gebildeter Bürger wie auch die effiziente Verbreitung von Informationen berücksichtigt. Daher appelliert EFNIL an die europäische Union, ihren Mitgliedsstaaten mehr Möglichkeiten zu entsprechenden Rege-lungen für ihre eigenen Sprachen zu bieten, um ausreichende soziale Gleichheit zu ermöglichen.
6. EFNIL bietet seine Expertise an, um politischen Entscheidungsträger bei der Entwicklung und Überprüfung von Maßnahmen auf diesem Gebiet zu unterstützen und darauf zu achten, dass nationale und regionale Sachlagen und Befindlichkeiten hinreichend berücksichtigt werden.

**el**

# ΔΙΑΚΥΡΗΞΗ ΤΗΣ ΛΙΣΣΑΒΟΝΑΣ ΓΙΑ ΤΗ ΧΡΗΣΗ ΤΗΣ ΓΛΩΣΣΑΣ ΣΤΙΣ ΕΠΙΧΕΙΡΗΣΕΙΣ ΚΑΙ ΤΟ ΕΜΠΟΡΙΟ ΣΤΗΝ ΕΥΡΩΠΗ

*Εγκρίθηκε από τη Γενική Συνέλευση της EFNIL στις 14/11/2008*

1. Η EFNIL αναγνωρίζει ότι η γλωσσική ικανότητα και οι επικοινωνιακές δεξιότητες καθίστανται ολοένα και περισσότερο κομβικοί παράγοντες για τις επιχειρήσεις και το εμπόριο στην Ευρώπη και γενικότερα σε όλο τον κόσμο.
2. Η EFNIL προτρέπει σε μεγαλύτερη συνεργασία ανάμεσα στην Ευρωπαϊκή Ένωση και τα κράτη-μέλη όσον αφορά την ανάπτυξη πολιτικών που απαντούν σε αυτή την πρόκληση. Οι πολιτικές θα πρέπει να κατευθύνουν τη δράση τους ως εξής:
   - να αναπτύξουν την επίγνωση ότι οι γλώσσες και οι γλωσσικές δεξιότητες είναι σημαντικοί παράγοντες για την επιτυχία ή την αποτυχία στο περιβάλλον των επιχειρήσεων;
   - να ενθαρρύνουν και να χρηματοδοτήσουν την παραγωγή εργαλείων για γλωσσική επεξεργασία και εκμάθηση γλωσσών στο πλαίσιο των επιχειρήσεων;
   - να ενθαρρύνουν και να χρηματοδοτήσουν την παραγωγή προγραμμάτων εξειδικευμένης μάθησης για την αποτελεσματική χρήση των γλωσσών στις επιχειρήσεις, ευνοώντας ιδιαίτερα τις λιγότερο χρησιμοποιούμενες γλώσσες ανά τον κόσμο;
   - να υποστηρίξουν την επιστημονική έρευνα, ειδικότερα των παραγόντων που καθορίζουν πώς οι γλώσσες και οι γλωσσικές δεξιότητες συμβάλλουν στη διαδικασία της δημιουργίας αξίας.
3. Οι πολιτικές δράσεις και τα αντίστοιχα μέτρα πρέπει να δώσουν τη δέουσα προσοχή στη σημασία:
   - των δεξιοτήτων στην *εθνική γλώσσα* (και όχι μόνο των δεξιοτήτων σε ξένες γλώσσες) ως κομβικών παραγόντων στο πλαίσιο της επικοινωνίας των επιχειρήσεων;
   - όλων των ευρωπαϊκών γλωσσών (και όχι μόνο των περισσότερο ομιλούμενων) ως εργαλείων για την ανάπτυξη των τοπικών αγορών;
   - των γλωσσών των ξένων αγορών εκτός Ευρώπης, με παράλληλη υποκίνηση της αμοιβαιότητας, με την έννοια ότι οι μη ευρωπαϊκές επιχειρήσεις θα πρέπει να δώσουν αντίστοιχη προσοχή στις ευρωπαϊκές γλώσσες;
   - της γλωσσικής ικανότητας των μεταναστών εργατών;
   - της ικανότητας χρήσης μιας ξένης γλώσσας σε εξειδικευμένα πεδία και στόχους ως αναπόσπαστα τμήματα της επαγγελματικής εκπαίδευσης και κατάρτισης
   - της μετάφρασης (αυτόματης και μη) και της ορολογίας ως απαραίτητης βοήθειας για την ανάπτυξη των τοπικών αγορών και την προσαρμογή τους στις ξένες αγορές και στους πελάτες τους.

4. Η EFNIL προτρέπει την Ευρωπαϊκή Επιτροπή να ιδρύσει μια υπηρεσία παροχής πληροφοριών και τεκμηρίωσης σε ευρωπαϊκό επίπεδο για τις εταιρίες και τους δημόσιους διαχειριστές και να προωθήσει τη βέλτιστη εφαρμογή της.
5. Η EFNIL θεωρεί ότι το ζήτημα της χρήσης της γλώσσας στις επιχειρήσεις δεν θα πρέπει να προσεγγίζεται αποκλειστικά από την οπτική του ελεύθερου εμπορίου αλλά και από την οπτική των δικαιωμάτων των καταναλωτών και των εργατών, αφήνοντας χώρο να τεθούν, παράλληλα, κοινωνικά ζητήματα όπως οι ίσες ευκαιρίες, ο κίνδυνος των κοινωνικών διακρίσεων απέναντι στους λιγότερο μορφωμένους πολίτες και η αποτελεσματική διάδοση της πληροφορίας. Γι' αυτό τον λόγο η EFNIL προτρέπει την Ευρωπαϊκή Ένωση να προσφέρει περισσότερες ευκαιρίες στα κράτη-μέλη ώστε αυτά να προβούν σε ρυθμίσεις προς όφελος της γλώσσας/των γλωσσών τους προκειμένου να δοθούν εγγυήσεις για κοινωνική ισότητα σε μια ικανοποιητική βάση.
6. Η EFNIL καταθέτει την εμπειρία της στην υπηρεσία όσων χαράσσουν γλωσσικές πολιτικές ανάπτυξης και παρακολούθησης προγραμμάτων σε αυτά τα πεδία προκειμένου να διασφαλίσει ότι λαμβάνονται υπόψη δεόντως οι εθνικές και τοπικές συνθήκες και ιδιαιτερότητες.

**et**

## Lissaboni Resolutsioon Keelekasutuse Kohta Äritegevuses Ja Kaubanduses Euroopas

*Vastu võetud EFNILi peaassambleel 14. novembril 2008*

1. *Euroopa Rahvuslike Keeleinstitutsioonide Föderatsioon* (EFNIL) mõistab, et keelte- ja suhtlusoskus on nii Euroopas kui kogu maailmas muutumas äris ja kaubanduses üha olulisemaks teguriks.
2. EFNIL soovitab suurendada koostööd Euroopa Liidu ja liikmesriikide vahel sellele vajadusele vastava poliitika väljatöötamisel. See peaks hõlmama järgmisi tegevuspunkte:
   - suurendada teadlikkust keelte ja keelteoskuse kui ärikeskkonnas edu saavutamist või läbikukkumist mõjutavate tegurite tähtsusest;
   - edendada ja rahastada äritegevuses kasutatavate keeletöötluse ja keeleõppe vahendite väljatöötamist;
   - edendada ja rahastada spetsiifiliste õppeprogrammide väljatöötamist eesmärgiga tagada äritegevuses keelte tõhus kasutamine, eelistades just vähem kasutatavaid keeli;
   - toetada teadusuuringuid, eriti nende tegurite uurimist, mis mõjutavad keelte ja keelteoskuse panust väärtuse loomise protsessi.
3. Poliitiliste meetmete võtmisel tuleks pöörata vajalikku tähelepanu järgmiste aspektide olulisusele:
   - riigikeele oskus (mis lisandub võõrkeelte oskusele) kui oluline tegur ärialases suhtlemises;
   - kõik Euroopa keeled (mitte ainult suuremad keeled) kui lokaliseerimise vahendid;
   - väljaspool Euroopat asuvatel turgudel kasutatavad keeled; vastastikkuse edendamine (s.t Euroopa-välised ettevõtted peaksid pöörama samaväärset tähtsust Euroopa keeltele);
   - võõrtööliste keeleoskus;
   - valdkonna- ja ülesandekeskne (võõr-)keelteoskus kui kutseõppe ja hariduse lahutamatu osa;
   - tõlkimine (tõlkijad ja automatiseeritud tõlkimine) ja terminoloogia kui vältimatud abivahendid lokaliseerimisel ning välisturgude ja sealsete klientidega kohandumisel.
4. EFNIL kutsub Euroopa Komisjoni üles looma üle-euroopalist teabe- ja dokumenditeenistust nii ettevõtete kui ka riigiasutuste tarbeks ning edendama häid tavasid.

5. EFNIL on seisukohal, et äritegevuses keelte kasutamise küsimust ei tohiks vaadelda ainult vabakaubanduse seisukohalt, vaid ka tarbijate ja töötajate õiguste seisukohalt, võttes seega arvesse sotsiaalseid kaalutlusi, nagu võrdsed võimalused, vähem haritud inimeste sotsiaalse diskrimineerimise oht ja teabe tõhus levitamine. Seetõttu kutsub EFNIL Euroopa Liitu üles pakkuma liikmesriikidele rohkem võimalusi piisava sotsiaalse võrdsuse tagamiseks oma riigikeelt (riigikeeli) soosivate õigusaktide kehtestamiseks.
6. EFNIL pakub oma teadmisi poliitikakujundajate abistamiseks kõnealuse valdkonna poliitika väljatöötamisel ja selle rakendamise jälgimisel ning asjaomase riigi ja piirkonna olukorra ja tundlike aspektide arvessevõtmise tagamisel.

**en**

# Lisbon Resolution on Language Use in Business and Commerce in Europe

*Approved by the EFNIL General Assembly: 14 November 2008*

1. The *European Federation of National Institutions for Language* (EFNIL) acknowledges that language competence and communication skills are increasingly key factors for business and commerce in Europe and the world.

2. EFNIL urges greater collaboration between the European Union and the Member States in the development of policies that address this challenge. These should include as action points:
   - to raise awareness of the importance of languages and language skills as factors for success or failure within the business environment;
   - to encourage and finance the development of tools for language processing and language learning within the business environment;
   - to encourage and finance the development of specific learning programmes for the effective use of languages in business, especially favouring less widely used languages;
   - to support scientific research, especially into the factors which determine how languages and language skills contribute to the process of value creation.

3. Policy actions and measures should pay due attention to the importance of:
   - *national language* skills as key factors in business communication (and not only foreign language skills);
   - all European languages as instruments for localisation (and not only the larger ones);
   - the languages of foreign markets outside Europe, stimulating also reciprocity, i.e. that non-European business should pay comparable attention to European languages;
   - the language competence of migrant workers;
   - domain- and task-specific (foreign) language competence as integral parts of professional training and education;
   - translation (both human and automated) and terminology work as an indispensable aid to localisation and adaptation to foreign markets and their customers.

4. EFNIL urges the European Commission to establish a Europe-wide information and documentation service for both companies and public administrators and to promote best practice.

5. It is EFNIL's view that the issue of language use in business should not be considered exclusively from the point of view of free trade but also from the perspective of consumers' and workers' rights, thus allowing for social considerations such as equal opportunities, the danger of social discrimination against less highly educated citizens and the efficient dissemination of information. Therefore EFNIL urges the European Union to offer more opportunities for regulation by Member States in favour of their own language(s) in order to guarantee sufficient social equality.
6. EFNIL offers its expertise to assist policy makers in the development and monitoring of policies in this field and to ensure that national and regional circumstances and sensibilities are duly taken into account.

**es**

# Resolución de Lisboa sobre el Uso de las Lenguas en Europa para los Negocios y el Comercio

*Aprobada por la EFNIL en su Asamblea General de 14 de noviembre de 2008*

1. La *Federación Europea de Instituciones Nacionales de la Lengua* (EFNIL) reconoce que la competencia lingüística y las destrezas comunicativas son factores cada vez más determinantes para los negocios y el comercio en Europa y en el mundo.
2. EFNIL pone en evidencia la necesidad de una colaboración mayor entre la Unión Europea y los Estados miembros en el desarrollo de políticas que den respuesta a semejante compromiso. Ello debería incluir como acciones puntuales las siguientes:
   - acrecentar el reconocimiento de la importancia de la lengua y las destrezas lingüísticas como factores de éxito o de fracaso en el ámbito de los negocios.
   - alentar y financiar el desarrollo de herramientas para el intercambio lingüístico y el aprendizaje de lenguas en el ámbito de los negocios.
   - alentar y financiar el desarrollo de programas de aprendizaje específicos para el uso eficaz de las lenguas en los negocios, favoreciendo en especial a los idiomas con menor uso generalizado.
   - apoyar la investigación científica, especialmente sobre los factores que determinan en qué medida las lenguas y las destrezas lingüísticas contribuyen a los procesos de creación de valor.
3. Las acciones políticas y sus medios consiguientes deberían prestar atención a la importancia de:
   - las destrezas específicas en los idiomas nacionales como factores clave en la comunicación relacionada con los negocios (y no solamente el manejo competente de las lenguas extranjeras);
   - todos los idiomas europeos como instrumentos para la localización (y no solamente los más grandes);
   - las lenguas de los mercados extranjeros fuera de Europa, con el propósito de estimular también la reciprocidad; es decir, la medida en que los ámbitos no europeos de negocios prestan la misma atención a las lenguas europeas.
   - la competencia lingüística de los trabajadores inmigrantes.
   - la competencia lingüística (en la lengua extranjera) específicamente relacionada con el sector y la tarea del trabajador como parte integrante de su entrenamiento y formación profesional.
   - el trabajo en los campos de la traducción (tanto humana como automatizada) y la terminología como un apoyo indispensable para el arraigo y adaptación a los mercados extranjeros y a sus clientes.

4. EFNIL insta a la Comisión Europea para que establezca un servicio de información y documentación de ámbito europeo para asesorar a las compañías y a los administradores públicos, y para promocionar las mejores prácticas por parte de unas y otros.

5. Es criterio de EFNIL que la cuestión del uso de las lenguas en el ámbito de los negocios no debería ser considerada exclusivamente desde el punto de vista del libre mercado, sino también desde la perspectiva de los derechos de los consumidores y los trabajadores, para favorecer así consideraciones sociales como la igualdad de oportunidades, el peligro de discriminación social contra ciudadanos con menos educación superior y la circulación eficiente de la información. Por lo tanto, EFNIL urge que la Unión Europea ofrezca más oportunidades, por parte de los Estados Miembros, para una regulación favorecedora de que los idiomas propios de cada uno de ellos garanticen una igualdad social suficiente.

6 EFNIL ofrece su experiencia para ayudar a los políticos en el desarrollo y seguimiento de las decisiones de gobierno tomadas en este oredn, y para asegurar que las circunstancias y sensibilidades nacionales y regionales se tomen en cuenta adecuadamente.

fi

## Lissabonin Julkilausuma Yritysten Ja Kaupan Kielenkäytöstä Euroopassa

*Hyväksytty EFNILin yleiskokouksessa 14. marraskuuta 2008*

1. *Euroopan kansallisten kielentutkimuslaitosten yhteistyöelin* (EFNIL) toteaa, että kielellinen kompetenssi ja kielitaito ovat enenevässä määrin liiketoiminnan ja kaupan avaintekijöitä Euroopassa ja maailmassa.

2. EFNIL kehottaa Euroopan unionia ja jäsenvaltioita laajempaan keskinäiseen yhteistyöhön niiden toimintatapojen kehittämisessä, jotka vastaavat tähän haasteeseen. Näitä toimenpiteitä tulisi edistää ainakin seuraavin tavoin:

   - parantamalla tietoisuutta kielten ja kielitaidon tärkeydestä yritysten toimintaympäristön menestysten tai epäonnistumisten tekijänä;
   - edistämällä ja rahoittamalla kielen prosessoinnin ja kielenoppimisen välineiden kehittämistä liiketoimintaympäristössä;
   - edistämällä ja rahoittamalla erityisten oppimisohjelmien kehittämistä, jotta kieliä käytettäisiin tehokkaasti liiketoiminnassa, erityisesti suosimalla vähemmän käytettyjä kieliä;
   - tukemalla tieteellistä tutkimusta, erityisesti niitä tekijöitä, jotka määrittelevät, kuinka kielet ja kielitaito vaikuttavat lisäarvon muodostumiseen.

3. Kielipoliittisessa toiminnassa tulisi kiinnittää asianmukaista huomiota seuraavien seikkojen tärkeyteen:

   - *kansalliskielten* hallinta avaintekijänä liike-elämän viestinnässä (ei vain vieraiden kielten hallinta);
   - kaikki Euroopan kielet kotouttamisen instrumentteina (ei vain suurimmat kielet);
   - ei-eurooppalaiset kielet, kannustaen myös vastavuoroisuuteen, so. että ei-eurooppalaisen liike-elämän tulisi osoittaa vastaavaa huomiota Euroopan kieliä kohtaan;
   - vierastyöläisten kielitaito;
   - ala- ja tehtäväkohtainen (vieraan) kielen kompetenssi ammatillisen koulutuksen ja jatkokoulutuksen integroivana osana;
   - kääntäminen, konekääntäminen ja termistötyö kotouttamisen ja vieraisiin markkinoihin ja niiden asiakkaisiin sopeuttamisen välttämättömänä apuna.

4. EFNIL kehottaa Euroopan komissiota luomaan Euroopan laajuista informaatio- ja dokumentaatiopalvelua sekä yrityksille että julkiselle hallinnolle ja edistämään parhaita käytänteitä.

5. EFNILin näkemyksen mukaan liike-elämän kielenkäyttöä ei pitäisi tarkastella yksinomaan vapaan kaupankäynnin näkökulmasta, vaan se tulisi nähdä myös asiakkaiden ja työntekijöiden oikeuksien näkökulmasta, ottaen siten huomioon sosiaaliset seikat, kuten yhtäläiset mahdollisuudet, vähemmän koulutettujen kansalaisten sosiaalisen syrjinnän uhan ja tiedon tehokkaan levittämisen. Siksi EFNIL vetoaa Euroopan unioniin, että se tarjoaa jäsenvaltioilleen enemmän mahdollisuuksia siihen, että jäsenvaltiot voisivat säädellä omien kieltensä suosimista ja siten taata riittävän sosiaalisen tasa-arvon.
6. EFNIL tarjoaa asiantuntemuksensa poliittisten toimijoiden tueksi kehitettäessä ja arvioitaessa tämän kentän toimia ja varmistaakseen, että kansalliset ja alueelliset olot ja erikoispiirteet otetaan asianmukaisesti huomioon.

**fr**

# Résolution de Lisbonne sur l'emploi des langues dans les affaires et le commerce en Europe

*Adoptée par l'assemblée générale de la FEILIN le 14 novembre 2008*

1. La *Fédération européenne des institutions linguistiques nationales* (FEILIN) considère que les compétences linguistiques et la capacité à communiquer en plusieurs langues constituent de plus en plus des facteurs-clés pour les affaires et le commerce en Europe et dans le monde.
2. La FEILIN préconise une collaboration plus étroite entre l'Union européenne et les Etats membres pour favoriser la mise en oeuvre de politiques qui répondent à ce défi. Cette collaboration devrait conduire à:
   - renforcer la prise de conscience de l'importance des langues et des compétences linguistiques, qui peuvent être un facteur de réussite ou d'échec dans le milieu des affaires;
   - encourager et soutenir le développement dans le milieu des affaires d'outils consacrés au traitement de la langue et à son apprentissage;
   - encourager et soutenir le développement de programmes d'apprentissage spécifiquement destinés à l'usage des langues dans le milieu des affaires, au profit notamment des langues moins largement diffusées;
   - soutenir la recherche scientifique, notamment pour déterminer dans quelle mesure les langues et les compétences linguistiques contribuent à la création de valeur.
3. Les actions et les mesures d'ordre politique devraient prêter une attention particulière à l'importance:
   - des compétences dans la langue nationale (et pas seulement dans les langues étrangères), qui jouent un rôle clé pour la communication dans les affaires;
   - de l'ensemble des langues européennes (et pas seulement les plus diffusées), en tant que vecteur de localisation;
   - des langues en usage dans les marchés extra-européens, que les milieux d'affaires des pays européens devraient encourager, dans un esprit de réciprocité, en leur prêtant une attention comparable aux langues européennes;
   - des compétences en langue des travailleurs migrants;
   - des compétences en langue (y compris étrangère) par domaines et par métiers, qui font partie intégrante de la formation professionnelle et de l'éducation;
   - de la traduction (à la fois humaine et automatique) et de la terminologie, qui constituent un appui indispensable à la localisation et à l'adaptation aux marchés étrangers et à leurs clients.

4. La FEILIN incite la Commission européenne à mettre en place un vaste service d'information et de documentation au profit des décideurs, des sociétés privées aussi bien que du secteur public, et à promouvoir les bonnes pratiques.
5. La FEILIN estime que la question de l'emploi de la langue dans les affaires ne devrait pas être exclusivement appréhendée du point du vue de la liberté du commerce, mais aussi dans la perspective des droits des consommateurs et des travailleurs. Indépendamment du risque de discrimination sociale envers les citoyens les moins éduqués et formés, des considérations telles que l'égalité des chances et l'accès à l'information pourraient ainsi davantage être prises en compte. Aussi, la FEILIN incite l'Union européenne à fournir aux Etats membres un cadre plus propice à des mesures en faveur de leur propre langue, qui soient de nature à garantir une égalité sociale suffisante.
6. La FEILIN propose son expertise pour aider les responsables à développer et à piloter des politiques dans ce champ et pour veiller à ce qu'ils tiennent bien compte des différentes spécificités et sensibilités aux plans national comme local.

**ga**

# Rún Liospóin Maidir Le húsáid Teangacha Sa Ghnó & Sa Tráchtáil San Eoraip

*Glactha leis ag Mór-Thionól EFNIL: 14 Samhain 2008*

1. Aithníonn an *European Federation of National Institutions for Language* (EFNIL) go bhfuil ag méadú ar an tábhacht atá le cumas teanga agus scileanna cumarsáide mar eochairthosca gnó agus tráchtála san Eoraip agus ar fud an domhain.
2. Molann EFNIL comhoibriú breise idir an Aontas Eorpach agus na Ballstáit chun beartais a fhorbairt a thabharfaidh aghaidh ar an dúshlán seo. Ba chóir go n-áireofaí iontu na gnímh seo:
   - feasacht a ardú ar thábhacht na dteangacha agus na scileanna teanga mar thosca ratha nó teipthe sa timpeallacht ghnó;
   - tacaíocht agus maoiniú a chur ar fáil d'fhorbairt uirlisí le haghaidh próiseáil focal agus foglaim teangacha sa timpeallacht ghnó;
   - tacaíocht agus maoiniú a chur ar fáil d'fhorbairt sainphacáistí foghlama le haghaidh úsáid éifeachtach teangacha sa ghnó, agus cúram ar leith a dhéanamh de theangacha neamhfhorleathana;
   - tacaícocht a thabhairt don taighde eolaíoch, go háirithe taighde ar na tosca a chinntíonn conas mar a chuireann teangacha agus scileanna teanga leis an bpróiseas trína gcruthaítear luach breise.
3. Ba chóir do ghníomhaíochtaí agus do bhearta beartais an aird chuí a thabhairt ar:
   - *Scileanna sa teanga náisiúnta* mar eochairthosca i gcumarsáid ghnó (agus ní hamháin scileanna na dteangacha iasachta);
   - na teangacha Eorpacha ar fad mar mhodhanna logánaithe (seachas na teangacha móra);
   - theangacha na margaí iasachta lasmuigh den Eoraip, le cómhalartacht a spreagadh chomh maith, i.e. go mbeadh an saol neamh-Eorpacha gnó ag tabhairt airde i gcomhréir ar na teangacha Eorpacha;
   - chumas teanga na n-oibrithe inimirceacha;
   - chumas i sainréimsí agus saintascanna teangacha (iasachta) mar dhlúthchodanna den ghairmoiliúint agus den ghairmoideachas;
   - obair an aistriúcháin (idir aistriúchán daonna agus ríomhaistriúchán) mar chabhair don logánú agus don oiriúnú do mhargaí iasachta agus dá gcuid custaiméirí, cabhair nach féidir déanamh dá ceal.
4. Molann EFNIL don Aontas Eorpach gréasán uile-Eorpach eolais agus cáipéisíochta a bhunú le freastal ar chomhlachtaí agus ar riarthóirí poiblí araon agus leis an dea-chleachtas a chur chun cinn.

5. Is é tuairim EFNIL nár cheart saincheist úsáid na dteangacha sa ghnó a bhreathnú ó thaobh saorthrádála amháin, ach ó thaobh chearta tomhaltóirí agus oibrithe chomh maith. Sa tslí sin chuirfí san áireamh cúrsaí sóisialta ar nós cothromaíocht deiseanna, baol ar leatrom sóisialta i gcoinne saoránach nach bhfuil ardchaighdeán ar fad oideachais orthu agus scaipeadh éifeachtach eolais. Dá réir sin molann EFNIL don Chomhphobal Eorpach níos mó deiseanna rialúcháin a thairiscint do na Ballstáit i bhfabhar a gcuid teanga(cha) féin chun a dheimhniú go mbainfí cothromaíocht shóisialta amach.

6. Tá EFNIL ag tairiscint a chuid saineolais a chur ar fáil do lucht ceaptha beartas chun beartais a fhorbairt sa réimse seo agus monatóireacht a dhéanamh orthu seo chun a dheimhniú go gcuirfear san áireamh mar is cóir tosca agus íogaireachtaí náisiúnta agus réigiúnacha.

**is**

## Lissabonyfirlýsingin um málnotkun í verslun og viðskiptum í Evrópu

1. *Samtök evrópskra málræktarstofnana* (EFNIL) viðurkenna að færni í tungumálum og samskiptahæfileikar séu í vaxandi mæli lykilatriði fyrir verslun og viðskipti í Evrópu og í heiminum.

2. EFNIL leggur áherslu á aukið samstarf milli Evrópusambandsins og aðildarríkja þess við mótun málstefna til að mæta þessari áskorun. Þær ættu að innihalda a.m.k. þessa aðgerðarliði:

   - að auka meðvitund um mikilvægi tungumála og tungumálafærni sem áhrifaþætti í velgengni eða mistök innan viðskiptaumhverfisins;
   - að hvetja til og fjármagna þróun verkfæra til að nota við vinnu með tungumál og til tungumálanáms í viðskiptalífinu;
   - að hvetja til og fjármagna þróun sérstakra námsáætlana fyrir árangursríka tungumálanotkun í viðskiptum, með sérstaka áherslu á tungumál með minni útbreiðslu;
   - að styðja vísindalegar rannsóknir, sérstaklega á þeim þáttum sem ákvarða hvernig tungumál og tungumálafærni stuðla að sköpun verðmæta.

3. Aðgerðir og ráðstafanir samkvæmt málstefnunum ættu að gæta að mikilvægi:

   - *móðurmálsfærni* sem lykilþætti í viðskiptasamskiptum (og ekki aðeins færni í erlendum tungumálum);
   - allra Evrópskra tungumála sem verkfæra fyrir staðfærslu og aðlögun (og ekki eingöngu hinna stærri);
   - tungumála á erlendum mörkuðum utan Evrópu og örva gagnkvæmar aðgerðir (þ.e. að fyrirtæki utan Evrópu ættu að veita Evrópskum tungumálum sambærilega athygli;
   - tungumálafærni farandverkafólks;
   - færni í (erlendum) tungumálum innan sérstakra umdæma og verkefna sem kjarnaþátta í þjálfun og menntun fagmanna;
   - þýðinga (bæði manngerðra og sjálfvirkra) og íðorðavinnu sem ómissandi hjálpartæki til staðfærslu og aðlögunar að erlendum mörkuðum og viðskiptavinum þeirra.

4. EFNIL hvetur Evrópuráðið til að koma á fót upplýsinga- og gagnaskráningarþjónustu sem nær yfir alla Evrópu og gagnast á bæði fyrirtækjum og opinberum aðilum og hefur að leiðarljósi bestu verklagaðferðir.

5. EFNIL lítur svo á að spurninguna um málnotkun í verslun og viðskiptum eigi ekki eingöngu að hugleiða út frá sjónarhorni frjálsrar verslunar heldur einnig með réttindi neytenda og verkafólks í huga og skapa með því rými fyrir félagsleg umhugsunarefni eins og jöfn tækifæri, hættuna á félagslegri mismunun minna menntaðra borgara og skilvirka miðlun upplýsinga. Þess vegna hvetur EFNIL Evrópusambandið til að bjóða aðildarríkjunum aukin tækifæri til að setja reglugerðir sem styðja við eigin tungumál í því skyni að tryggja fullnægjandi félagslegan jöfnuð.
6. EFNIL býður fram sérfræðiþekkingu sína til að aðstoða stefnumótandi aðila við þróun og eftirlit með stefnum á þessu sviði og tryggja að aðstæðum og úrlausnarefnum einstakra þjóða og svæða sé sýnd nægileg athygli.

**it**

# Risoluzione di Lisbona Sull'Uso delle Lingue nelle Attività Produttive e Commerciali in Europa

*Approvata dall'Assemblea Generale EFNIL il 14 November 2008*

1. La *Federazione Europea delle Istituzioni Linguistiche Nazionali* (EFNIL) riconosce la competenza linguistica e le capacità comunicative come fattori chiave di importanza crescente per le attività produttive e commerciali in Europa e nel mondo.
2. La EFNIL sollecita una maggiore collaborazione fra l'Unione Europea e gli Stati Membri nello sviluppo di politiche che affrontino questa sfida. Esse devono comprendere i seguenti punti:
   - suscitare la consapevolezza dell'importanza delle lingue e delle capacità linguistiche come fattori di successo o di insuccesso nell'ambito delle attività economiche;
   - incoraggiare e finanziare lo sviluppo di strumenti per il trattamento e per l'apprendimento delle lingue nell'ambito delle attività economiche;
   - incoraggiare e finanziare lo sviluppo di programmi specifici di apprendimento per l'uso effettivo ed efficace delle lingue nel lavoro, favorendo specialmente le lingue di uso meno comune;
   - sostenere la ricerca scientifica, specialmente in relazione ai fattori che determinano il contributo delle lingue e delle capacità linguistiche al processo di creazione di valore.
3. Le azioni e le misure di politica linguistica dovrebbero prestare la dovuta attenzione:
   - alla padronanza della *lingua nazionale* (e non solo delle lingue straniere) come fattore chiave della comunicazione nelle attività economiche;
   - a *tutte* le lingue europee (e non solo alle maggiori) come strumenti di rapporto col territorio;
   - alle lingue dei mercati stranieri al di fuori dell'Europa, stimolando anche la reciprocità, nel senso che gli ambienti economici non europei dovrebbero prestare una corrispondente attenzione alle lingue europee;
   - alla competenza linguistica dei lavoratori migranti;
   - alla competenza linguistica specifica per settore e per tipo di lavoro come parte integrante della preparazione professionale;
   - alla traduzione (sia umana, sia automatica) ed alla creazione terminologica come aiuto indispensabile al rapporto col territorio e all'adattamento ai mercati e ai clienti stranieri.

4. La EFNIL sollecita la Commissione Europea a istituire un servizio europeo di informazione e di documentazione sia per le aziende, sia per le pubbliche amministrazioni, ed a promuovere le prassi migliori.

5. La EFNIL ritiene che il problema dell'uso del linguaggio nelle attività economiche non debba essere considerato esclusivamente dal punto di vista del libero mercato, ma anche nella prospettiva dei diritti dei consumatori e dei lavoratori, dando perciò spazio a considerazioni sociali quali le pari opportunità, il pericolo di discriminazioni sociali ai danni dei cittadini meno istruiti e la necessità di una diffusione efficiente dell'informazione. Perciò la EFNIL sollecita l'Unione Europea ad offrire agli Stati Membri maggiori possibilità di regolamentazione in favore della loro lingua o delle loro lingue, allo scopo di garantire un'adeguata parità di condizioni nella società.

6. La EFNIL offre la propria consulenza per assistere i responsabili politici nello sviluppo e nel monitoraggio delle politiche in questo campo e per far sì che siano debitamente tenute in conto le circostanze e le sensibilità nazionali e regionali.

**lv**

# Lisabonas Rezolūcija par Valodu Lietošanu Uzņēmējdarbībā un Komercdarbībā Eiropā

*Pieņemta EFNIL Ģenerālajā asamblejā 2008. gada 14. novembrī*

1. *Eiropas Nacionālo valodu institūciju federācija* (EFNIL) apstiprina, ka valodu zināšanas un komunikācijas prasme kļūst par aizvien izšķirīgāku faktoru uzņēmējdarbībā un komercdarbībā gan Eiropā, gan visā pasaulē.

2. EFNIL rosina aizvien plašāku sadarbību gan Eiropas Savienībā, gan starp tās dalībvalstīm rīcībpolitikas izstrādē šajā jomā. Tai jāietver šādi pasākumi:

   – jāpilnveido zināšanas par valodu un to prasmi kā nozīmīgu faktoru panākumiem vai zaudējumiem uzņēmējdarbības vidē;

   – jārosina un jāfinansē valodu apguves līdzekļu un programmatūru izstrāde uzņēmējdarbības videi;

   – jāveicina un jāfinansē īpašas valodu apguves programmas efektīvai valodu izmantošanai uzņēmējdarbībā, īpaši atbalstot mazāk lietotās valodas;

   – jāatbalsta zinātniski pētījumi, īpašu uzmanību pievēršot to faktoru izpētei, kas nosaka valodu un valodu prasmes ieguldījumu pievienotās vērtības radīšanā.

3. Veidojot politiku, īpaša uzmanība jāpievērš:

   – valsts (nacionālās) valodas prasmei (un ne tikai svešvalodu prasmei) kā izšķirīgam faktoram komunikācijā;

   – visām Eiropas valodām (un ne tikai vairāk lietotajām valodām) kā uzņēmējdarbības lokalizācijas instrumentam;

   – ārpus Eiropas lokalizētajos tirgos lietotajām valodām, veicinot arī Eiropas valodu lietošanu šajos tirgos, t.i., adekvātu Eiropas valodu lietošanu citvalstu uzņēmējdarbībā;

   – viesstrādnieku valodas prasmei;

   – valodas un svešvalodu speciālā lietojuma prasmei, to atzīstot par neatņemamu profesionālās izglītības sastāvdaļu;

   – tulkošanai (arī mašīntulkošanai) un terminoloģijas attīstībai kā neatņemamam faktoram veiksmīgā uzņēmējdarbības pielāgošanā gan vietējai videi, gan ārvalstu tirgiem un patērētājiem.

4. EFNIL aicina Eiropas Komisiju izveidot Eiropas mēroga informācijas un dokumentācijas dienestu, kas apkalpotu gan uzņēmējsabiedrības, gan valsts iestādes un atbalstītu veiksmīgas prakses izplatīšanu.

5. EFNIL uzskata, ka valodu lietojums uzņēmējdarbībā ir nozīmīgs ne tikai saistībā ar brīvo tirgu, bet arī saistībā ar patērētāju un nodarbināto tiesībām, šādi veicinot sociālo taisnīgumu – radot vienlīdzīgas iespējas, novēršot mazāk izglītotu pilsoņu sociālo diskrimināciju, nodrošinot efektīvu informācijas izplatīšanu. Tāpēc EFNIL aicina Eiropas Savienību piešķirt plašākas iespējas dalībvalstīm pašām regulēt valodu lietošanu, atbalstot savu oficiālo valodu, lai garantētu sociālo vienlīdzību.
6. EFNIL dalībvalstu politikas veidotājiem piedāvā ekspertu pakalpojumus, lai palīdzētu rīcībpolitikas izstrādē un monitoringā un lai nodrošinātu valstu un reģionu apstākļu un īpatnību ievērošanu šajā politikas jomā.

**le**

# Resolutioun vu Lissabon iwwert de Sproochegebrauch an der Ekonomie an am Handel an Europa

*Approuvéiert vun der Assemblée Générale vun der EFNIL de 14. November 2008*

1. D'*European Federation of National Institutions for Language* (*Europäesch Federatioun vun den Nationale Sproochen-Instituter* – EFNIL) weist drop hin, datt Sproochekompetenz a Kommunikatiounsfähegkeet ëmmer méi zu Schlësselelementer fir den Handel an d'Ekonomie an Europa a weltwäit ginn.
2. D'EFNIL fuerdert méi eng grouss Zesummenaarbecht tëschent der Europäescher Unioun an hire Memberstaaten bei der Konzeptioun vun enger Politik, déi dëser Erausfuerderung Rechnung dréit. Esou eng Politik sollt ënnert anerem déi elei Aktiounsmomenter enthalen:
   - d'Bedeitung vu Sproochen a vu Sproochkompetenz als Elementer fir de Succès oder den Echec an der Ekonomie méi däitlech erausstellen;
   - d'Entwécklung vun Instrumenter fir den Ëmgank mat an d'Léiere vu Sproochen am ekonomeschen Ëmfeld encouragéieren a finanzéieren;
   - d'Entwécklung vu spezielle Léierprogrammer fir en effiziente Gebrauch vu Sproochen an der Ekonomie encouragéieren a finanzéieren, an dobäi déi manner gebrauchte Sprooche besonnesch favoriséieren;
   - d'wëssenschaftlech Fuerschung ënnerstëtzen, speziell am Kader vun de Facteuren, déi bestëmmen, wéi Sproochen a Sproochkompetenzen zu der Realisatioun vu Plus-valuen bäidroen.
3. Bei politeschen Aktiounen a Moossnamen sollten déi elei Aspekter adequat beuecht ginn:
   - d'Kompetenzen an der *Nationalsprooch* als Schlësselelement fir d'Kommunikatioun an der Geschäftswelt (an net nëmmen d'Kompetenzen a Friemsproochen);
   - all europäesch Sproochen als Instrumenter fir eng Lokaliséierung (an net nëmmen déi grouss Sproochen);
   - d'Sprooche vun auslännesche Mäert baussent Europa, woubäi och d'Géigesäitegkeet sollt stimuléiert ginn, d.h. datt d'Ekonomië baussent Europa hirersäits déi europäesch Sprooche grad esou beuechte sollten;
   - d'Sproochekompetenz vu Migranten;
   - secteur- a missiounsspezifesch (Friem-)Sproochekompetenzen als integrale Bestanddeel vun enger berufflecher Aus- a Weiderbildung;
   - (mënschlech an automatiséiert) Iwwersetzungs- an Terminologieaarbecht als onverziichtbar Hëllef fir eng Lokalisatioun an eng Adaptatioun u friem Mäert an hir Konsumenten.

4. D'EFNIL fuerdert d'Europäesch Kommissioun op, en uniounswäiten Informatiouns- an Dokumentatiounsservice fir Entreprisen grad ewéi fir Administratiounen opzebauen a confirméiert Praktiken ze ënnerstëtzen.

5. D'EFNIL ass der Opfaassung, datt d'Fro vum Sproochegebrauch an der Ekonomie net nëmmen ënnert dem Aspekt vum fräien Handel sollt considéréiert ginn, mee och aus der Perspektiv vun de Rechter vum Konsument a vum Salarié, woumadder d'Méiglechkeet geschafe gëtt, sozial Considératiounen wéi d'Chancegläichheet, d'Gefor vu sozialer Diskriminatioun vis-à-vis vu Mënsche mat manner Formatioun an eng effizient Informatiounsverbreedung mat anzebezéien. D'EFNIL fuerdert dofir d'Europäesch Unioun op, méi Méiglechkeete fir eng Regulatioun duerch d'Memberstaaten zugonschte vun hirer eegener Sprooch respektiv hiren eegene Sprooche virzegesinn, fir datt genuch sozial Gläichheet gerantéiert ka ginn.

6. D'EFNIL offréiert hir Expertise, fir déi politesch Décideuren bei der Entwécklung an Iwwerwaachung vu politesche Moossnamen an dësem Beräich ze ënnerstëtzen a fir sécherzestellen, datt nationalen a regionalen Ëmstänn a Sensibilitéiten adequat Rechnung gedroe gëtt.

**lt**

# Lisabonos rezoliucija dėl kalbos vartojimo versle ir prekyboje Europoje

*Priimta EFNIL generalinės asamblėjos 2008 m. lapkričio 14 d.*

1. *Europos Sąjungos nacionalinių kalbos institucijų federacija* (EFNIL) pripažįsta, kad kalbinė kompetencija ir bendravimo įgūdžiai tampa vis svarbesniais verslo ir prekybos veiksniais Europoje ir pasaulyje.

2. EFNIL ragina Europos Sąjungą ir šalis nares glaudžiau bendradarbiauti tam, kad būtų sukurta veiklos strategija šiam uždaviniui spręsti. Ji turėtų apimti šias veiklos kryptis:
   - skatinti kalbų ir kalbos įgūdžių, kaip sėkmę ar nesėkmę verslo aplinkoje lemiančių veiksnių, svarbos supratimą;
   - skatinti ir finansuoti lingvistinės informacijos apdorojimo ir kalbos mokymo verslo aplinkoje priemonių kūrimą;
   - skatinti ir finansuoti specialių veiksmingo kalbų vartojimo versle mokymo programų kūrimą, pirmenybę teikiant ne taip plačiai vartojamoms kalboms;
   - remti mokslinius tyrimus, ypač tuos, kuriais siekiama nustatyti, kaip kalbos ir kalbų įgūdžiai prisideda prie vertės kūrimo.

3. Pasirenkant veiksmus ir priemones reikėtų atkreipti dėmesį į svarbą šių dalykų:
   - *nacionalinių kalbų* įgūdžių (ne tik užsienio kalbų įgūdžių), kaip lemiamų verslo ryšių veiksnių;
   - visų Europos kalbų (ne tik didžiųjų kalbų), kaip lokalizacijos priemonių;
   - už Europos ribų esančių užsienio rinkų kalbų, skatinant abipusiškumą, t.y. panašų ne Europos verslo dėmesį Europos kalboms;
   - migruojančių darbuotojų kalbinės kompetencijos;
   - su tam tikra sritimi ar darbu susijusios kalbinės (užsienio kalbos) kompetencijos, kaip būtinos profesinio mokymo dalies;
   - vertimo (žmogaus atliekamo ar automatinio) ir terminologijos darbo, kaip būtinos lokalizavimo ir prisitaikymo prie užsienio rinkų ir jų klientų priemonės.

4. EFNIL ragina Europos Komisiją įkurti visos Europos informacijos ir dokumentacijos tarnybą, dirbančią su įmonėmis ir valstybės tarnautojais, ir skatinti geriausios patirties diegimą.

5. EFNIL mano, kad kalbos vartojimo versle klausimas turėtų būti svarstomas ne vien tik laisvosios prekybos požiūriu, bet ir vartotojo ir darbuotojo teisių požiūriu, tokiu būdu atsižvelgiant į tokias socialines aplinkybes, kaip lygios galimybės, mažiau

išsilavinusių piliečių socialinės diskriminacijos pavojus ir veiksminga informacijos sklaida. EFNIL skatina Europos Sąjungą suteikti daugiau galimybių jos šalims narėms pirmenybę teikti jų pačių kalboms tam, kad būtų užtikrinta pakankama socialinė lygybė.

6. EFNIL siūlo savo žinias ir patirtį, kurios padėtų strategijos kūrėjams rengti ir kontroliuoti šios srities veiklos strategiją ir užtikrintų, kad būtų deramai atsižvelgta į nacionalines ir regionines aplinkybes.

**hu**

# Lisszaboni állásfoglalása az Európai üzleti és kereskedelmi nyelvhasználatról

*Az EFNIL közgyűlésének 2008. november 14-i jóváhagyásával*

1. A *Nemzeti Nyelvi Intézetek Európai Szövetsége* (EFNIL) elismeri, hogy Európában és a világban egyre jelentősebb szerephez jutnak a nyelvi kompetenciák és kommunikációs készségek a kereskedelmi és üzleti élet területén.

2. Az EFNIL szorosabb együttműködésre szólítja fel az Európai Uniót és a tagállamokat olyan intézkedések kidolgozása érdekében, amelyek válaszolnak e kihívásokra. Ez a következő tevékenységeket foglalná magában:

   - tudatosítsák a nyelveknek és nyelvi készségeknek az üzleti sikerekben betöltött szerepét;
   - nyújtsanak szellemi és anyagi támogatást az üzleti környezetben alkalmazható nyelvfeldolgozó és nyelvtanulást segítő eszközök fejlesztéséhez;
   - nyújtsanak szellemi és anyagi támogatást célzott, a hatékony üzleti nyelvhasználat elsajátítását segítő programokhoz, különösen a kevésbé használt nyelvek esetében;
   - támogassák a tudományos kutatásokat, különösen azokat, amelyek azt vizsgálják, hogyan vesznek részt a nyelvek és nyelvi készségek az értékteremtés folyamatában.

3. Szükséges, hogy a politikai döntések és intézkedések kellő figyelmet fordítsanak

   - az idegen nyelvi készségeken túl *a nemzeti nyelvi* készségek, mint az üzleti kommunikációban meghatározó készségek fontosságára;
   - arra, hogy a termékek és szolgáltatások helyi igényekhez és piacokhoz igazítása (lokalizáció) során valamennyi európai nyelv (és nem csak a nagy nyelvek) megjelenjenek;
   - az Európán kívüli külföldi piacok nyelvének fontosságára, s ezáltal arra, hogy a kölcsönösség jegyében az Európán kívüli üzleti szféra is hasonló figyelmet fordítson az európai nyelvekre;
   - a migráns munkavállalók nyelvi kompetenciájára;
   - a szakmához és feladathoz kapcsolódó (idegen)nyelvi kompetenciára, mint a szakmai képzések és továbbképzések elengedhetetlen részére;
   - a (gépi és emberi) fordításra és a terminológiai munkára, amely elengedhetetlen a lokalizáció és a külföldi piacokhoz és vásárlókhoz való alkalmazkodás során.

4. Az EFNIL kezdeményezi, hogy az Európai Bizottság hozzon létre egy olyan európai szintű információs- és dokumentációs szolgáltatást, amelyet mind a vállalati, mind a közszféra igénybe vehetne, és amely a bevált gyakorlatokat terjesztené.

5. Az EFNIL meggyőződése, hogy az üzleti nyelvhasználat kérdését nem kizárólag a szabad kereskedelem felől kell megközelíteni, hanem a fogyasztók és dolgozók jogai felől is. Így teret kaphatnak olyan szociális tényezők is, mint az esélyegyenlőség, a kevésbé tanult emberek negatív szociális megkülönböztetésének veszélye és az információ hatékony terjesztése. Ezért az EFNIL arra szólítja fel az Európai Uniót, hogy a megfelelő mértékű szociális egyenlőség garantálása érdekében több lehetőséget adjon a tagállamoknak a saját nyelvüket/nyelveiket érintő szabályozások terén.

6. Az EFNIL felajánlja szakértelmét, hogy segítse a politikai döntéshozókat az e területeket érintő intézkedések megalkotásában és nyomon követésében, és biztosítsa, hogy a nemzeti és regionális tényezők és sajátosságok megfelelő figyelmet kapjanak.

**mt**

# Ir-riżoluzzjoni ta' Liżbona dwar l-użu tal-lingwa fin-negozju u l-kummerċ fl-Ewropa

*Approvata mill -Assemblea Ġenerali ta' EFNIL fl-14 ta' Novembru 2008*

1. *Il-Federazzjoni Ewropea tal-Istituzzjonijiet Nazzjonali għal-Lingwa* (EFNIL) tagħraf li l-kompetenza lingwistika u l-ħiliet fil-komunikazzjoni, kull ma jmur qed isiru fatturi iktar kruċjali fin-negozju u l-kummerċ fl-Ewropa u fid-dinja.

2. L-EFNIL tirrakomanda lill-Unjoni Ewropea u lill-Istati Membri li jikkollaboraw iżjed bejniethom biex jiżviluppaw politika li tindirizza din l-isfida. Bħala punti ta' azzjoni din il-politika għandha, fost ħwejjeġ oħra:

   - tqajjem kuxjenza fl-ambjent kummerċjali dwar l-importanza tal-lingwi u tal-ħiliet lingwistiċi bħala fatturi għas-suċċess jew għall-falliment;
   - tinkoraġġixxi u tiffinanzja l-iżvilupp ta' għodod għall-ipproċessar u t-tagħlim tal-lingwa fl-ambjent kummerċjali;
   - tinkoraġġixxi u tiffinanzja l-iżvilupp ta' programmi speċifiċi ta' tagħlim għall-użu effettiv tal-lingwi fil-kummerċ, u tiffavorixxi b'mod speċjali l-lingwi inqas mifruxa;
   - tappoġġja r-riċerka xjentifika, l-aktar dik li tistudja l-fatturi li jiddeterminaw x'sehem għandhom il-lingwi u l-ħiliet lingwistiċi fil-proċess li bih jinħoloq il-valur.

3. L-interventi u l-miżuri ta' din il-politika għandhom jitfasslu fid-dawl tal-importanza ta' dawn li ġejjin:

   - il-ħiliet fil-*lingwa nazzjonali* bħala fatturi kruċjali fil-komunikazzjoni għall-kummerċ (u mhux biss il-ħiliet fil-lingwi barranin);
   - il-lingwi Ewropej kollha bħala strument għal-lokalizzazzjoni (u mhux biss il-lingwi l-kbar);
   - il-lingwi tas-swieq barranin 'l hinn mill-Ewropa, u għandhom jistimulaw ukoll ir-reċiproċità, jiġifieri li l-kummerċ non-Ewropew għandu jagħti l-istess attenzjoni lill-ilsna Ewropej;
   - il-kompetenza lingwistika tal-ħaddiema migranti;
   - il-kompetenza fil-lingwi (barranin) f'oqsma u f'xogħlijiet speċifiċi, bħala parti integrali mit- taħriġ u l-edukazzjoni professjonali;
   - ix-xogħol fit-traduzzjoni (kemm dik umana kif ukoll dik awtomatika) u fit-terminoloġija bħala għajnuna indispensabbli għal-lokalizzazzjoni u adattament għas-swieq barranin u għall-klijenti tagħhom.

4. Lill-Kummissjoni Ewropea, l-EFNIL tirrakomandalha bil-qawwa li tistabbilixxi servizz ta' informazzjoni u dokumentazzjoni mifruxa mal-Ewropa għall-benefiċċju kemm ta' kumpanniji u kemm ta' amministraturi pubbliċi, u li tippromwovi l-aħjar prattika.

5. L-EFNIL hija tal-fehma li l-kwistjoni tal-użu tal-lingwa fil-kummerċ m'għandhiex titqies biss mill-punt di vista tal-kummerċ ħieles, imma anki mill-perspettiva tad-drittijiet tal-konsumatur u tal-ħaddiem, biex jinħoloq spazju għall-konsiderazzjonijiet soċjali bħalma huma l-opportunitajiet indaqs, il-periklu tad-diskriminazzjoni soċjali kontra dawk iċ-ċittadini li m'għandhomx edukazzjoni għolja, kif ukoll it-tixrid effiċjenti tal-informazzjoni. Għaldaqstant l-EFNIL tirrakkomanda lill-Unjoni Ewropea li toffri iktar opportunitajiet lill-Istati Membri biex jgħaddu miżuri favur il-lingwa/i tagħhom bil-għan li jiggarantixxu ugwaljanza soċjali suffiċjenti.

6. L-EFNIL qed toffri l-kompetenza tagħha biex lil dawk li jfasslu l-politika, tgħinhom jiżviluppaw u jimmonitorjaw il-prinċipji politiċi f'dan il-qasam, u biex tiżgura li ċ-ċirkostanzi u s-sensibilitajiet nazzjonali u reġjonali jkunu meqjusin kif imiss.

**nl**

# Resolutie van Lissabon over het gebruik van talen in het zakenleven in Europa

*Goedgekeurd door de Algemene Vergadering van EFNIL op 14 november 2008*

1. De *Europese Federatie van Nationale Taalinstellingen* (EFNIL) erkent dat taalkennis en communicatieve vaardigheden voor bedrijfsleven en commercie in Europa en de wereld in toenemende mate sleutelfactoren zullen blijken te zijn.
2. EFNIL pleit voor een nauwere samenwerking tussen de Europese Unie en de Lidstaten wat betreft de ontwikkeling van beleid op dat gebied. Dat moet o.a. de volgende actiepunten bevatten:
   - het bewustzijn te versterken van het belang van talen en taalvaardigheid als factoren voor succes of mislukking in het bedrijfsleven;
   - de ontwikkeling van op het bedrijfsleven gerichte tools voor taalverwerking en taalonderwijs te bevorderen en te financieren;
   - de ontwikkeling van specifiek op de behoeften van het zakenleven gerichte taalleerprogramma's te bevorderen en te financieren, en er daarbij op te letten dat ook de minder grote talen voldoende aan bod komen;
   - het wetenschappelijk onderzoek te bevorderen, vooral naar de factoren die de bijdrage van talen en taalvaardigheden aan het (economische) waardeproces bepalen.
3. Beleidsmaatregelen en -acties moeten aandacht besteden aan het belang van:
   - een goede beheersing van de moedertaal als sleutelfactor in het zakenleven (en niet alleen de beheersing van vreemde talen);
   - alle Europese talen als noodzakelijke middelen voor lokalisatie (en niet alleen de grotere talen);
   - de talen van vreemde markten buiten Europa, waarbij wederkerigheid wordt aangemoedigd, namelijk dat niet-Europese bedrijven vergelijkbare aandacht schenken aan Europese talen;
   - de taalcompetenties van allochtone arbeidskrachten;
   - domein- en taakspecifieke taalbeheersing als integraal onderdeel van beroepsopleiingen en -onderwijs;
   - vertaling (zowel door mensen als machinaal) en terminologie als onmisbare hulpmiddelen voor het aanpassen van producten en diensten aan vreemde markten en consumenten.
4. EFNIL verzoekt de Europese Unie om een Europese informatie- en documentatievoorziening op te zetten voor zowel bedrijven als overheidsdiensten en daarbij goede praktijkvoorbeelden te verspreiden;

5. Het is de overtuiging van EFNIL dat de kwestie van het taalgebruik in het bedrijfsleven niet alleen beschouwd mag worden vanuit het standpunt van vrije handel maar ook vanuit het perspectief van de rechten van consumenten en werknemers, waarbij sociale overwegingen in acht genomen moeten worden, bijvoorbeeld over gelijke kansen, het risico van sociale discriminatie van lager geschoolden, efficiënte informatieverspreiding e.d. Daarom verzoekt EFNIL de Europese Unie om de Lidstaten hiertoe meer ruimte te geven voor regelgeving ten voordele van hun eigen nationale taal.
6. EFNIL biedt beleidsmakers haar kennis en ervaring aan, om hen te ondersteunen met beleidsontwikkeling en -toetsing en er daarbij voor te zorgen dat nationale en regionale omstandigheden en gevoeligheden voldoende worden verdisconteerd.

**no**

# Lisboaresolusjonen om språkbruk i handel og næringsliv i Europa

*Vedtatt av Efnils generalforsamling 14. november 2008*

1. *Den europeiske sammenslutning av europeiske språkinstitutter*, Efnil (European Federation of National Institutions for Language) er av den oppfatning at språklig kompetanse og evnen til å kommunisere blir stadig viktigere nøkkelfaktorer i Europa og verden for øvrig.
2. Efnil oppmuntrer til økt samarbeid mellom den Europeiske union og dens medlemsstater for å utvikle strategier for å møte denne utfordringen. Strategiene bør omfatte følgende tiltak:
   - å øke bevisstheten om språk og språkferdigheter som viktige faktorer for å lykkes eller mislykkes i næringslivet;
   - å oppmuntre til og finansiere utvikling av verktøy for språkbehandling og språkinnlæring i næringslivet;
   - å oppmuntre til og finansiere utvikling av spesifikke undervisningsprogram for effektiv anvendelse av språk i næringslivet, der spesielt mindre anvendte språk bør støttes;
   - å støtte forskning, særlig når det gjelder slike forhold som avgjør hvordan språk og språkferdigheter bidrar til den verdiskapende prosessen.
3. Når det gjelder retningslinjer og metoder, bør det legges vekt på
   - kunnskaper i nasjonale språk som nøkkelfaktorer når det gjelder forretningsspråk (og ikke bare kunnskaper i fremmedspråk);
   - alle europeiske språk som lokaliseringsinstrument (og ikke bare de større);
   - språkene på utenlandske markeder utenfor Europa og stimulering til gjensidighet, det vil si oppmuntre til at det i ikke-europeisk handel gis samme oppmerksomhet til europeiske språk;
   - språkkompetansen til innvandrerarbeidere;
   - bransje- og fagspesifikk språkkompetanse som en vesentlig del av yrkesutdannelsen;
   - oversettelse (både menneskelig og automatisert) og terminologiarbeid som en uunnværlig hjelp ved lokalisering og tilpassing til utenlandske markeder og kunder.
4. Efnil henstiller til Europakommisjonen å opprette en europeisk informasjons- og dokumentasjonstjeneste for både firmaer og myndigheter og fremme gode forbilder.

5. Efnil mener spørsmålet om språkanvendelse innen næringslivet ikke bare må ses ut fra et frihandelsperspektiv, men også ut fra et forbruker- og arbeidsrett-perspektiv, for på den måten å kunne ta hensyn til sosiale forhold som like muligheter, faren for sosial diskriminering mot borgere med lavere utdannelse og effektiv spredning av informasjon. Efnil henstiller derfor til Den europeiske union å tilby medlemslandene bedre muligheter for å støtte egne språk, for dermed å kunne garantere tilstrekkelig sosial likhet.
6. Efnil tilbyr sin ekspertise som hjelp til å utvikle og overvåke tiltak på dette området og for å sikre at nasjonale og regionale forhold blir tatt tilstrekkelig hensyn til.

**pl**

## Rezolucja lizbońska w sprawie używania języka w biznesie i handlu w Europie

1. Europejska Federacja Narodowych Instytucji na rzecz Języka (EFNIL) uznaje, że kompetencja językowa i sprawność w komunikowaniu się w coraz większym stopniu stają się czynnikami zasadniczymi dla biznesu i handlu w Europie.

2. EFNIL wzywa do ściślejszej współpracy między Unią Europejską a krajami członkowskimi UE w kształtowaniu zasad postępowania odpowiadających temu wyzwaniu. Zasady te powinny uwzględniać następujące działania:
   - rozbudzać świadomość ważności języków i sprawności językowej jako czynników sukcesu lub porażki w otoczeniu biznesowym;
   - zachęcać do finansowania i doskonalenia narzędzi przetwarzania języka i uczenia się języków w środowisku biznesowym;
   - zachęcać do finansowania i doskonalenia właściwych programów nauki skutecznego używania języków w biznesie ze szczególnym uwzględnieniem języków mniej używanych;
   - wspierać badania naukowe zwłaszcza nad czynnikami, które decydują o tym, jak języki i sprawności językowe uczestniczą w procesie tworzenia wartości.

3. Zasady i środki działania powinny zwracać należytą uwagę na ważność:
   - sprawności używania języka narodowego (a nie tylko języka obcego) jako kluczowego czynnika komunikacji biznesowej;
   - wszystkich (a nie tylko większych) języków europejskich jako narzędzi lokalności;
   - języków z obcych rynków spoza Europy, powodujących na zasadzie wzajemności porównywalne uwzględnianie języków europejskich przez pozaeuropejski biznes;
   - kompetencji językowej gastarbeiterów;
   - znajomości języka (obcego) stosownej do dziedziny i zadań jako integralnej części zawodowego szkolenia i kształcenia;
   - przekładu (tak osobowego, jak i automatycznego) oraz pracy nad terminologią jako niezbędnej pomocy w lokalizacji i dostosowaniu do zagranicznych rynków i ich klientów.

4. EFNIL wzywa Komisję Europejską do powołania ogólnoeuropejskich służb informacji i dokumentacji dla przedsiębiorstw i administracji publicznej, a także do popierania najlepszych rozwiązań praktycznych.

5. Zdaniem EFNIL-u kwestia używania języka w biznesie nie powinna być rozpatrywana wyłącznie z punktu widzenia wolnego handlu, ale także z perspektywy praw konsumentów i pracowników, tak by umożliwić społeczne rozważania takich tematów, jak równe szanse, niebezpieczeństwo społecznej dyskryminacji mniej wykształconych obywateli czy skuteczne rozpowszechnienie informacji. Stąd EFNIL wzywa Unię Europejską, by stworzyła państwom członkowskim większe możliwości regulacji na rzecz ich własnego języka(ków) w celu zagwarantowania dostatecznej równości społecznej.
6. EFNIL oferuje swoje doświadczenie, by wesprzeć polityków w rozwijaniu i monitorowaniu takich zasad działania w tej dziedzinie, by zapewniały, że narodowe i regionalne uwarunkowania i uczucia są należycie uwzględnione.

pt

## Resolução de Lisboa línguas e negócios na Europa

1. *Federação Europeia de Institutos Nacionais de Língua* (EFNIL) reconhece que as competências linguística e comunicativa, quer nas línguas nacionais quer nas línguas estrangeiras, são factores decisivos para o incremento dos negócios na Europa e no mundo.
2. A EFNIL reclama uma maior colaboração entre a União Europeia e os Estados-Membros para o desenvolvimento de políticas que implementem este desafio. A saber:
   - consciencializar todos os Estados Membros da importância das línguas e da sua aprendizagem como factores de sucesso ou de insucesso no mundo dos negócios;
   - encorajar e financiar o desenvolvimento de instrumentos que agilizem o ensino e aprendizagem de línguas na área dos negócios;
   - encorajar e financiar o desenvolvimento de programas de ensino e aprendizagem específicos da área dos negócios, que favoreçam especialmente o uso alargado das línguas;
   - apoiar a investigação científica, especialmente com a finalidade de ser determinado o valor económico das diversas línguas.
3. As medidas e acções desta política deverão chamar a atenção e incidir para a relevância dos seguintes aspectos:
   - as competências nas línguas nacionais são factores determinantes para a comunicação no mundo dos negócios (e não só as competências em línguas estrangeiras);
   - todas as línguas da Europa são importantes (e não só as maiores) e devem ser respeitadas nas suas especificidades, quer linguísticas quer culturais;
   - os mercados estrangeiros fora da Europa também deverão atribuir importância às línguas europeias;
   - a competência comunicativa dos trabalhadores migrantes;
   - a aprendizagem de linguagem técnica em línguas estrangeiras como parte integrante da educação e formação profissional;
   - a tradução (humana e automática) e glossários terminológicos como ajudas indispensáveis para a compreensão das características específicas e adaptação aos mercados estrangeiros e seus clientes.
4. A EFNIL deseja que a Comissão Europeia crie um serviço europeu alargado de informação e documentação para empresas e administradores públicos e promova boas práticas.

5. A EFNIL está convicta de que esta temática, o uso das línguas nos negócios, deve ser considerada não só do ponto de vista do mercado livre mas também na perspectiva dos direitos dos consumidores e dos trabalhadores, dando especial atenção às questões sociais que se relacionam com a igualdade de oportunidades, o combate à discriminação social e uma eficaz divulgação da informação. Assim, a EFNIL pugna junto da EU para que esta proporcione mais oportunidades aos Estados Membros para que possam regulamentar em favor das suas próprias línguas com o propósito de serem garantidas as igualdades sociais.
6. A EFNIL disponibiliza-se para apoiar a criação, desenvolvimento e monitorização destas medidas e também para assegurar o respeito pelas características e especificidades, quer linguísticas quer culturais, nacionais e regionais

ro

# Rezoluția de la Lisabona cu privire la utilizarea limbilor în afaceri și comerț în Europa

*Adoptată de Adunarea generală a FEILIN din 14 noiembrie 2008*

1. Federația europeană a instituțiilor lingvistice naționale (FEILIN) consideră competențele lingvistice și capacitatea de a comunica în mai multe limbi ca fiind din ce în ce mai mult factori- cheie pentru domeniul de afaceri și comerț în Europa și în lume.
2. FEILIN preconizează o colaborare mai strânsă între Uniunea Europeană și statele membre pentru a favoriza realizarea unor politici care să răspundă unei asemenea provocări. Această colaborare ar trebui să conducă la:
   - conștientizarea deplină a importanței limbilor și competențelor lingvistice care pot fi un factor de reușită sau de eșec în mediul de afaceri;
   - încurajarea și susținerea dezvoltării în mediul de afaceri a unor instrumente consacrate utilizării limbilor și învățării lor;
   - încurajarea și susținerea dezvoltării de programme de învățare specifice destinate folosirii limbilor în mediul de afaceri, favorabile îndeosebi limbilor de mai mică circulație;
   - susținerea cercetării științifice, mai ales pentru a determina în ce măsură limbile și competențele lingvistice contribuie la crearea de valoare.
3. Acțiunile și măsurile de ordin politic ar trebui să acorde o atenție deosebită:
   - competențelor în limba națională (și nu numai în limbile străine), care joacă un rol cheie în comunicarea de afaceri;
   - ansamblului limbilor europene (și nu numai a celor de largă circulație), ca fiind vectori de localizare;
   - limbilor folosite pe piețele extra-europene pe care mediile de afaceri din țările europene ar trebui să le încurajeze, într-un spirit de reciprocitate, dându-le o atenție asemănătoare cu cea acordată limbilor europene;
   - competențelor de limbă ale muncitorilor imigranți;
   - competențelor de limbă (inclusiv străină) pe domenii și meserii, care fac parte integrantă din pregătirea profesională și din educație;
   - traducerii (în același timp umană și automată) și terminologiei, care constituie un sprijin indispensabil pentru localizare și adaptare la piețele străine și la clienții acestora.
4. FEILIN propune Comisiei europene să realizeze un vast serviciu de informare și documentare pentru factorii de decizie, societățile private, ca și pentru sectorul public, și să promoveze bunele practici.

5. FEILIN consideră că problema folosirii limbii în afaceri nu ar trebui să fie abordată exclusiv din punctul de vedere al libertăţii comerţului, ci şi din perspectiva drepturilor consumatorilor şi muncitorilor. Independent de riscul discriminării sociale faţă de cetăţenii mai puţin educaţi şi formaţi, ar putea fi luate mai mult în considerare egalitatea şanselor şi accesul la informaţie. De asemenea, FEILIN propune Uniunii europene să ofere statelor membre un cadru propice pentru luarea unor măsuri în favoarea propriilor lor limbi, astfel încât să poată fi asigurată o minimă egalitate socială.
6. FEILIN propune să-şi ofere expertiza pentru a ajuta factorii de răspundere să dezvolte şi să piloteze politicile din acest domeniu şi pentru a veghea ca aceştia să ţină într-adevăr cont de diferitele specificităţi şi sensibilităţi atât pe plan naţional, cât şi pe plan local.

**sk**

# Lisabonská rezolúcia o používaní jazyka v hospodárstve v Európe

*Prijatá na generálnom zhromaždení EFNILu 14. novembra 2008*

1. *Európska federácia národných jazykových inštitúcií* (EFNIL) je presvedčená, že jazyková kompetencia a komunikačné zručnosti sa stávajú čoraz kľúčovejšími faktormi pre obchod a podnikanie v Európe i vo svete.

2. EFNIL kladie dôraz na užšiu spoluprácu medzi Európskou úniou a jej členskými štátmi pri uskutočňovaní politických krokov týkajúcich sa tejto výzvy. Do uvedenej oblasti obchodnej sféry by mohli patriť tieto ciele:

   - lepšie spoznať význam jazykov a jazykových zručností ako činiteľov ovplyvňujúcich úspech alebo neúspech v obchodnom prostredí;
   - podporovať a financovať šírenie pomôcok na jazykovú prípravu a jazykovú výučbu v obchodnom prostredí;
   - podporovať a financovať rozvoj špeciálnych vyučovacích programov na efektívnu jazykovú prípravu v obchodnom styku s osobitným dôrazom na menej používané jazyky;
   - podporovať vedecký výskum predovšetkým tých faktorov, ktoré podmieňujú prínos jazykov a jazykových zručností pri procesoch tvorenia hodnôt.

3. Jazykovopolitické akcie a opatrenia by mali venovať pozornosť predovšetkým:

   - ovládaniu príslušných národných jazykov (nielen cudzích jazykov) ako kľúčových predpokladov v obchodnej komunikácii;
   - všetkým európskym jazykom (nielen významnejším) ako prostriedkom lokalizácie (užitočným v istých lokalitách)
   - jazykom mimoeurópskych trhov stimulujúc takto reciprocitu s cieľom, aby podobnú pozornosť venovali aj mimoeurópski obchodní partneri európskym jazykom;
   - jazykovej zdatnostii migrantských zamestnancov;
   - regionálnej a špecifickej (cudzo)jazyčnej kompetencii ako integrálnej súčasti profesného vzdelávania;
   - humánnemu a strojovému prekladaniu terminológie ako nevyhnutnej pomoci pri lokalizácii a prispôsobovaní sa cudzím trhom a ich klientom.

4. EFNIL nabáda Európsku komisiu, aby založila celoeurópsku informačnú a dokumentačnú službu, ktorú by mohli využívať firmy a verejná správa, a aby zabezpečila jej čo najlepšie využívanie v praxi.

5. EFNIL je tej mienky, že na používanie jazyka v hospodárstve by sa nemalo hľadieť výlučne z hľadiska voľného obchodu, ale dôležité je aj hľadisko práv spotrebiteľov a zamestnancov, lebo tak sa zapoja aj sociálne aspekty ako rovnosť šancí, ktorých porušenie hrozí najmä pri skupine menej vzdelaných občanov. Tiež by sa malo prihliadať na vhodný spôsob šírenia informací. Preto EFNIL apeluje na Európsku úniu, aby poskytovala viac možností členským štátom v otázke regulovania svojich vlastných jazykov s cieľom zabezpečiť adekvátnu sociálnu rovnosť.
6. EFNIL ponúka svoje expertízy na podporu politických rozhodovateľov pri tvorbe a monitorovaní opatrení v tejto oblasti, pričom je dôležité, aby sa v dostatočnej miere brali do úvahy národné i regionálne okolnosti a špecifiká.

**sl**

# Lizbonska resolucija o rabi jezikov v poslovanju in trgovanju po Evropi

*Sprejeta na občnem zboru EFNIL-a 14. novembra 2008*

1. *Evropska zveza državnih jezikovnih ustanov* (EFNIL) se zaveda, da so jezikovna zmožnost in sporazumevalne spretnosti čedalje pomembnejši dejavniki za poslovanje in trgovanje po Evropi in svetu.

2. EFNIL priporoča večje sodelovanje med Evropsko zvezo in državami članicami pri razvijanju politik, ki odgovarjajo na ta izziv. Vključevati bi moralo naslednje glavne dejavnosti:

   - večanje zavesti o pomenu jezikov in jezikovnih spretnosti kot dejavnikov za uspeh ali neuspeh v poslovnem okolju;
   - spodbujanje in financiranje razvoja orodij za obravnavanje in učenje jezikov v poslovnem okolju;
   - spodbujanje in financiranje razvoja posebnih učnih programov za učinkovito rabo jezikov v poslovanju, s posebnim poudarkom na manj uporabljanih jezikih;
   - podpiranje znanstvenih raziskav, posebno o tistih dejavnikih, ki vplivajo na to, kako jeziki in jezikovne spretnosti pripomorejo k ustvarjanju dodane vrednosti.

3. Pri političnih dejavnostih in ukrepih naj se namenja ustrezna pozornost pomembnosti naslednjega:

   - spretnosti v državnem oziroma domačem jeziku (in ne samo spretnosti v tujih jezikih) so ključni dejavnik pri poslovnem sporazumevanju;
   - vsi evropski jeziki (ne samo največji) so sredstva za lokalizacijo – prilagajanje določenemu kulturnemu okolju;
   - jeziki zunajevropskih tujih trgov spodbujajo tudi vzajemnost, tako da bi moralo neevropsko poslovanje nameniti primerljivo pozornost evropskim jezikom;
   - jezikovne zmožnosti gostujočih delavcev;
   - tujejezične zmožnosti za posebna področja in naloge kot sestavine strokovnega šolanja in izobraževanja;
   - prevajanje (človeško in strojno) ter terminološko delo kot nenadomestljiva pomoč za lokalizacijo in prilagajanje tujim trgom in tamkajšnjim strankam.

4. EFNIL priporoča Evropski komisiji, da ustanovi vseevropsko službo za informiranje, dokumentiranje in promocijo dobrih jezikovnih praks, namenjeno tako podjetjem kot tudi javni upravi.

5. EFNIL meni, da se o jezikovni rabi v poslovanju ne bi smelo razmišljati izključno iz zornega kota proste trgovine, temveč tudi iz zornega kota uporabnikovih in delavčevih pravic; to bi omogočilo družbene premisleke o enakih priložnostih, nevarnosti družbene diskriminacije manj izobraženih državljanov in učinkovitem širjenju informacij. EFNIL zato poziva Evropsko zvezo, naj državam članicam ponudi več priložnosti, da bodo lahko ukrepale v prid lastnih jezikov in zagotovile zadostno družbeno enakopravnost.
6. EFNIL ponuja svoje strokovno znanje v pomoč snovalcem politike pri razvoju in spremljanju programov na tem področju ter pri zagotavljanju ustreznega upoštevanja narodnih in območnih razmer in občutljivih posebnosti.

SV

# Lissabondeklarationen om språkbruk inom handel och näringsliv i Europa

*Antagen av Efnils generalförsamling i Lissabon den 14 november 2008*

1. *Samarbetsorganisationen för språkråd i EU-stater*, Efnil (European Federation of National Institutes of Language), vill framhålla att språklig kompetens och kommunikationsfärdigheter är allt viktigare nyckelfaktorer i Europa och världen i övrigt.
2. Efnil manar till ökad samverkan mellan Europeiska unionen och dess medlemsstater för att utveckla strategier för att möta denna utmaning. Dessa strategier bör innefatta följande:
   - att väcka medvetenhet om språk och språkfärdigheter som viktiga faktorer för framgång eller misslyckande inom affärsområdet;
   - att uppmuntra och finansiera utvecklandet av verktyg för språkbehandling och språkinlärning inom affärsområdet;
   - att uppmuntra och finansiera utvecklandet av specifika undervisningsprogram för en effektiv användning av språk inom affärsområdet, varvid speciellt mindre använda språk bör gynnas;
   - att stödja forskning, i synnerhet om faktorer som avgör hur språk och språkfärdigheter bidrar till den värdeskapande processen.
3. Vid uppställande av riktlinjer och metoder bör man ge akt på vikten av:
   - kunskaper i nationella språk som nyckelfaktorer när det gäller affärskommunikation (och inte bara kunskaper i främmande språk);
   - alla europeiska språk som lokaliseringsinstrument (och inte bara de större);
   - språken på utländska marknaden utanför Europa, och samtidigt uppmuntra till att icke-europeisk handel skall ge motsvarande uppmärksamhet till europeiska språk;
   - språkkompetensen hos invandrad arbetskraft;
   - bransch- och fackspecifik språkkompetens som en väsentlig del i yrkesutbildning;
   - översättning (både mänsklig och automatiserad) och terminologiarbete som en oumbärlig hjälp vid lokalisering och anpassning till utländska marknader och kunderna där.
4. Efnil uppmanar Europeiska kommissionen att inrätta en europeisk informations- och dokumentationstjänst för såväl företag som myndigheter och att främja goda förebilder.

5. Enligt Efnil bör frågan om språkanvändning inom näringslivet inte enbart ses utifrån ett frihandelsperspektiv utan också utifrån ett konsumenträtts- och arbetsrättsperspektiv, för att på så sätt ta hänsyn till sociala förhållanden såsom lika möjligheter, faran för social diskriminering gentemot medborgare med lägre utbildning och effektiv spridning av information. Därför uppmanar Efnil Europeiska unionen att erbjuda fler möjligheter för medlemsstaterna att stödja staternas egna språk i syfte att garantera tillräcklig social jämlikhet.

6. Efnil erbjuder sin expertis som hjälp för att utveckla och övervaka åtgärder på detta område och för att säkerställa att nationella och regionala omständigheter vederbörligen beaktas

## Contacts

Guy Berg: <guy.berg@europarl.europa.eu>

Sophie Bressé: <sophie.bresse@cee-recherche.fr>

František Čermák: <frantisek.cermak@ff.cuni.cz>

Janez Dular: <janez_dular2@t-2.net>

José Paulo Esperança: <Jose.Esperanca@iscte.pt>

Stephen Hagen: <Stephen.Hagen@uwe.ac.uk>

Guðrún Kvaran: <gkvaran@hi.is>

Corina Cilianu-Lascu: <lascu_corina@yahoo.fr>

Pirkko Nuolijärvi: <pnuolija@kotus.fi>

Walery Pisarek: < uwpisare@cyf-kr.edu.pl>

Charlotte Rønhof: <chr@di.dk>

Marius Sala: <marsalamar@yahoo.com>

Martin Stegu: <Martin.Stegu@wu.ac.at>

Gerhard Stickel: <stickel@ids-mannheim.de>

Lisbeth Verstraete-Hansen: <lvh.ikk@cbs.dk>

## European Federation of National Institutions for Language (EFNIL): Members and associate member institutions

For detailed information on EFNIL and its members see www.efnil.org

### 1. Member institutions grouped by country

| | |
|---|---|
| Austria: | ***Österreichisches Sprachen-Kompetenz-Zentrum***, Graz<br>Austrian Centre for Language Competence |
| | ***Bundesministerium für Unterricht, Kunst und Kultur***, Wien<br>Federal Ministry for Education, Art, and Culture |
| Belgium: | ***Service de la langue française***, Bruxelles<br>French Language Service |
| | ***Nederlandse Taalunie***, Den Haag<br>Dutch Language Union (Flanders and The Netherlands) |
| Bulgaria: | ***Българска академия на науките, Институт за български език***, Sofia<br>Bulgarian Academy of Sciences, Institute for Bulgarian Language |
| Czech Republic: | ***Ústav Českého národního korpusu Univerzity Karlovy***, Praha<br>Institute of Czech National Corpus, Charles-University |
| Denmark: | ***Dansk Sprognævn***, København<br>Danish Language Council |
| Estonia: | ***Eesti Keelenõukogu***, Tallin<br>Estonian Language Council |
| | ***Eesti Keele Instituut***, Tallin<br>Institute of the Estonian Language |
| Finland: | ***Kotimaisten kielten tutkimuskeskus / Forskningscentralen för de inhemska språken***, Helsinki/Helsingfors<br>Research Institute for the Languages of Finland |
| France: | ***Délégation Générale à la langue française et aux langues de France***, Paris<br>General Delegation for the French Language and the Languages of France |
| Germany: | ***Deutsche Akademie für Sprache und Dichtung***, Darmstadt<br>German Academy for Language and Literature |
| | ***Institut für Deutsche Sprache***, Mannheim<br>Institute for the German Language |

| | |
|---|---|
| Greece: | ***Κέντρο Ελληνικής Γλώσσας***, Thessaloniki<br>Centre for the Greek Language |
| Hungary | ***Magyar Tudomános Akadémia, Nyalvtudományi Intézet***, Budapest<br>Hungarian Academy of Sciences, Research Institute for Linguistics |
| | ***Oktatási és Kulturális Minisztérium***, Budapest<br>Ministry for Education and Culture |
| Ireland | ***Foras na Gaeilge***, Dublin<br>(the all-island body for the Irish language) |
| Italy | ***Accademia della Crusca***, Firenze<br>(the central academy for the Italian language) |
| | ***CNR – Opera del Vocabolario Italiano***, Firenze<br>The Italian Dictionary |
| Latvia | ***Valst valodas komisija***, Riga<br>State Language Commission |
| | ***Valsts valodas aģentūra***, Riga<br>State Language Agency |
| Lithuania | ***Lietviu Kalbos Institutas***, Vilnius<br>Institute of the Lithuanian Language |
| | ***Valstybine Lietuviu Kalbos Komisija***, Vilnius<br>State Commission for the Lithuanian Language |
| Luxembourg | ***Institut Grand-Ducal, Section de linguistique***, Luxembourg<br>Grand Ducal Institute, Linguistic Section |
| | ***Conseil permanent de la langue luxembourgeoise***, Luxembourg<br>Permanent Council of the Luxembourgish language |
| Malta | ***Kunsill Nazzjonali ta'l-Ilsien Malti***<br>National Council of the Maltese language |
| Netherlands/Belgium | ***Nederlandse Taalunie***, Den Haag<br>Dutch language Union (The Netherlands and Flanders) |
| Poland | ***Rada Jezyka Polskiego***, Warszawa<br>Council for the Polish Language |
| Portugal | ***Instituto Camões, Lisbõa***<br>(the institution for the promotion of Portuguese language and culture) |
| Romania | ***Academia Română, Institutul de Lingvistica***, Bucureşti<br>Romanian Academy, Institute of Linguistics |
| | ***Academia de Studii Economice Bucureşti***<br>Bucharest Academy of Economic Studies |

| | |
|---|---|
| Slovakia | ***Jazykovedný ústav Ľudovíta Štúra Slovenskej***, Bratislava<br>Slovak Academy of Sciences, Ludovit Stúr Institute of Linguistics |
| Slovenia | ***Ministrstvo za kulturo - Sektor za slovenski jezik***, Ljubljana<br>Ministry of Culture, Section for the Slovenian language |
| Spain | ***Real Academia Española***, Madrid<br>Royal Spanish Academy |
| Sweden | ***Språkrådet***, Stockholm<br>The Swedish Language Council |
| United Kingdom | ***Oxford English Dictionary***, Oxford<br>***British Council*** |

## 2. Associate member institutions

| | |
|---|---|
| Iceland | ***Íslensk málnefnd***, Reykjavik<br>Icelandic Language Council |
| Norway | ***Språkrådet***, Oslo<br>Norwegian Language Council |

**DUISBURGER ARBEITEN ZUR SPRACH- UND KULTURWISSENSCHAFT**
**DUISBURG PAPERS ON RESEARCH IN LANGUAGE AND CULTURE**

Herausgegeben von
Ulrich Ammon, René Dirven und Martin Pütz

Band 1 René Dirven / Yvan Putseys (Eds.): A User's Grammar of English: Word, Sentence, Text, Interaction - Part A. The Structure of Words and Phrases. 1989.

Band 2 René Dirven / Richard A. Geiger (Eds.): A User's Grammar of English: Word, Sentence, Text, Interaction - Part B. The Structure of Sentences. 1989.

Band 3 René Dirven / Wolfgang Zydatiß / Willis J. Edmondson (Eds.): A User's Grammar of English: Word, Sentence, Text, Interaction - Parts C & D. The Structure of Texts / The Structure of Interaction. 1989.

Band 4 René Dirven: (Ed.): A User's Grammar of English: Word, Sentence, Text, Interaction - Compact Edition. 1989.

Band 5 Martin Pütz / René Dirven (Eds.): Wheels within Wheels. Papers of the Duisburg Symposium on Pidgin and Creole Languages. 1989.

Band 6 Ulrich Schmitz / Rüdiger Schütz / Andreas Kunz (Eds.): Linguistic Approaches to Artificial Intelligence. 1990.

Band 7 Friedrich Lenz: Organisationsprinzipien in mündlicher Fachkommunikation. 1989.

Band 8 Luc Van Doorslaer (Hrsg.): Niederländische Literatur im Spiegel niederländischer Kultur. Aufsätze zur Gastprofessur von Prof. Dr. Marcel Janssens (Universität Löwen) in Duisburg, Sommersemester 1988. 1990.

Band 9 Frank Lüschow / Marita Pabst-Weinschenk (Hrsg.): Mündliche Kommunikation als kooperativer Prozeß. Sprechwissenschaftliche Arbeitsfelder. Festschrift für Elmar Bartsch. 1991.

Band 10 Susanne Niemeier: Ein Fall im Medienvergleich: Film- und Fernsehversion von "A Streetcar Named Desire". Beitrag zur Annäherung an eine Mediensemiotik. 1990.

Band 11 Paul Kent Andersen: A new look at the passive. 1991.

Band 12 Richard Kremer: The efficiency of English language teaching in smaller countries: Denmark. Basic English language teaching in Denmark and its wider context. 1991.

Band 13 Frank Lüschow: Sprache und Kommunikation in der technischen Arbeit. 1992.

Band 14 Günter Kellermann / Michael D. Morrissey (Eds.): Diachrony within Synchrony: Language History and Cognition. Papers from the International Symposium at the University of Duisburg 26-28 March 1990. 1992.

Band 15 Wim Waumans (Hrsg.): Mit fremden Augen. Niederländisch: eine Sprache, verschiedene Kulturgemeinschaften. 1993.

Band 16 Eberhard Klein: Konditionalität in didaktischen und pädagogischen Grammatiken des Englischen. Prinzipien zur Erstellung von Lehr- und Lerngrammatiken. 1993.

Band 17 Xiaoan Zhu: "Wenn sich das Gras bewegt, dann muß auch der Wind blasen!" Studien zur Metapher in der deutschen politischen Pressesprache – unter besonderer Berücksichtigung der China-Berichterstattung. 1993.

Band 18 Fritz Ponelis: The Development of Afrikaans. 1993.

Band 19 Martin Pütz: Sprachökologie und Sprachwechsel. Die deutsch-australische Sprechgemeinschaft in Canberra. 1994.

Band 20 Heiner Pürschel (Ed.); Co-Editors: Elmar Bartsch, Peter Franklin, Ulrich Schmitz, Sonja Vandermeeren: : Intercultural Communication. Proceedings of the 17th International L.A.U.D. Symposium. Duisburg, 23-27 March 1992. 1994.

Band 21 Dominiek Sandra: Morphology in the reader's mental lexicon. 1994.

Band 22 René Dirven: Metaphor and Nation. Metaphors Afrikaners live by. 1994.

Band 23 Ralph Bisschops: Die Metapher als Wertsetzung. Novalis, Ezechiel, Beckett. 1994.

Band 24 René Dirven / Johan Vanparys (Eds.): Current Approaches to the Lexicon. A Selection of Papers Presented at the 18th LAUD Symposium, Duisburg, March 1993. 1995.

Band 25 Michael Schloßmacher: Die Amtssprachen in den Organen der Europäischen Gemeinschaft. Status und Funktion. 1996. 2., durchges. Aufl. 1997.

Band 26 Johan Vanparys: Categories and Complements of Illocutionary Verbs in a Cognitive Perspective. 1996.

Band 27 Hideaki Takahashi: Die richtige Aussprache des Deutschen in Deutschland, Österreich und der Schweiz nach Maßgabe der kodifizierten Normen. 1996.

Band 28 Angela Heidemann: The visualization of foreign language vocabulary in CALL. 1996.

Band 29 Kazuma Matoba: Referenzperspektive in Sprechakten. Ihre Funktion und Entwicklung in der deutschen und japanischen Sprache. 1997.

Band 30 Olaf Jäkel: Metaphern in abstrakten Diskurs-Domänen. Eine kognitiv-linguistische Untersuchung anhand der Bereiche Geistestätigkeit, Wirtschaft und Wissenschaft. 1997.

Band 31 Birgit Smieja / Meike Tasch (Eds.): Human Contact through Language and Linguistics. 1997.

Band 32 Martin Pütz (Ed.): The Cultural Context in Foreign Language Teaching. 1997.

Band 33 Andrea Gerbig: Lexical and Grammatical Variation in a Corpus. A Computer-Assisted Study of Discourse on the Environment. 1997.

Band 34 Helga Bister-Broosen: Sprachkontakte und Sprachattitüden Jugendlicher im Elsaß und in Baden. Vergleichende soziolinguistische Untersuchungen in Colmar (Frankreich) und in Freiburg und Müllheim (Deutschland). 1998.

Band 35 Helga Bister-Broosen (Hrsg.): Niederländisch am Niederrhein. 1998.

Band 36 Alicja Sakaguchi: Interlinguistik. Gegenstand, Ziele, Aufgaben, Methoden. 1998.

Band 37 Benjamin Biebuyck / René Dirven / John Ries (Eds.): Faith and Fiction. Interdisciplinary Studies on the Interplay between Metaphor and Religion. A Selection of Papers from the 25th LAUD-Symposium of the Gerhard Mercator University of Duisburg on 'Metaphor and Religion'. 1998.

Band 38 Ulrich Ammon (Hrsg.): Sprachförderung. Schlüssel auswärtiger Kulturpolitik. 2000.

Band 39 El Hadj Ibrahima Diop: Das Selbstverständnis von Germanistikstudium und Deutschunterricht im frankophonen Afrika. Vom kolonialen Unterrichtsfach zu eigenständigen Deutschlandstudien und zum praxisbezogenen Lernen. 2000.

Band 40 Herman M. Batibo / Birgit Smieja (Eds.): Botswana: The Future of the Minority Languages. 2000.

Band 41 Harald Haarmann: Die Kleinsprachen der Welt – Existenzbedrohung und Überlebenschancen. Eine umfassende Dokumentation. 2001.

Band 42 Dirk Scholten: Sprachverbreitungspolitik des nationalsozialistischen Deutschlands. 2000.

Band 43 Riana Roos Paola: Pro-active Language Teacher Education in a Multicultural Society. 2001.

Band 44 Angelika Daniel: Lernerwortschatz und Wortschatzlernen im bilingualen Unterricht. 2001.

Band 45 Edel O'Halloran: Ist Mode englisch? Französische und englische Einflüsse auf die deutsche Mode- und Gemeinsprache im 20. Jahrhundert. 2001.

Band 46 Maya Khemlani David (Ed.): Methodological and Analytical Issues in Language Maintenance and Language Shift Studies. 2002.

Band 47 Martin Praxenthaler: Die Sprachverbreitungspolitik der DDR. Die deutsche Sprache als Mittel sozialistischer auswärtiger Kulturpolitik. 2002.

Band 48 Ulrich Ammon / Grant McConnell: English as an Academic Language in Europe. A Survey of its Use in Teaching. 2002.

Band 49 Birgit Smieja: Language Pluralism in Botswana - Hope or Hurdle? A sociolinguistic survey on language use and language attitudes in Botswana with special reference to the status and use of English. 2003.

Band 50 Carlos Inchaurralde / Celia Florén (Eds.): Interaction and Cognition in Linguistics. 2003.

Band 51 Andreas Ross: Europäische Einheit in babylonischer Vielfalt. Die Reform des Sprachenregimes der Europäischen Union im Spannungsfeld von Demokratie und Effizienz. 2003.

Band 52 Michael Anton Böhm: Deutsch in Afrika. Die Stellung der deutschen Sprache in Afrika vor dem Hintergrund der bildungs- und sprachpolitischen Gegebenheiten sowie der deutschen Auswärtigen Kulturpolitik. 2003.

Band 53 Martin Pütz / JoAnne Neff-van Aertselear / Teun A. van Dijk: Communicating Ideologies. Multidisciplinary Perspectives on Language, Discourse, and Social Practice. 2004.

Band 54 Yuko Sugita: Gesprächserwartungen. Eine kontrastive Studie über die Gesprächsführung in deutschen und japanischen Telefonaten. 2004.

Band 55 Eithne B. Carlin: A Grammar of Trio. A Cariban Language of Suriname. 2004.

Band 56 Maya Khemlani David (Ed.): Teaching of English in Second and Foreign Language Settings. Focus on Malaysia. 2004.

Band 57 Rita Brdar-Szabó / Elisabeth Knipf-Komlósi (Hrsg.): Lexikalische Semantik, Phraseologie und Lexikographie. Abgründe und Brücken. Festgabe für Regina Hessky. 2004.

Band 58 Claudia Kunschak: Language Variation in Foreign Language Teaching. On the Road to Communicative Competence. 2004.

Band 59 Allan Turner: Translating Tolkien. Philological Elements in *The Lord of the Rings*. 2005.

Band 60 Markus Motz (Hrsg.): Englisch oder Deutsch in Internationalen Studiengängen? 2005.

Band 61 Birte Kellermeier-Rehbein: Areale Wortbildungsvarianten des Standarddeutschen. Beiuntersuchung zum *Variantenwörterbuch des Deutschen*. 2005.

Band 62 Maya Khemlani David / Hafriza Burhanudeen / Ain Nadzimah Abdullah (Eds.): The Power of Language and the Media. 2006.

Band 63 Vít Dovalil: Sprachnormenwandel im geschriebenen Deutsch an der Schwelle zum 21. Jahrhundert. Die Entwicklung in ausgesuchten Bereichen der Grammatik. 2006.

Band 64 Sara Hägi: Nationale Varietäten im Unterricht Deutsch als Fremdsprache. 2006.

Band 65 Albert Weideman / Birgit Smieja (eds.): Empowerment through Language and Education. Cases and Case Studies from North America, Europe, Africa and Japan. 2006.

Band 66 Iraide Ibarretxe-Antuñano / Carlos Inchaurralde / Jesús-M. Sánchez-García (eds.): Language, Mind, and the Lexicon. 2007.

Band 67 Roswitha Reinbothe: Deutsch als internationale Wissenschaftssprache und der Boykott nach dem Ersten Weltkrieg. 2006.

Band 68 Fredericka van der Lubbe: Martin Aedler and the *High Dutch Minerva*. The First German Grammar for the English. 2007.

Band 69 Frank Polzenhagen: Cultural Conceptualisations in West African English. A Cognitive-Linguistic Approach. 2007.

Band 70 Augustin Simo Bobda (ed.): Explorations into Language Use in Africa. 2008.

Band 71 Johannes Eckerth / Sabine Siekmann (eds.): Task-Based Language Learning and Teaching. Theoretical, Methodological, and Pedagogical Perspectives. 2008.

Band 72 Laura Sicola: *No, they won't 'just sound like each other'*. NNS-NNS Negotiated Interaction and Attention to Phonological Form on Targeted L2 Pronunciation Tasks. 2009.

Band 73 Gerhard Stickel (ed.): National and European Language Policies. Contributions to the Annual Conference 2007 of EFNIL in Riga. 2009.

Band 74 Daniel Klaaß: Untersuchungen zu ausgewählten Aspekten des Konsonantismus bei österreichischen Nachrichtensprechern. 2009.

Band 75 Javier Herrero Ruiz: Understanding Tropes. At the Crossroads between Pragmatics and Cognition. 2009.

Band 76 Javier Valenzuela / Ana Rojo / Cristina Soriano (eds.): Trends in Cognitive Linguistics. Theoretical and Applied Models. 2009.

Band 77 Maya Khemlani David / James McLellan / Shameem Rafik-Galea / Ain Nadzimah Abdullah (eds.): Code Switching in Malaysia. 2009.

Band 78 Gerhard Stickel (ed.): Language Use in Business and Commerce in Europe. Contributions to the Annual Conference 2008 of EFNIL in Lisbon. 2010.

www.peterlang.de

www.ingramcontent.com/pod-product-compliance
Ingram Content Group UK Ltd.
Pitfield, Milton Keynes, MK11 3LW, UK
UKHW022100051026
15623UKWH00003B/585

9 783631 588031